Colin McLaren was one of Australia's finest detectives; he travelled the world on high-end investigations during the 1980s and 1990s. He faced down the underbelly of Australian crime and his work has been the subject of many police genre documentaries and television series. A film of his hugely successful first book, *Infiltration*, the true story of his efforts as an undercover cop, was made in 2011. Colin writes constantly and is a regular advisor to TV and cinema productions. His investigation into JFK's death has been exhaustive: he spent 4.5 years on his cold case study and forensic analysis of all the testimonies and police reports to uncover the truth. He made a powerful US-based documentary about JFK's murder that screened worldwide in November 2013 – the fiftieth anniversary of the president's death.

ALSO BY COLIN MCLAREN

Infiltration
On the Run
Sunflower
Underbelly: The Golden Casket

JFK

THE SMOKING GUN

COLIN McLAREN

hachette
AUSTRALIA

*To Howard Donohue, a man who epitomised
the very reason we demand dedicated and precise
forensic science at the forefront of unravelling
complex crime. Despite his arduous 25-year study
he was snubbed and ultimately silenced by official
suits and lawsuits. His ballistic expertise, his astute
opinions and his skill live on through my story.*

hachette
AUSTRALIA

First published in Australia and New Zealand in 2013
by Hachette Australia
(an imprint of Hachette Australia Pty Limited)
Level 17, 207 Kent Street, Sydney NSW 2000
www.hachette.com.au

This edition published in 2016

10 9 8 7 6 5 4 3 2 1

National Library of Australia
Cataloguing-in-Publication data:

McLaren, Colin, author.

JFK: the smoking gun/Colin McLaren.

ISBN: 978 0 7336 3641 7 (paperback)

Kennedy, John F. (John Fitzgerald), 1917–1963 – Assassination.
Presidents – Assassination – United States.
Conspiracies – United States – History – 20th century.

973.922092

r, Dallas Times Herald Collection/

CONTENTS

JOINING THE DOTS

'Truth is like the sun.
You can shut it out for a time,
but it ain't goin' away.'

ELVIS PRESLEY, 1964

There's nothing more tantalising than a scandal. Spellbound television audiences ogle nightly as mannequin-faced presenters offer complex, at times convoluted theories behind what might have been a straightforward death. Our media has drawn to its bosom the adage 'never let the truth get in the way of a good story'. Hardly a week in the world of current affairs journalism passes without a healthy dose of joining the dots. Sprinkling a rumour or two of a bizarre murder/terrorist/love-rat tryst whets the appetites of the rapacious gossip readers. Our weekend newspapers wouldn't be the same without at least one juicy conspiracy story between their pages every now and again.

Our consumption of conspiracy-based thrillers is just as voracious, outselling the once clear-cut page-turning whodunits. The contrived, often tortuous scenarios of our modern novels can be as long as the book itself, with scant scope left for logic or realism. So sensational are some of today's writings that it is unlikely an Edgar Allan Poe or Agatha Christie would make a living with their style of whodunits. And we need our bad guy to be a mix of terrorist or left-over Soviet, Muslim fundamentalist, or surviving fascist linked to a serial killer, renegade, bent cop, corrupt judge or sexually rampant priest veiled behind the order of Saint John or between the walls of the Vatican or on the pages of the Koran!

Going to the cinema is no longer an easy Hitchcockian experience either. The crime genre film now inevitably takes in a labyrinth of technology and weaponry interwoven with myriad suspects and subplots, culminating in often ludicrous outcomes that compete to surpass their predecessors in complexity. No one suffers a simple death any more. Rarely does a victim in a novel or on the big screen get shot with a single bullet. Nor does the killer drop the murder weapon to the ground and flee the scene. The cliché of an open-and-shut case is well gone, and the more celebrity attached to the victim, the more dots there are to join and the more outlandish the theories.

The thought process of a seasoned detective at a crime scene seldom involves considering the complexities of a conspiracy. Most murders are the act of an individual perpetrator and, while sometimes gruesome, are often easily explained. Forensics and years of detective training and experience, coupled with witnesses, exhibits and circumstantial evidence aid in solving the crime. In the arena of misadventure, accidents causing death are mostly due to malfunction, mishap or a series of events rolling together to a tragic outcome.

So, when did the conspiracy theory graduate from a rarely posed question by a detective while mulling over the facts to an unbridled and excessively used alternative? At what point in our history did the conspiracy theorist grow legs and run on to become what they are today: a regular intruder in the black and white world of investigation?

It's hard to imagine a diligent Scotland Yard detective, in the heady days of nineteenth-century investigation, adrift on a conspiracy whim. The tenets of the Westminster system led to the flourishing of investigation as a science: practical answers to felonies using tried and tested crime scene principles, initial action procedures and forensic examination. A hundred years ago, catching a crook was uncomplicated. Fingerprints put the suspect at the scene or the murder weapon in their hand. Blood typing, blood splattering, soil tracing and a myriad other techniques underpinned the conviction that every contact leaves its trace. This went with that and before long the perpetrator was signing an admission, case closed. Then police got even smarter and forensic science matured. Before long the worldly tool kit for a detective was all-inclusive: gunshot residues; hair and ultimately DNA sampling; telephone intercepts; and, by the 1970s, listening devices.

It's also interesting to note the parallel growth of the media. In the late 1800s, news travelled slowly and by its only medium, the daily broadsheet newspaper. Reporting on a crime was based on facts acquired by a reporter who would converse directly with the inspector or sergeant in charge of an investigation, or occasionally with a witness still lingering at the scene. It was rare for a reporter to pose an answer to a tragedy that hadn't yet seen a courtroom. But, as the saying goes, you can't stand in the way of progress. By the twentieth century the business of delivering news had become serious. A number of media innovations simmered in the background, allies that would ultimately dominate; black and white text was enhanced by the introduction of photography. Marconi invented the radio and by the 1920s his invention was delivering bulletins faster than any printer could arrange his typesetting. Television followed in a natural progression of sorts, the square box finding a place of honour in lounge rooms around the globe in the 1940s and '50s. Both these innovations were instrumental in popularising the conspiracy theory. By the late 1950s the phenomenon called the tabloid newspaper had entered the race. Stories became features, serialised over many weeks. For the first time detectives were under pressure to be interviewed, questioned and probed. Investigations were scrutinised and juries were pre-armed with a little bit of knowledge that was often dangerous. All of a sudden the dots on the horizon began to tempt the journalist. Storytelling was being consumed just as much as hard-nosed news and, as everybody knows, a good story needs colour.

As if a perfect catalyst to the changing face of journalism, the 1960s exploded with a 'make love, not war' attitude to life. Individual expression through music, prose, drugs and freedom of speech became dominant. Out of nowhere the world seemed to be sprinting. The slow old days of only a decade earlier were a mere memory. The time was ripe to listen to the conspiracy theorist, wordsmiths vehemently chasing down quotes to complete their copy. Society became tantalised.

As an aside to the advent of the swinging '60s, it's worth mentioning the tragic death of James Dean in 1955, at a time when conspiracy theorists had not yet flexed their muscle. Dean was travelling alone in his silver Porsche Spyder on a Californian highway when he crashed. Fatally wounded, the screen idol, heartthrob of three blockbuster films, was at the top of his game – a celebrity in every sense of the word, gifted with good looks and an intriguing private life. He was homosexual. Had he died ten years later, any number of scenarios may well have played out in the media proffering what 'actually' happened on Highway 466 that afternoon. Instead, the world accepted that he died as the result of a tragic accident caused by excessive speed. There were no allegations of a perverse homosexual clique or a cocktail of drugs or of tampering with the mechanics of the car or criminal involvement by any rival film company!

Even more could have been made of 'the day the music died' in 1959 when an aircraft crashed, killing the Big Bopper, Buddy Holly and Richie Valens. With the rise of conspiracy theorists still to come, the tragedy was written up as just a plane crash. Questions over the deaths of Buddy Holly and his fellow travellers, like that of James Dean and virtually all high-profile fatalities prior to the 1960s, have definitive answers, detailed from court judgements, judges' comments or police department media releases. Very much like the old era itself, the cause of death was black and white. The public read the article then turned the page.

How times have changed. The birth of the conspiracy has allowed the plotter to choose a suspect that best suits the case under scrutiny, much like another phenomenon of the 1960s, the supermarket. The theorist goes down aisles full of options when they construct their story, selecting the juiciest, tastiest morsels to add to their cart. Not limited by restrictions in the areas of truth or correctness or, in the case of the supermarket, budget, theorists can shop to their hearts' content, adding whatever condiments or spices they need to pepper their stew. A quick meal knocked together in no time, the finished tidbit sitting appropriately alongside the bare-breasted page-three girl. Interestingly, the conspiracy theory as a plausible solution to a sensational crime found the American people at a time when that nation first embraced fast food, celebrity, pornography, consumerism and popular culture.

Conspiracy theorists evolved to become slick and racy, as ribald as the rest of society. By the 1960s popular culture ruled. Hedonism was evident in every facet of the arts, from fashion and painting to architecture and music. Excess was spread thick on the ground. Those same extremist tendencies soon became prevalent throughout the media, the conspiracy theorists' logical collaborator. Comfortable livings were made presenting pseudo-documentaries, magazine and television programs proffering the most absurd explanations behind the death of anybody in the public eye. Such stories weren't limited to pop singers or movie stars; they included politicians and sportspeople, indeed anyone with a public persona. By the 1980s 'conspiracy' had become an accepted outcome to a tragedy. Regardless of the lack of factual support, the dots became text and that was enough to satisfy the reader. The real outcome, sometimes straightforward, often dull, was irrelevant, as in all likelihood something a little bit more exciting, a little bit more intriguing, would come along and sell more copies.

A clever conspiracy theorist will select their facts at random or convenience and weave a yarn that will ultimately create a tapestry that is impossible to unpick. In time, the story offered sits as the truth, often quoted as the definitive answer years after first being woven. The only watchdog, the laws of libel and defamation, has proven easy to challenge, too expensive to implement or long-winded and ineffective. Few cases ever result in compensation or public apology. The result is tacit encouragement for grander and more hideous theories. It's as if something that once started as a twitch of an idea and developed to a slight scratch on the arm of factual reporting has since festered into an abscess, infecting honest journalism.

In an era of internet, Twitter, Reddit, instant information and split-second communications, the conspiracy theory has found a cosy home in a culture that can change as quickly as it started. The bottom-of-the-alphabet generations expect their information to come at them brief, hard, and with as much colour and intrigue as possible. And there are plenty behind their computer, phone or tablet ready to upload directly from the action.

With the popularity of search engines such as Google and Bing, conspiracy theorists can chart, plot and write in one working shift. In an instant the search engine will throw back results, in the case of someone famous often thousands of hits. A writer lacking ideas or facts just needs to link the hits, join the dots and further add to the theorists' maze. Journalism has changed since the times of the Watergate scandal, when a conspiracy investigation could topple governments and ruin a president. Conspiracies have blurred practical investigative landscapes so much that the public is sometimes dubious of a simple explanation of a death and bewildered by a minefield of alternatives thrown up by the theorists, none of whom are qualified investigators, and few with the character of a Carl Bernstein or Bob Woodward: in the pursuit of truth. Conspiracy is now the cheap trick in journalism, just like the Wonderbra is to a woman's vanity, Botox is to ageing and reality television to entertainment. None are likely to fade away in a world that now demands quantity, not quality. We can expect the conspiracy theories to become an even more powerful obstruction to truth in the future. In fact, we are already seeing the search for truth as the ultimate victim in many tragedies.

JFK: The Smoking Gun looks at one death, a killing on a perfect Texan autumn day in 1963. A death in the public arena, surrounded by a complex set of circumstances that lasted less than six seconds yet caused the tragedy to fall into a category all its own, the most tragic event of its type. This ending of a human life would ultimately be brushed with countless conspiracy theories, suffer from more conjecture, more speculation and hypothesis than any other death in our global history. Interestingly, the case still remains unsolved in the minds of the masses and some of the solutions levelled towards the victim's fate are among the most ridiculous and foolhardy ever conjured. In the case of the demise of the 35th President of the United States, John Fitzgerald Kennedy, conspiracies have thickly coated the facts since the moment he and Governor John Connally were shot. JFK's death has become the Holy Grail of conspiracy theories, a label that may never fade. Not only has his name and reputation been muddied, so too have those of many of the bit players in the saga, a ruse to cover up the real cause of death and the identity of the individuals behind the killing.

'Who killed JFK?' is a question that might never be satisfactorily answered, so rightfully cynical is the public of the official version of events in Texas that afternoon. It could well be argued that 22 November, 1963, was the day the truth died, along with JFK. Certainly the official version of what happened was dead in the water before it was even printed and disseminated to a waiting nation. Paradoxically, 22 November, 1963 could be viewed as the day conspiracy theories were born.

Yet, to a seasoned detective, the death of JFK can be explained, as long as the investigator takes the time to read all the available evidence and testimony. That is an enormous task in itself. The case is the perfect example of a riddle wrapped in an enigma and shrouded in mystery. And the solution is far more disturbing than any fanciful conspiracy could ever be.

Colin McLaren

CHAPTER 1
INTO THE WELL

With the passing of half a century, the identity of the killer(s) of John Fitzgerald Kennedy, 35th President of the United States, remains the world's most talked about mystery. A recent survey conducted in America revealed that well over 70 per cent of the nation's citizens believe a conspiracy was behind the assassination. Only 12 per cent deem that they have been told 'the truth, the whole truth and nothing but the truth' on the subject. And most don't subscribe to the theory that lone gunman Lee Harvey Oswald was responsible. But if these suspicions are correct, then where is the truth to be found?

As a kid in short pants at the time of the assassination I have only vague, black and white recollections of the atrocity. I was too young to sense the impact, too young to recall where I was on the day the shocking news broke of the killing of a president. Yet, a few years after the crime I found myself doing school projects on the not dissimilar death of JFK's brother Bobby Kennedy, and my interest in the siblings was sparked. I'd collect clippings from the Sunday newspapers and before long I was a ten-year-old Kennedy family aficionado. I believed what I read in the newspapers. I was certain that communists were behind the assassination of the American President and that Lee Harvey Oswald hadn't acted alone. I believed that mafia mobsters or Russian spies probably had a hand in the killing and I saw the merit in levelling blame at Fidel Castro. On and on the suspect list went, another month, another theory and another suspect; the stories seemed to be endless. I believed them all mostly because I heard the snippets so often and no one was telling me any different. Certainly everyone I knew accepted that there was a conspiracy entwined there somewhere. The 'one man, one gun' theory didn't seem to wash with my pre-pubescent mind and all the 'facts' that I read kept reinforcing the conspiracy angle. But, that's how rumour can become truth. If repeated often enough, especially if the voice of the teller is charismatic, authoritative and earnest, just about any story will gain credibility. Mud, as they say, sticks. Repetition and reinforcement, over and over – it's the way propaganda works, too: keep beating the same drum and eventually the majority will believe. There are many examples of this phenomenon in history. One only has to remember how Adolf Hitler convinced an uncertain Germany that he and fascism were the answer. Or how 918 followers of lunatic evangelist Jim Jones clung so tightly to the dreams he promised that they were convinced to kill themselves in the Jonestown horror of 1978. Repetition, rhetoric and the clever use of selected material are the keys to convincing people, the stuff conspiracy theorists thrive on.

In the case of the death of JFK, if one is to accept the conspiracy theorists, one is to accept that a communist subgroup with hidden ties to the Las Vegas mafia assisted Lee Harvey Oswald in the assassination; that a second shooter lay in wait behind the grassy knoll or high in the tree tops on Elm Street as the motorcade rolled along; that the driver of the President's convertible was in on the play, as was the CIA, who aided Oswald with false identities, travel documents, as well as an introduction to a sleeper spy posing as a strip club owner cum double agent, Jack Ruby, who was in cahoots with the FBI and Vice President LB Johnson, in a plot that was hatched in Cuba at the instigation of Fidel Castro after the botched Bay of Pigs invasion, and that the Dallas Police Department acquiesced in the killing of the century, clearing their streets of detectives to permit the Secret Service to cover up the whole sordid affair. Phew! For me it's a tad too busy, too fat on plot. Surely there's a simpler answer? Yet, conspiracy theorists will actually try to sell this, or parts thereof, and many of them make a fine living plying their absurd threads of 'fact'. Interestingly, none of them are qualified detectives.

The real casualty in all this is not only John F Kennedy, but also the truth. The American people have become so bogged down in fanciful explanations that they are missing the purity of evidence. They haven't had the opportunity to read the facts, study the real back-story. As a story it's a fine blend of the logical, the black and white recollections, and the memory recall of the hundreds of people who were at the Dealey Plaza on the day of the killing. The story is in the witness statements, fascinating and understandable, straightforward and easy to comprehend. It's just that no one has presented their stories . . . yet.

By the time I reached my twenties and marched out of the police academy, my awareness of the granddaddy of all cold cases had sharpened. But it was not until I had undertaken years of crime scene courses and law modules and had begun specialising as a detective that solving the death of JFK entered my psyche. My police career had escalated into the world of major crime – rape, drug trafficking, police killings and homicides – and, in time, I became one of Australia's most experienced task force investigators, with an eighteen-year career in my hometown of Melbourne, a city of four million people, of four million stories, many of them criminal. The more I learnt my craft of detecting, solving and unravelling, the more crimes I was charged with tackling. Murder and attempted murder by gunshot and knives were commonplace, head shot wounds part of the injuries, fatal or otherwise, that made up my workload. I will never forget being one of the chosen few to investigate what is still one of Australia's most agonising crimes, the slaying of two policemen. One had his head near blown away, the other, his body ruined with rounds from his own hand gun. Nor shall my memory ever completely fade of being the first detective at a live and bloody crime scene, dozens of bullets whizzing in all directions, as a crazed gunman blasted seven victims to death, before succumbing to his own cowardly demise, leaving behind multiple murder scenes, each coated in blood splatters, dozens of deeply shocked survivors and human flesh at every step, every glance.

Or, the following year, the torching of a high-rise apartment and the attempted murder of six residents as they fled, on fire, by a physically powerful man hell-bent on revenge. I also investigated one of Australia's worst killers, a gangland figure who murdered ten petty criminals, mostly with gunshots. On my crime scene tally went, a vast number of crime scenes attended, and investigated, many hundred by career end. Eclipsing my investigative career was my role overseeing the investigation into the bombing of the office of the National Crime Authority building by an organised crime target. The office was blown to smithereens, causing the execution of one of the nations' finest detectives and seriously injuring many other law enforcement staff. It seemed the crime scenes became more ferocious, more complex to unravel, as my career went on.

Throughout, the Kennedy case sort of sat on my shoulder. I would be drawn back in time and again with the folly of the latest conspiracy theory: they always featured in prime-time news coverage.

Midway through my career I took a few weeks off. I'd just completed a team leader role in a task force investigation into the murder of a little girl and the serial rape of many others. This required me to revisit and reinvestigate dozens of old crime scenes. By the end I was exhausted, troubled by the abhorrent crimes I had uncovered and in need of some time off. I chose New York City as my escape destination for a change of scenery and it was that trip that forever changed my thinking on the killing of JFK. I became fascinated with how bold American culture was compared with my own. Walking in and out of the dodgy knife and bong shops in Times Square, browsing, mostly sticky-beaking, I walked into a bookstore specialising in true crime. In search of a good read for an upcoming flight, I pushed aside the customary mafia books on offer, drawn to a book by Bonar Menninger on the research of ballistics expert Howard Donahue entitled *Mortal Error: The Shot that Killed JFK*. It was a discount copy due to poor sales; apparently it was too technical for most. I devoured the book on my flight to

Chicago, couldn't put it down. Donahue thought he had found the answer to the world's greatest mystery. For 25 years he applied his technical skills, finally concluding that a second shooter had to have been at the scene of the crime. He was convincing and his science was sound; however, he was working with one hand tied behind his back. He didn't have the opportunity to study the back-story at will. Testimony and documents on the investigation into the assassination were still being held under restrictive use provisions. Donahue was missing the purity of witness evidence. Here was a great ballistics theory but with no supportive evidence or, as detectives say, 'all meat and no potatoes' – no forensic analysis of the testimonies to support his premise.

I carried the book in my cabin luggage when I winged my way homeward. By the time I arrived in Australia I had read it again and was charged with a desire to undertake a cold-case forensic study into the killing of the 35th President of the United States. I wanted to apply my trade and uncover the truth behind the mystery. I wanted to lend help to Howard Donahue and his theory. I wanted it so badly that I could almost taste it. But, it was 1992 and as charged as I was, I soon realised that there was no way an Australian detective, or any detective for that matter, could ever have access to the case files. They were locked away, part of another time, another world, where secrets were stamped 'Top Secret', dust gathering on files under the secrecy provisions that shrouded the official investigation into the assassination. At least that's what I thought.

Reality hit as my plane touched down and many more years of Australian crime scenes took precedence. I spent the last half of my career as a detective sergeant, team leader on murder task forces and at the National Crime Authority, Australia's premier investigative agency. In all I investigated some of the most horrific and significant crimes of my time, capping off my career as a lecturer at the prestigious detective training school. I instructed rookie investigators in the art of working a crime scene: what to do and what not to do. I wrote a new investigator's course, *Field Investigations: the how, why, when and where of managing crime scenes and gathering forensic evidence*. I lectured hundreds of student detectives, sharing my ways, offering advice. Then it was time to resign. When I did, I was at the top of my game.

Most detective training classrooms around the world give the JFK assassination a run, if not as a dedicated study, certainly as a case to debate at the end of a long day of law and investigative procedures. It's more than the ultimate whodunit; it's a fascinating look at the myriad mindsets that can bump into an investigator working a case. Tunnel vision, lack of resources, poor crime scene management, jumping the gun and playing to the media were all ticked off by the Dallas boys in blue in November 1963. How, I remember thinking as a detective, could they have got it so wrong? No wonder the conspiracy theorists flourished – the errors by the real investigators left so many stones unturned, so many avenues unvisited, it was always going to be the crime to attract the crazies!

On the day of the shooting, schools across America dismissed their students early and half of the country's workers downed tools. Citizens stopped in their tracks, unable to go on; many wept openly, others suffered nervousness, anxiety, had difficulty sleeping and a lesser few festered in rage at the atrocity. A week after the death the general public was still reeling from the attack on their democracy. Newspaper reporters, television commentators and anchors from local and international networks devoted entire segments to the premature death of a man who had charmed his people. A grieving populace was seeking answers to far too many questions, but the only answers seemed to be coming from the conspiracy theorists.

FBI Director J Edgar Hoover announced to his staff that he, too, wanted action, 'something issued so we can convince the public that Oswald is the real assassin'. His prejudicial pitch was not the ideal opening ball to any game; nevertheless, the US Government announced the formation of possibly the largest criminal investigative body assembled anywhere in the world at that time, the Warren Commission. At the helm was Chief Justice Earl Warren, a highly skilled and well-regarded man of the courts. He was to hear evidence from and cross-examine 552 witnesses as well as receive exhibits, images, photographs, affidavits and sworn statements.

In late September 1964, ten months after its inception, the Commission released a public report on its discoveries. This became known as the front volume of the 'Warren Commission Report'. Hastily published and released for general reading, it was still a long time coming. The 726-page report was a document free of secrecy and promised to provide all the answers. Anyone could buy a copy; even the *New York Times* offered texts for sale. The months that followed saw the report top the bestsellers list; everyone wanted a copy; every sitting room had one, an important part of the home library. But after digesting the pages, the public appetite remained far from sated; many were left wondering whether this really was the definitive answer to the killing of their president. Unfortunately for those who needed more, the 'front volume' acted as more of a tease than a solution. Sitting down to a canapé when you thought you had been invited to a degustation.

Twenty-six additional volumes of factual comment were printed, making up the sum total of all evidence uncovered. So vast was this leatherbound material that when standing side by side the tomes of print would run to a length of over three metres, the equivalent of more than 100 normal-sized novels. Held in text libraries, these volumes were not for general perusal. In the middle of the cold war and just after the end of McCarthyism, the last thing Americans needed was secrets regarding the death of their handsome young leader. Here was the perfect scenario for the conspiracy theorist. Their 'information' was readily available, free to air and free to read. And it was relentless, wild story after illogical rationale, each week another edition, another 'expert' proffering fantastic explanations. In the absence of any counter-fact from law enforcement agencies or government the stories grew wilder and the fantastic soon became ridiculous. Few knew what to believe and even fewer believed the Warren Commission Report.

•

There is one type of evidence that a detective will always turn to, evidence so powerful that its presence can lead to convictions: the paper trail. A witness statement, contemporaneous notes, affidavit, sworn testimony, recording or transcript of observations and spoken words are invaluable. There's nothing better for a detective than to see, touch, read and study verbatim comments made by a witness who has raised the Bible and sworn to tell the truth, the whole truth and nothing but the truth. The fear of perjury charges, the worry of public humiliation, the fright of being exposed as a liar brings out the best in a witness. At least that would have been the case back in the conservative days of the early 1960s. And every detective knows the best sort of written evidence is that which is taken as soon as practicable after a crime and tested in a court of law, exactly the sort of evidence that the mysterious back volumes were likely to contain.

By 1993 the US Senate caved to public pressure and instigated a rethink on the secrecy provisions that held the 'secret' Warren Commission material, and a whole range of other documents under the 'JFK' banner. Hey presto and the back volumes of the biggest hearing in US criminal history were finally available, but only as photocopied documents. Able to be read, yes, but only at an excruciatingly slow pace and only if you could get to somewhere that held a copy, such as libraries or an archival research library. The sheer effort required to wade through the stuffy volumes coupled with the cumbersome manner of cross-referencing meant few bothered to satisfy their thirst for knowledge. And so it prevailed for some time.

These were the early days of the internet being widely accessible, and it was a few more years before software was developed that permitted limited access to the reports. Eventually a breakthrough came about with the invention of PDF technology and Adobe readers, and the rest is history. The new millennium opened the door to the aged yet fascinating material. PDF technology offered enthusiasts the ideal tool to study at leisure all 8124 pages, more than 6000 photographs, statements, images and witness testimony, without the restriction of library times, the burden of joining a queue or suffering unnecessary scrutiny. It also allowed the researcher the chance to go back and forth, to labour over points of interest, to copy and compare and to properly analyse the many thousands of files. Thank God for PDF!

So, with the free spirit of one who knows not what lies ahead, I wiped my reading glasses and commenced my research in early 2009, determined to hunt out all the information, online or in hard copy from the bookshops. My local bookstore owner beamed with delight at my request. I'm sure she was mentally calculating her percentage on the 1000 related titles on JFK that had at one time or another been in print. And would I like some of those sent to my home address? she asked. I politely declined and turned my attention to what was available at the library and online. It wasn't proving to be easy, with more than 800 publications on the death of JFK! I spent weeks scouring websites, drinking lattes till the wee hours, lifting documents, eating take-away pizzas, reading reports and stories on the assassination, studying witness accounts and getting the 'job' inside my thinking. Social invitations soon dropped off as I dined alone on DVDs and breakfasted with videos of TV dramatisations and JFK feature films. I digested everything there was on the cyberspace menu and was left decidedly unsatisfied.

By then I had secured a copy of the 'retail' front volume of the Warren Commission Report, one of the items I had bought from eBay. I scanned a few pages as I walked home from the post office. Once back in my ergonomic chair I settled in to read. I'd heard enough to indicate that before the first interviewee had even stepped into the witness box, Earl Warren's team had been much maligned. I was curious to find out why. It was a properly constituted commission, akin to the Supreme Court of the United States, with a chairman, six representatives and fifteen assisting counsel. The chairman or his assistant would hear the evidence and one or more counsellors would do the lawyer work, hunt the truth. It reminded me of some of the task forces with which I had been involved, so why the doubt? Although the front volume report lay to rest many questions it was clearly just a briefing paper of what went before the Commission in its ten months of sitting. Obviously the story was bigger than this volume. I needed to get my hands on the unabridged account, the transcripts that contained every word by each witness, not an edited version. I needed access to the 'back volumes', all twenty-six of them.

I wanted to pore over the written words of the 552 American people who were there, the ones who heard the shots, saw the movement and felt the horror. I needed to read the testimony and affidavits and decipher the truth. When the opportunity presented itself to turn my own investigative know-how and extreme level of patience to finding an outcome, I had little hesitation. Trouble was, I also had no forewarning that like an investigative junkie I'd be drawn into a labyrinth of untruths, uncertainties, lies, courtroom twists and turns, the unravelling of which would see me burn the midnight oil for four and a half long years. So enslaved I became to finding the facts that I would stare at my laptop screen, greedily sampling one testimony after another for an estimated 4000 hours, criss-crossing the thousands of pages of Olivetti transcript. It was like falling head-first into a bottomless well of information. I would need to visit my optometrist six monthly and gradually increase the magnitude of my reading glasses by an overall three levels. Such was the intensity of the task, the strain to my eyes; such was the volume of information and the hold my forensic mission had on me.

Interestingly, as I read, I was always conscious of the many JFK websites that offered direct lifts, shortcuts through the maze of information and summaries and indexes that might have helped my task. Certainly the websites might have made life a tad easier, the task quicker, but there is one thing detectives tend to ignore: abridged versions of facts. However tempting it is to take the shortcut, the path itself is often dangerous. Who knows if the documents on the websites have been edited, the transcripts corrected or altered to suit the argument that is often the basis of the website's very existence. When I did surf the web and read some of the dozens of sites, I came away concerned at their selectivity, their ignorance of many of the facts, their lack of investigative know-how, their inability to see the forest, through their own trees. It was obvious many of the sites existed solely to push an opinion, promote a position on the death of a president. Sadly, a good number of the sites were scathing, if not insulting, in their blog comments concerning anyone who chose to mount an argument that differed from their own. It was as if some of the websites had claimed ownership on the subject of the assassination of JFK. The only sites I seemed to be able to rely upon, to double-check the occasional event or incident, were: jfkassassination.net and the comprehensive site by Vince Palamara, a man who has turned a hobby into an important virtual library of data on JFK. And the exemplary 'History Matters' website that holds copies of all testimony, affidavits and statements.

Midway through the reading and research process, I found another database. It was a mini version of the Warren Commission documents in the form of the Assassination Records Review Board (ARRB) documents, the transcript testimonies of the pathologists, medical assistants and photographers who performed the autopsy on John Fitzgerald Kennedy on the night of 22 November, 1963. Their evidence, vital to the understanding of what really happened on that fateful day, proved just as riveting a read as the Warren Commission Report. Another (almost) 1500 pages of testimony amounting to thousands of questions and answers gathered during an extraordinary hearing undertaken between the years 1995 and 1998, more than thirty years after the assassination. This commendable anthology of evidence from those (still living) members of the autopsy team can best be described as the icing on the cake. And the Warren Commission heard virtually none of the revelations.

•

The following pages are a forensic analysis of the entire Warren Commission Report as well as the Assassination Records Review Board hearings of 1995 to 1998. During the course of the narrative I will chart the journey, movement, actions and reactions of key witnesses following verbatim testimony of the sights they saw that afternoon in Dallas, Texas. I will note what they heard and the words they uttered as I knit the narrative together, one line at a time, like a long scarf of truth. To save on repetition I have quoted only one witness to a fact unless the comment is a revelation important enough to the story and to the flow. Collectively, this is the witnesses' story, good, bad or indifferent. Facts, until now largely unacknowledged, from affidavits, sworn testimony and cross-examination bring to life the (mostly) now dead citizens who had the bravery to step forward and the decency to raise their hand and tell the world what they knew. And as every detective knows, the way to find the truth behind a crime is invariably through the witnesses.

Where required, the narrative will cover pertinent events leading up to the assassination. In the case of Marina and Lee Harvey Oswald, I commence the story as far back as the late 1950s to allow the reader into the early life of the man who was undeniably in possession of a rifle and on the sixth floor of the Texas Bookshop Depository on 22 November, 1963. I have made sure to quote the exact words of Marina and the family and colleagues of Lee Harvey Oswald, and not to overstate with prose. The set-up chapters are there for one very good reason: history tends to have been rewritten on the subject of the death of JFK. The real story has suffered a mighty blow at the hands of sensationalism. I present the facts; the *truth* has long ago been pushed aside to make room for the fanciful, the exaggerated and the invented. The back-stories of Lee Harvey Oswald and his connections are fascinating in themselves, and they need to be read to be properly informed and see the broader picture.

I also provide an insight into the workings of the JFK autopsy procedure, the details of which may shock some readers. The rest is a narrative related to the crime scene analysis and the two facts that must be proved in any homicide investigation, motive and causation – the same two things that all conspiracy theories fail to deliver.

While stunned at my own findings, I now know why the truth has been concealed for so long; why this homicide, one of the most devastating in modern-day history, has been mired in absurd conspiracy theories for 50 years.

Here is the result . . . I hope you, too, can see the smoking gun.

CHAPTER 2

THE PRETTY RUSSIAN

Russia, 17 July, 1941. A baby girl is born to simple peasant folk and given the beautiful name of Marina Nikolaevna Prussakova. Tragically, World War Two claimed the life of her father soon after her birth, a man whose memory the pretty daughter would hold dear, learning at a tender age to live with sorrow. As a youngster she stayed close by her mother in their small house in Arkhangelsk, on the edge of the White Sea, where eventually a stepfather completed the family.

From her tiny bedroom window, Marina would gaze out at the tall, snow-capped mountains of Finland. She knew that the US was on the other side, out there somewhere far beyond. And like most of the new generation of Soviets, she dreamed of warmer climes, fields of daisies and Hollywood matinee idols. It was always so chilly in Northern Russia. Like the climate, her 1950s childhood saw relations between Russia and the US hit sub-zero, with both superpowers losing themselves to a Cold War. How President Eisenhower loved to throw this term around as he waved his finger at the Big Bear of Northern Europe. Perceived as an era of spying and political skulduggery, the intrigue was largely at government level. Most Russian workers needed to focus on keeping a fire burning, putting food on the table and enduring communism to be obsessed with any John le Carré-like fancies.

As the decade progressed, the teenage Marina and her family moved to Leningrad. With a learning institution on every corner and the finest ballet dancers in the world, Marina immersed herself in culture, history and Marxism, gaining a diploma in pharmacology. Soon afterwards, she began boarding with her uncle and aunt in picturesque Minsk. Uncle Prussakova was not only kindly towards his niece, he was a man with connections. As a colonel in the Interior Ministry Security Service and head of the local lumber industry, he was fortunate. His home was warm, a classic renaissance apartment nestled amid wide boulevards and seventeenth-century architecture. Marina adored her new world and secured a job in the pharmacy of a local hospital. Arm-in-arm with after-work friends, she delighted in long walks along the green-banked river that snaked through her city. Life was good and luxuries were plentiful, yet Marina, like many of her age group, believed that only in America would she be delivered all of life's answers.

With striking dark features, Marina blossomed like a Russian orchid, taking her first interest in the opposite sex. A portion of her meagre salary was spent on lipstick and the occasional bottle of French perfume, and heads were turning. She took to daydreaming of better tomorrows, cashmere twin sets, pearls and country drives in stylish European roadsters. At nineteen, independent and quite the young lady, she didn't know it but she was one step closer to her dream. It was then that a brash young Texan named Lee Harvey Oswald sashayed into her life. Of thin, almost weedy build, Lee had quit his capitalist homeland a year and a half earlier, lured east by a flirtation with Marxism. Ironically, he believed that Russia held all his answers.

As a teenager in the US Marines, Oswald was disliked by most. He rarely went drinking or left the base to socialise with others and failed to develop any significant friendships. None of his fellow marines ever saw him in the company of a woman; a few even thought him homosexual. Having achieved only slightly above the minimum rating required to become a sharp shooter, Lee managed to wound himself in the arm with a bullet from his own .22 calibre pistol while sitting in his barracks, an embarrassment for a kid who envisioned himself in the role of a weapons trainer. He was a loner and a sufferer, spending most of his free time poring over books. Conjuring a fascination for all things Soviet, Lee had even taught himself the Russian language. He confided to his sergeant that as a child he often went hungry and was tired of being 'kicked around', hence his manner towards his superiors was often belligerent.

In 1958 Oswald declared a desire to go to the Sierra Maestra to help Cuban rebel leader Fidel Castro train his troops. Idolising Castro's ways, Lee began to champion himself in the role of a revolutionary more than a communist. One of his few army acquaintances was nicknamed 'Hidell', a name that Oswald often jested sounded a lot like 'Fidel'. This was clearly a name he thought would come in handy, for later use. By the time he left the armed services in September 1959, Lee had managed to obtain the higher qualification of marksman, having scored in the 'high expert' range. This was the only notable achievement in an otherwise ordinary and short career. While the title sounded impressive, in reality the qualification was mediocre in the serious world of military weaponry.

With his sights firmly set on Russian culture and choosing defection over a holiday, the dishonourably discharged nineteen-year-old soldier ran from his southern American roots and landed in Moscow, full of optimism, believing that only in the Soviet Union could he unravel life's puzzles.

Upon arrival, the only work he could find was that of an unskilled factory worker. On a fast track to amounting to very little, his smooth-talking American drawl managed to charm an unworldly and naive Russian girl seeking discovery. East met West at a local dance hall where an ensemble of neighbourhood musicians played too many variations on the polka and the brash courted the shy. Instantly, Marina was smitten. But no sooner had the music stopped than her cowboy fell ill and was admitted to hospital. Dressed in her Soviet starched pharmaceutical uniform, Marina made regular visits to his bedside. Without a game plan, and facing the harsh reality of Russian life, Lee fell back on what he did best: he sweet-talked his big-eyed girl and exaggerated his achievements. He boasted of involvement in guerrilla warfare, blowing up bridges, derailing trains and manufacturing bombs. These racy escapades were more colourful in his mind than in reality: Lee had never undertaken any stealth combat training.

The sub-zero temperatures in the sterile hospital ward thawed as the Russian Florence Nightingale nursed her Texan radical back to health. Suddenly everything seemed possible for both of them. Lee proposed marriage, promising his bride the world. Marina's family was as besotted as their intended, believing her young, fresh-faced man to be fine husband material. Not everyone, it seemed, was obsessed with global politics – even the stiff-necked colonel encouraged the frivolity, happy with his niece's choice of beau. Marina and Lee were married ten days later and the band played on.

Within a month the groom tested the loyalty of his in-laws, announcing a change of heart that no one saw coming. His hankering for a Russian lifestyle, his romance with the Soviet mystery, had turned sour. Reality had hit. The weather was bleak, money scarce and factory work was proving to be hard toil. Having recovered from one illness, he was now homesick for the star-spangled banner. Of course Lee planned to take his new wife with him. Crestfallen, the colonel tried valiantly to dissuade Lee from leaving. Anxiety brewed in their Russian home as other elders began to look on Lee with less admiring eyes. Cracks were appearing in the man's façade and doubt reigned. Not the ideal sentiment for a union, especially in 1961 when conformity and family acceptance were the underpinning of a marriage, whether in the land of the bear or the eagle.

Few people of the time travelled between the US and Russia; in fact, few people travelled anywhere. And if they did choose the Soviet Union, they undertook the task after much consideration and planning – otherwise, nervous authorities might require answers to long lists of questions. The now-pregnant Marina sided with her husband. The couple packed their bags, remaining on Russian soil only long enough to give their first-born child, June, a Soviet birthright.

Traditional celebrations prevailed as extended family put aside their misgivings and rejoiced with the new parents. In a gesture of goodwill the colonel assisted with the expediency of their visa applications to the US, calling in some favours from his diplomatic connections. The three were away, a young family of mixed backgrounds and fluctuating ideals. Moscow via Poland via Germany via Holland, destination America.

Walking down the gangway of the SS *Rotterdam* in the height of a New York summer, Marina scanned the landscape for her statue of freedom. But all Lee offered was a two-dollar room in a dive off Times Square and a handbasin that became a baby bath for one long miserable night. It was 1962 and Marina's girlhood fantasies of movie stars and romance were fading with the burden of motherhood and immigrant isolation. While Lee disappeared onto the dark, violent streets, Marina changed nappies and stared out onto a rusted fire escape. Broadway, the boulevard of dreams, felt an eternity away. There were no lights shining on this Russian wife who slowly realised her horizons had been lost, for good.

The following afternoon the family boarded a jet airliner bound for a tarmac in dusty Dallas, Texas. Whistling tumbleweeds greeted the young family, and the rumbling of an idling Oldsmobile. At the wheel was Robert Oswald, Lee's brother, with whom they would room unhappily for the next two months. Things didn't get any better with the next batch of family-hopping. Lee's impossibly difficult mother, Marguerite, saw no shine in her son's choice of bride. By September, Lee's boast of booming opportunity in the land of democracy had amounted to nothing more than a job as an unskilled metalworker at a dollar twenty-five an hour. But at least he was able to move his family into a rundown apartment, where Marina attempted to create her haven, albeit subject to copious unwanted visits from the often sneering Marguerite.

The purchase of a little luxury for the home, a black and white television, delighted the new bride, but marital bliss, if it ever existed, was short-lived. Lee's mood changed almost overnight, from congenial to angry tyrant. He came home early one day to find Marina attempting to learn English from an afternoon soap opera. Agitated, he pulled the plug, picked up the television and returned it to the department store. From that time onwards the Oswald home suffered long bouts of silence broken only by baby June's cries as her kitchen-bound mother attempted to rock the child to sleep.

Marina tried to battle through by seeking out fellow Russian immigrants, people who could offer her company and the simple joy of conversation in her native language. She took to creating her own world, arranging coffee mornings at her home, smiling, and nurturing new acquaintances, relishing the simple pleasure of preparing a plate of sandwiches or a sponge cake to share. Lee, on the other hand, pursued a path of isolation and withdrawal into himself. The two opposites, the Russian and the American, were now in their own domestic cold war.

Lee became an obsessive reader of serious texts, selecting mostly works from American history, Marxism and various staid biographies of eminent statesmen. Before long, he came to regard Russian immigrants as miserable souls. He failed to understand or appreciate the need for betterment, to be able to buy into a slice of a lifestyle that they felt only the US could offer them. His love of Russia had deteriorated to disdain and Marina sensed that same feeling brewing towards her. Her husband had become enthralled by renewed interest in another world issue: Cuba.

Marina's reaction was to focus on her child and her own independence. The dour Texan didn't take kindly to his wife's resilience, expecting her to be needy, more wanting of her man. He declared that he didn't want Marina to have any contact with the outside world, labelling his wife's friends as 'fools' for having left Russia, and 'traitors' attempting to dissuade her from any meaningful friendships. If this irrational jealousy wasn't enough for Marina to bear, Lee would often take to beating her if he saw her administer any discipline to their daughter. For all his hardline ways, Lee was extremely possessive of June, and doted on her. It was a weakness Marina exploited. She would have Lee believe she was venturing out to buy something for 'his baby', something important, only to run to a girlfriend and seek refuge for a few hours. The great American dream was fast being replaced by fear. Yet, the good Russian wife persevered, desperately trying to find a middle ground in a marriage that was clearly doomed.

An unexpected knock on the door provided the ideal distraction for a man dulled by marriage and seeking escapism. Two lowly FBI agents stood on his threshold, grey suited and poker faced. They were on the most basic administrative task, an immigration enquiry relating to the newly arrived Russian. In true Cold War fashion all Russian migrants were routinely assessed. The bureau had sent the agents to the Oswald home for the sole purpose of establishing that the young woman was, in fact, cohabiting with her husband. As uninteresting and brief as their duty was, Lee saw adventure in their visit, his imagination running wild. The two suits sat and completed their flick-and-tick paperwork while the metalworker's mind filled with intrigue. He waylaid the attention of the FBI for two long hours, going into enormous detail on his visit to Russia and offering up his political opinions. Lee had the perfect opportunity to spice up his profile, to embellish his persona: from a man of no skills to a person of interest. Indeed, a man of importance to the government. When the agents had left, Lee recounted his version of the meeting to his wife in his reasonable turn of the Russian language. He insisted that the agents had attempted to enlist him as a spy. In actuality the agents had formed the opposite viewpoint while suffering Lee's long-winded story, and no recruitment took place. But in Lee's delusional mind, jealousy and fear had joined hands with madness in what was the onset of the decline of a man struggling with life, battling reality. His bewildered wife served a cold dinner to a chuffed husband lost to self-importance.

Of all the Russians to befriend Marina, the only one to take a shine to Lee was the elderly George de Mohrenschildt. A big, burly, matter-of-fact man, he'd been married four times, had several adult daughters and a pair of barking dogs. He also had a vivid imagination and a lot of stories to tell. Lee and George were bound to be buddies. Each time the men got together, the Oswald's quiet home was suddenly filled with boisterous discourse on politics, communism and world leaders. George's current wife, in a story that was as fanciful as Lee's spy recruitment program, would interject with her own boast of having once known the elegant Jacqueline Kennedy. Exaggeration was welcome in this group of friends. The talk between the two women would turn to the latest fashion gossip and invariably lead to discussions about the beautiful First Lady. Lee was rarely amused, more fascinated with talk of the hard political than tabloid tidbits. Unlike most of America, who along with Marina had formed a genuine affection for the handsome president and his stylish wife, Lee shared no such feelings.

Becoming the most reticent of the four during their chats, Lee would hold his jealousy tightly in check while the guests remained in his home. But once the front door was locked tight for the night, Lee offered his opinions on the Kennedys in a flamboyant show of anger. The union of these two opposites was in strife; separation was not only imminent but in the forefront of Marina's mind. Born with a strong disposition and an inability to tolerate abuse, she realised that she had married a man she did not know, a troubled man with a troubled mind. Her puzzle was how to find a way out of her escalating mess.

By 1962 the Oswalds were introduced to a woman by the name of Ruth Paine. Ten years Marina's senior, Ruth would become an enduring friend at a time when friendship was not only rare but frowned upon by Marina's husband. The two women bonded quickly and strong-willed Ruth sensed her young immigrant girlfriend was in strife and in need of support. Ultimately the one responsible for Marina's first steps into life as a single parent, Ruth offered Marina and June sanctuary in her shared apartment. Within weeks of their meeting, Marina felt not only the support of a real friend but relief at finding the freedom she was promised, albeit under very different circumstances.

An unimpressed Lee took a room at the YMCA in the centre of Dallas, reacquainting himself with a familiar comrade, isolation. The separation gave them both the opportunity to think. Marina was far from optimistic about reconciliation despite the efforts of her now apologetic husband. Keen to win back her affections, Lee had turned the charm on hot and strong. He changed jobs, from metalworker to photographic laboratory assistant, and his salary kicked up to a dollar forty an hour, the average wage for unskilled labour at a time when a packet of cigarettes was a dime and a dollar would take you on a Greyhound bus to the next state.

As a weekend father, Lee visited his girls on Saturdays when they would all venture out to a nearby lake for a picnic. Marina would prepare a packed lunch and a thermos and Lee would laugh and giggle, turning on his charm, delighting in the time spent with baby June. The disheartened mother couldn't help but smile at the lengths to which her husband was going to win her back; however, his pattern of unpredictable behaviour had her fully aware of his real traits. His anti-Russian and anti-religious sentiments meant Marina undertook the baptism of their daughter at a tiny local church without his knowledge.

The adage of distance allowing the heart to grow fonder worked for the Oswalds, for a time, with husband lying alone of a night, lost to thoughts of reconciliation, and wife exhausting herself with an active child. If they had one thing in common, it would be their poor communication skills. With Lee unable and unwilling to develop any meaningful friendships and Marina incapable of speaking English, their lives were oddly similar. Lee rented a tiny one-bedroom apartment in downtown Dallas for the going rate of sixty dollars a month and the Oswald family eventually reconciled, much to the annoyance of Ruth Paine, who had hoped Marina might continue to tough it out. Within days, Lee's foul moods returned. Almost from the time Marina's well-used suitcase landed on the doorstep, their new home was anything but harmonious. Marina could see that her breadwinner was displaying two distinct personalities. On the one hand he would show all the signs of being a devoted family man, quiet and helpful. Then, puzzlingly, he would turn into an ill-tempered tyrant over the most trivial of matters, perhaps dinner being five minutes late or if Marina omitted to put a butter dish on the table. Even a family outing proved difficult, as Lee was never able to drive a motorcar. His fix-all answer to his growing list of frustrations was to physically abuse his wife. Despite her attempts to hide her injuries beneath scarves, sunglasses and make-up, the tell-tale bruises were becoming obvious, with friends whispering, urging her to leave. Alienated by Lee's continuing anti-social behaviour, most of them drifted away. The only spark in their home came with old George, but he, too, was tiring of Lee's erratic manner so his visits dropped away.

The Russian with the lovely name had become a browbeaten, one-dimensional victim of suburbia. Her revolutionary road had come to a dead end. She took refuge with sympathetic neighbours, but inwardly she longed to return to her homeland, to a place of equality and a culture to which she belonged. She reached out to an old flame in Russia in a short letter, revealing her sadness and pondering how her life would have been had she married him instead. With true postal efficiency, the letter was returned to sender: the postage was one cent short. Lee opened the letter to read of his wife's raw, heartfelt pain. He saw it as the ultimate betrayal. Like a headmaster with a naughty child, Lee forced Marina to read the letter aloud, word for word, until tears saturated her cheeks. Then her husband's cruel hands came down on her, his fists beating her until once again she was submissive and repentant. Marina was left feeling ashamed, foolish and even more alone.

As an ideal distraction to the regular domestic violence, and perhaps as a blessing in disguise, Lee began studying English and typing three nights a week. He had no friends, so why or to whom he needed to type was anyone's guess. On the nights he wasn't at school, he would pore over history books, reading insatiably. From the time he walked in the front door at 5pm, he would sit alone and read, sometimes in the bath, other times on the back porch. Although Marina was safe from his temper while he followed his solitary pursuits, she was increasingly frustrated by her forced isolation and Lee's growing jealousy. She had begun to give serious contemplation to the issue of divorce, an extraordinarily rare occurrence at that time in American culture, more so for a migrant who hadn't yet satisfied all the immigration red tape and formalities, a fact that weighed heavily upon her.

Lee's chaotic response to his wife's predicament was to hand her a pen and paper and order her to request a visa to return to Russia. Spiralling further into psychosis, he was forever blaming his lot on external events, this time dissatisfaction with his life in the US. His ball had fallen into the other court again, as his nationalism flip-flopped to the other side once again.

In an attempt to have his dishonourable discharge from the marines reversed, Lee wrote to John Connally, the Secretary of the Navy at the time of his disgrace. Mr Connally had resigned his post a month earlier to become the Governor of Texas. The letter was reassigned, lost in the system. Frustrated by the lack of response Lee visited the new governor's office, wandering aimlessly in the reception area before giving up and morosely returning home.

His troubled mind considered the possibility of the family returning to Russia, where Marina could find work. Now exasperated by his behaviour, Marina staunchly rebutted the idea. She demanded Lee change his ways, citing his disturbed behaviour, not their country of residence, as the cause of their tensions. In true narcissistic fashion Lee rebuffed her, declaring that a good wife would accept him as he was. Marina then acquiesced: she would return to Russia if Lee would agree to divorce her. On this point he flatly declined. They applied to return to Russia but, unbeknown to Marina, Lee wrote to the Soviet Embassy asking for each submission to be treated separately.

It was March 1963 when Marina first saw a rifle propped in a corner of a room of their apartment in Neely Street. It was a small room that Lee kept private, where he locked away his secrets. He had instructed her never to enter and often shooed her away when she came near. When Marina objected to the presence of a rifle in her home, Lee became obstinate, replying it would, 'come in handy some time for hunting.' In shoot-em-up Texas a gun was not just a farmer's tool as in Marina's Russia, it was a symbol of manhood. And as such it needed to be held daily, cleaned regularly and sighted often. Lee would drape the firearm lovingly with a coat as if putting it to bed when he went out and, of course, it would go on to play a starring role in his future.

As Lee toyed with his Italian-made Carcano bolt-action rifle, Marina harboured a strange feeling in the pit of her stomach that he was preparing for something. He had become increasingly secretive and was coming and going at odd times from the family home with the rifle and a reflex camera. Old George, too, became an aficionado of the rifle and would occasionally accompany Lee to the local airport, quirkily named Love Field, for target practice. It was during one of Lee's many bouts of absenteeism that Marina uncovered photographs of an unknown residence tucked away in her husband's secret room. They were photographs of the home of General Edwin Walker, an army retiree who had entered politics. As far as Oswald was concerned, Walker was a 'hated right-wing activist' but when Marina challenged him to explain the photographs, he refused to comment. Little did she know that her husband was embroiled in amateur surveillance on the retired general, and that he was thinking of killing the man.

On a pleasant spring morning that same year, Marina took advantage of the sunshine to hang the washing on the line in their backyard. Toting his camera and the Carcano rifle, Lee emerged from the house dressed in his Sunday best. He was looking for attention and a few photographs of himself for posterity. He showed Marina how to operate the camera and posed for several studies holding his rifle and a .36 Smith & Wesson revolver, recently purchased from Klein's sporting goods store using his newly created alias, 'A Hidell'. Clearly not the man of intrigue he hoped to be just yet, Oswald had the gun posted to a post office box listed in his correct name. After the roll of film had been developed at the local drug store, Lee insisted that one of the photographs be kept in the family album for his beloved June.

After a routinely silent dinner at their humble kitchen table, Lee left the apartment, ostensibly to catch the bus to night school. Marina saw something odd in his eyes that night, a look that worried her as he slammed the flimsy front door. She believed there was more than night school on her husband's troubled mind. Her wariness caused her to think hard about the man, but did not prepare her for the note Lee had left behind.

Simply headed 'if I am arrested', it contained enough money for the family to get by for some time and a list of instructions detailing where the key to their post office box was kept. When Marina saw that the rifle was missing she felt shivers through her soul. The bewildered wife with very little English and no understanding of how to call for help sat shaken and scared, waiting for her husband's return. And return he did, very late that evening, looking stressed and pale. He had run several kilometres to catch a bus home in time to listen to radio news reports of his exploit. He claimed to have been out hunting, his prey: General Walker. Lee boasted of taking precise aim at his target, who stood oblivious at his window, looking into the night. Luckily for the retired officer, the confused ex-army soldier with his treasured Italian-made World War Two bolt action rifle was a poor shot. Marina was dumbstruck, her worst fear realised. She may well be married to a murderer.

As his nervous fingers tuned the radio, Lee was unaware that his bullet had only grazed a window frame where Walker had been standing, looking out; there was no death or injury, not even an awareness of the shot. Oswald was crestfallen, having hoped for radio news of his exploit, only to find rock 'n' roll music. No one knew of his deed. He would later work out that he had not, in fact, hit his target, and he took to brooding. Marina, however, was growing more frantic and felt trapped. She was unable to comprehend what to do, how to take action. She also trusted in the popularly held notion that a wife could not testify against her husband. Her concession to the incident was to obtain Lee's promise that it would not happen again. She tucked the note he had left for her between the pages of a cookbook and lay awake all night, reflecting on the mess in her life and what lay beside her.

In the morning Marina confronted Lee about his missing rifle. She had spent hours cradling baby June, pondering the safety of staying under the same roof as a killer. In a hauntingly matter-of-fact manner, Lee claimed that it was buried somewhere far away where the 'dogs couldn't find it'. Buried, in the bushland, perhaps near his prey, General Walker. Yet another heated argument ensued, a mix of yelled Russian and equally loud English and wild gesticulating of hands. Marina demanded to know why her husband would want to kill a man and what could any man have done to deserve such a fate. With his twisted logic, Lee replied '. . . what would you say if somebody got rid of Hitler at the right time? So if you don't know about General Walker, how can you speak up on his behalf?' Loosened up by his oratory, he told her he had been planning the shooting for two months. Boastfully, he pulled out the pictures of the mysterious house Marina had discovered weeks earlier, the pictures he had taken of the Walker residence. Lee also produced a private journal containing notations of surveillance related to the General's home as well as maps and sketches detailing his approach path and escape route. With the manner of a madman he placed one of the Walker photos in the family album alongside snaps of Leningrad, New Orleans and of himself in the army. Soon after, Lee began a set of private memoirs, nightly adding tidbits and comments, before tucking it away for safekeeping in his secret room.

A few days later, as she cleared away the afternoon tea, Marina overheard the tail end of a conversation with George, words leading her to speculate that perhaps the old man was as demented as her husband. '. . . Lee, how is it possible that you missed?' It appeared she must also doubt the integrity of her last remaining visitor, an elderly native of her beloved Russia and a man she had previously encouraged her husband to befriend.

It wasn't much later that Lee lost his job. For reasons unknown to his wife, he floated a notion to relocate the family to New Orleans. Marina jumped at the plan, seeing it as a way of preventing any further attempts on the life of General Walker and distancing him from old George, who seemed to have become a confidant of the wrong type. The couple was in agreement for the first time since leaving Minsk. So, in late April, Lee departed for New Orleans, knocking on the door of his aunt, Lillian Murret. Shortly after, to the great relief of his uncle and cousin who didn't ever warm to their relative, Lee secured a position at the Reilly Coffee Co at a dollar thirty-five an hour and found a small rental apartment. Marina and June stayed temporarily with Ruth Paine, who offered them free board in return for Russian language lessons, and later drove Marina and her baby to their new abode. Despite the generous nature of Marina's now best friend, Lee still considered her little more than a 'stupid woman'.

During their time in Louisiana Lee immersed himself deeper in left-wing politics, joining the Play Fair for Cuba Committee (PFCC), an inconsequential organisation made up largely of misfits and displaced persons. Clutching onto the East–West intrigue of the time the group members soon found themselves at the wrong end of the prying binoculars of the FBI.

A man with a newfound political agenda needed to communicate with his fold, so Lee rented a PO box, rolling out his preferred pseudonym, 'AJ Hidell', the one he had used to purchase the Smith & Wesson handgun. This was the first time Marina had heard Lee use the alias. He explained the link as derived from 'Fidel' and then laughed to himself. The wannabe communist activist never used his own name, always assuming the surname 'Hidell'. In time he obtained medications, had a smallpox vaccination and gathered a network of PO boxes in Dallas, all the time posing as 'A Hidell'. Perhaps his most elaborate creation was the forgery of a US Marine Corps identity card with the alias alongside his own photograph. Trouble was, for a spy he failed dismally, placing his actual name on the application forms and the PO box authority cards. While his mind was lost to the intrigue of double identities it would not be too difficult for any investigating detective to link the two names with matching handwriting, photographs and addresses, but Lee hadn't considered that in the slightest.

Lee Harvey Oswald found great comfort in standing on a lonely street corner handing out leaflets to blasé passers-by; for the first time in his life he had a cause. It was the aim of the Play Fair group to make US citizens aware of the plight of the Cubans, who had been subjugated four years earlier by Fidel Castro and his revolutionaries. Lee liked that word: revolutionary. It was in his history books and now in his mindset, so he printed 1000 handbills and stood on his corner.

During one of these handout days a scuffle ensued between Lee and some passers-by. He was arrested along with another man. After a night in jail he was interviewed by John Quigley, a street-level FBI agent given the mundane task of reporting on political strife. Lee relished the arrest. Released on bail after being charged with disturbing the peace and fined ten dollars, he saw the experience as elevating him in importance, making him a key player in his own little game of intrigue. Marina believed Lee had wanted to be arrested, photographed and written about in newspapers, to become 'known', to be famous. He hoped, as a result, that the Cuban government might welcome him to their country. He was right on one front: he did feature in the newspaper, standing alone with a handful of leaflets. But no one contacted him and no one seemed to care.

During the heat of that summer Lee distributed PFCC literature at the wharf where the warship USS *Wasp* was docked. A week later, without Marina's knowledge, he applied for a new passport. Lee had become more disoriented than ever and now desperately wanted to return to Russia.

In keeping with the blackness of his mood, Lee would sit on his porch alone after dark, nursing his rifle for hours on end, peering through the telescopic viewfinder. With his grandiose affectations fostering his sick imagination, he saw himself as an outstanding individual, claiming he would be 'prime minister in twenty years time'. Despite his confidence of obtaining high office he remained unable to hold down a simple job and was fired from the Reilly Coffee Co. in July 1963.

The impact of the dismissal was softened dramatically when a letter arrived from a communist philosopher based in New York, encouraging Lee's leaflet duties on the New Orleans streets. Apparently the philosopher had seen the picture in the paper and wanted to praise Lee. Lee embraced the praise as an accolade from a truly great individual, worth repeating over and over to his dulled wife. From what Marina surmised, his leaflet-handing duties were simply a waste of time, pulling him further away from reality. Lee persisted; he was being rebirthed. Then, as if he had undergone an epiphany, he announced that he was leaving for Cuba. All he knew of the tiny country in the Caribbean Sea came from what he had read in his outdated books, written many years before the revolution and of no value to anyone seeking to run in that direction. He hatched a scheme whereby he would travel to Cuba, fake the kidnapping of an aircraft and inform the newspapers. A tactical move, designed to gain notoriety. He began to check airline timetables from New Orleans to Cuba with a view to carrying out his plan. He became preoccupied with Fidel Castro, whom he adulated, and wrote a succession of letters to the PFCC branch in New York. One of his plans involved heading for Havana alone. It was as if he had graduated from leaflet duties to being the new Che Guevara, spring-boarding into an exciting new mission. In his mind, he too had become a revolutionary and his cause had become crystal clear: head for Cuba and join the revolution.

Marina declared that she and the baby weren't going; he would be alone on his communist jaunt. She wouldn't tolerate any further relocations and would have nothing of his nonsense. Furthermore, she had become so used to the ranting and raving of her delusional husband that she had taken to ignoring him completely, the only way she could cope. She now wanted just one thing from him: the occasional translation of a newspaper or magazine article on the popular President Kennedy, which Lee suffered without comment. He had learned to hide his jealousy well.

Despite having Lee's family in New Orleans, who were always very kind to Marina, not a soul came to visit them. No one sought the company of the confused young man from Dallas and no one understood the language of his Russian bride. Marina had fallen into utter isolation. She made attempts to learn English, thinking that at least in time she might be able to fend for herself. With her self-centred husband too absorbed in plotting his own communist tryst to assist his wife's efforts, she received no help or study materials.

A pleasant distraction for the now eight months pregnant Marina arrived with her friend Ruth, who appeared on the doorstep for a much-needed catch-up. Marina was delighted by Ruth's suggestion that they return to Dallas together and share Ruth's apartment in preparation for the birth. Lee was less than enthusiastic about babies or Texas. He was headed for Mexico, chasing his Cuban dream. For the second time Ruth would save her young friend, to the disdain of the brooding communist sympathiser. The trio of girls packed up and departed New Orleans in September 1963. Lee's only contribution was to care for his most important piece of luggage. He wrapped his rifle in a blanket and hid it in Ruth's car. Then Lee and Marina were away again, this time in opposite directions.

Upon arrival at Ruth's apartment, the first thing Marina did was to secrete the blanketed parcel in the garage. Ashamed of having to conceal the weapon from Ruth, she felt nonetheless unable to challenge Lee. His violent temper was best avoided.

Lee travelled to Mexico City, checking in at the Hotel del Comercio. He visited the Cuban Embassy to apply for permission to travel to Cuba, but his application was denied. Collecting his wits and gritting his teeth, he conjured his next move. His bag of confused thoughts held only one other option: a visa to the Soviet Union. When that, too, was refused, he headed back to Dallas, tail between his legs. Hopelessly stuck in an unfulfilled fantasy of political intrigue, the lone Texan was now a dejected man. Forced to return home minus a revolutionary hero's welcome he faced the doom of domesticity and a working life that offered a dollar forty an hour. Not surprisingly, Lee was secretive about his one-week round-trip to Mexico. He had to be, he had nothing to tell. To make amends he gave Marina a man's bracelet, proffering that he had bought it especially for her in Mexico. Lee was turning on the charm again. A less-than-delighted Marina was not responding, however, as she was certain she had seen an identical piece of cosmetic jewellery on the streets in New Orleans only weeks earlier.

In Lee's absence Ruth and Marina had cemented their friendship. Their living arrangement, in Ruth's apartment, gave Marina a sense of peace and an environment that provided the expectant mother the support she needed. In return, Marina continued to instruct Ruth in the Russian language. Lee hoped to take a bed in the apartment and to reconcile his differences with his wife, but the now more self-assured Marina was hesitant. Lee then rented a room and went in search of work.

His first room was at a boarding house run by Mary Bledsoe. The rent was seven dollars a week, but it was to be short-lived, in fact long enough only for the seven dollars to run out. Mary thought Lee was odd, saying, 'There was something about him', and chose to have a vacant room rather than Lee as a guest. He then knocked on the door of a boarding house run by Mrs Earlene Roberts and took a room on 14 October for an indefinite period. Oswald used an alias to his landlady, she only knew him as OH Lee. Earlene kept to herself, not bothering with the comings and goings of her guests, but she did observe that Lee 'never went out, always stayed at home'.

After a while and with the help of Ruth's neighbours, Lee was told of a job offer at the Texas School Book Depository.

Lee went for an interview, as an order-filler, the person who packs the boxes, for two hundred and thirty dollars a month. He was back to being nobody again, back to being normal, like everyone else. At least he still had his rifle hidden away in Ruth's garage. Apart from working at the Texas School Book Depository, his only activity was to visit his wife and family on weekends.

Lee Harvey Oswald was swinging like an out-of-balance pendulum. His imagination had brewed a deep level of paranoia insofar as he believed that the FBI was targeting him. He instructed Marina that they weren't, under any circumstances, to find out where he lived, and should an agent come looking for him she was to claim no knowledge, take down the licence plate number of the car and pass it on to him. In truth, the FBI had scant interest in the Oswalds, other than to finalise Marina's migration status. Lee continued to transcribe material into his 'secret' journal, jotting notes and ideas, treating it more as a diary than a set of memoirs. Most inscriptions developed a particular flavour: a distinct tang of FBI obsession.

On the crest of November, Lee suggested to Marina that she should dismiss any thoughts of returning to Russia and remain in the US, where she would be under the protection of the FBI. Marina could only sigh at his latest notion. One of Lee's diary entries read, 'I and my wife strongly protest tactics by the notorious FBI'. Lee had taken to referring to himself as a past secretary of the PFCC, a position he had never held. His wife thought him crazy.

When Marina gave birth to Audrey, their second child, Lee stayed at home with little June. He didn't phone the hospital during labour or after the birth, although on the one occasion he did visit, he had tears in his eyes, overwhelmingly proud and happy to be a father for the second time. He stayed over for two weekends when Marina and her baby returned home, travelling to and from his new workplace with his co-worker Wesley, who was sharing a house with his sister nearby.

The ranting of Lee Harvey Oswald finally started to catch up with him through November: a whisper filtered through to FBI agents Wilson and Hosty, who visited Ruth and Marina's home. Their enquiry related to Lee's possible involvement with a Cuban committee and they requested Marina pass on their telephone number to him. The agents also appealed to Ruth to ascertain Lee's private address, which she undertook to do. As instructed by her husband, Marina wrote down the vehicle's registration number in Lee's journal. At long last, Lee had truly found himself to be 'a person of interest'. Oddly, his reaction was not what might have been expected. He became upset and moody, almost fearful. A scared man, for the first time he showed signs of normalcy, as if he had been jolted back to reality. He became more involved with his children and more attentive to Marina, which pleased her. Marina even attempted to divert his grey moods by giving him driving lessons, and they went for walks with the babies. Lee begged her to return to living as a family unit again. Although he had started to treat her with more kindness than she could remember, and even flashes of affection, she remained hesitant. She was happier to remain apart. Lee was in limbo in a world of uncertainty, with a marriage hanging by a thread and a pending interrogation by his arch-enemy, that supremely secretive Federal Bureau of Investigation.

November 21, 1963, a normal day for the mother of two, more nappies and chores from dawn to dusk. Marina retired to her bedroom at 11.30pm, exhausted, having spent a busy night with the children. Lee had dropped over earlier expecting to stay the night. He arrived with cap in hand, again asking to reconcile the marriage. Suffering another refusal he fell back into his silent, dark mode. They did watch the news service together, though. Marina delighted in the footage of President Kennedy and his wife Jackie. The President was expected in Dallas the following day for a visit and motorcade; the world's attention would be on the dusty Texan town. Lee didn't stir. Marina seemed enthralled, captivated by the world's most important politician and commented with a delicious smile on how handsome he was and what a fine man America had for a leader. Lee continued to watch the news service in silence, observing his wife's adoration. He hurt badly. Marina sensed her husband's jealousy return, but this time she was lost to the black and white images of a smiling, smartly attired man.

Busy with dishes, Marina thought her husband had gone to bed sometime after 9.30pm. Ruth certainly had and the apartment was in darkness. When Marina rose the next morning, her estranged husband was long gone and the mood was steely quiet. But, something else was also gone. Marina had a feeling, an odd sense that all was not well, a feeling that had lasted all night. She checked the garage and discovered Lee's prized possession, his Carcano rifle, was missing, but the blanket was still there, flopped on the garage floor. And, with a mix of shock and relief, on the kitchen table she saw her husband's wedding ring.

CHAPTER 3

THE WORKMATE

DALLAS, SEPTEMBER 1963

Wesley Frazier was just nineteen years old when he blew into Dallas. Originally from Huntsville, to the south, he'd packed his Wrangler denims and Cuban-heeled boots and left the family home in search of work and big-city adventure. His first stop was his older sister, who lived with her partner and three toddlers in Irving, a suburb half an hour's drive outside town. She welcomed her kid brother, offered him a room. Wesley was neither educated nor savvy, but he was good-natured; he'd rather do a good turn than a bad one, and he adored his little nieces. Thankful for a soft bed and a good meal, he soon headed out to scout for work, to pay his way.

Knocking on doors of employment agencies, the boy with the ready smile and the hometown drawl soon landed a job at the Texas School Book Depository, filling orders. For a dollar twenty-five an hour all he had to do was match books to an invoice sheet, fill a box and close the lid. The hours were easy, 8am to 4.45pm, with forty-five minutes for lunch at noon. The depository warehouse was an imposing building, tall for the early 1960s, all of seven floors high. It stuck out on the landscape like a giant red brick monolith. As a workplace, the best thing about it was the expansive view, overlooking a grassy knoll and the city skyline.

Wesley fell into a comfortable daily routine. Rising at 6.30am, he'd be at the breakfast table by 7am, entertain his cheeky-monkey nieces in between mouthfuls till just on 7.20am. Then, scooping up his brown paper bag lunch and waving his sister goodbye, he'd be in his jalopy, pushing through the traffic to work. His custom extended to parking his car in the same lot, just a couple of doors up from the depository, and punching his time card at bang on 8am. He was fitting in nicely to the pattern of life, it was just the work that was dull. To compensate, management had allowed the employees to create a dominoes room on the ground floor, so the bored could play board games during their lunch break. And for those looking for less of a challenge the first-floor tearoom candy machine or the Dr Pepper soda dispenser was the place to drop a few dimes.

Over the evening meal one night in mid-October, Wesley's sister mentioned that a neighbour's friend was commencing work at the depository and that Wesley should keep a look out, say howdy. That friend was Lee Harvey Oswald. Ruth and Marina were living around the corner from the Fraziers and had been enjoying a little small talk over the back fence with Wesley's sister. So Wesley sought out Lee and introduced himself; he was keen to make new friends. Most people in the city, he had discovered, kept pretty much to themselves; they'd pass you by rather than stop and chat. He learnt that Lee was also new to town and had taken a room in the city, where he stayed during the week. On weekends he'd visit his wife and small children. As odd as that arrangement seemed, Wesley wasn't the sort to pry. The oddity that piqued his interest was that Lee couldn't drive a car, although he did say he was taking lessons and intended to buy a vehicle one day. Wesley learnt quickly that Lee often seemed to have intentions to do this or that.

Each Friday after work Lee would accept a lift home with Wesley to Irving, spend the weekend at his wife's place and return on Monday morning with Wesley to the depository. Wesley learnt very little about his mate on those trips, other than that Lee adored his baby girls and had travelled to Germany, France and Russia. He never spoke of his wife being Russian; in fact, he never spoke much of anything. Lee attempted a discourse on Marxism and communism once, but the subject matter was incomprehensible to the small-town driver. About the only thing that the two co-workers had in common was that both took a brown paper bag cut lunch each day, and both chose to eat their lunch at their desks, Lee on the upper level where he worked and Wesley on the lower, both filling orders.

Life was oh-so predictable. Thursday 21 November rolled around quickly. It was coming up to the sixth weekend that Wesley had played chauffer and his passenger hadn't once put his hand in his pocket for fuel. Still, always up for a chat and some company, when Lee tapped him on the shoulder as he packed his boxes and asked for a lift to Irving that night, Wesley was glad to oblige. It seemed Lee was going to visit his wife to pick up some curtain rods and do a little decorating at his rooming house. As they motored home together, Wesley asked Lee if he'd like a lift the following night also, seeing as it was the weekend and all. Lee declined the lift, saying he was not intending to visit his family that weekend.

The following morning Wesley checked the weather from the kitchen window before settling down to one of his sister's hearty breakfasts. It was shaping up to be a fine day for the edge of winter: light drizzle, supposed to fade in the late morning to mild sunshine. When he glanced at the wall clock it was just past 7.15am. His sister was cutting his lunch and grinning at the antics at the breakfast table. It was a happy kitchen. His mother was in town and the flock were together again. All of a sudden his mother gave a start, at an odd face peeping through the kitchen window. Lee Harvey Oswald had arrived early. Wesley signalled calm, kissed his mother on the cheek and accepted his brown bag from his sister as she wiped her hands on her apron. With his usual wave he headed out the back door, the two co-workers jumped in the car and drove away.

As they were moving off Wesley noticed a package on the back seat. A metre long, maybe longer, and about six inches wide. It was wrapped like you would groceries, in heavy brown paper. 'What's the package, Lee?' he queried. The monotone reply from his chum was simply, 'Curtain rods', nothing more. The comment was enough for Wesley to recall the purpose of Lee's need for a lift the previous night. Little else was said of the parcel on the back seat; in fact, little else was said for the entire ride other than a throwaway line or two about the weather. Wesley attempted to start up a dialogue, noticing that Lee had no lunch bag. But Lee simply replied that he would be buying lunch. At the end of their journey, Wesley steered the car into the car park and the two men walked silently into the building together, Lee all businesslike with his parcel slung under his arm, and Wesley full of energy, heading straight for the work bench.

It was an uneventful morning. There wasn't anything remarkable in packing boxes. Wesley was running up and down from his workstation on the first floor to the upper floors where Lee worked. There was a lot of gossip around the six-storey depository. He heard it at every desk. Lee buzzed past him a couple of times and the general atmosphere was one of mild excitement. Most of the staff were lost to chatter about the President's motorcade, due to cruise right past their workplace bang on lunchtime, presenting the perfect alternative to dominoes. Wesley was keen to see the President, after all, '... it's not every day in your life that you get to see the President.' So at twelve noon on the button, he raced to take a front-stalls position on the steps of the building overlooking Elm Street. Billy Lovelady and a few of his co-workers from the upper levels milled around also. They craned their necks and focused their eyes to watch the motorcade slowly snake its way through the throng of waving mums, dads and excited schoolkids. The last time Wesley saw Lee Harvey Oswald he was somewhere upstairs, on either the fifth or sixth floor; it was nearly lunchtime. The workmate took little notice of the man he had come to accept was a loner and went to watch the parade.

CHAPTER 4

BOSSMAN

Roy Truly was a man who made it to the top through hard work and persistence. Having started on the shop floor, at fifty-three years of age he now held the title of company director of the Texas School Book Depository. He was on the board of directors and acted in the role of operations superintendent. In other words he virtually ran the show. He was, as his workers called him, the 'bossman'. The workers liked their bossman; they respected his ways and achievements. Many of his staff were 'coloured' folk, most of them unskilled. It was dull work; all they did was pack books into boxes and move orders throughout the seven-storey building. And look out the window, often.

Life hadn't always been so prosperous for the bossman. As a young man he had dragged himself through the Depression, turning his hand to almost anything. He walked the floor of his parents' cafe in Dallas serving soup and black char coffee to the strugglers. He even did a spell at a local cotton company driving an old lorry till the work ran out and he ended up behind the wheel of a laundry truck, criss-crossing the streets of the city he adored. Texan born and bred, he had his sights set far beyond the Depression. When the tides of misery finally turned and the economy lifted, suddenly it was as if everybody wanted to read. Books, novels and journals became popular. Roy sensed a future in publishing, so the high school graduate took a job at the newly formed Texas School Book Depository. His path to success was only interrupted during the war years when he volunteered at the Arlington aviation plant, taking charge of shipping and dispatch, all to aid the war effort.

In 1963, after some thirty years, his approach hadn't changed. Bossman still knew the value of the personal touch. He worked alongside nineteen staff and led by example, managing to garner genuine respect for his fair-handed style and the dollar twenty-five an hour he paid.

When on 15 October Roy took a phone call from a woman named Ruth Paine, he offered her, as was his way, a fair hearing. She was looking for a favour; in fact, she was ringing out of desperation. Mr Truly was just one of a string of company executives she was contacting in an effort to find work for the husband of a friend of hers. The man's name was Lee Harvey Oswald and he had a pregnant wife and toddler. The bossman felt saddened. It was in his nature to give a man a fair go so he suggested to Ruth that Lee come in immediately for an interview.

Roy's initial impression of Lee Harvey Oswald was that of a nice fellow, a recent ex-marine who claimed an honourable discharge and, oddly, a man who always ended his sentences with 'Sir'. A leftover from his army days. However, there was no mention of overseas travel or a visit to Russia; the applicant just skimmed over his life in double-quick time. Lee proffered that he had no police history and was looking for any sort of work, as his baby's birth was imminent. He was desperate and, even though Mr Truly had no current vacancies, he created a job to help out the clean-cut young man.

Lee was to pack boxes on the sixth floor in the area known as reserve stock. His job required him to work alone beneath a run of windows overlooking the parkway and beautiful boulevards of Houston and Elm streets. He caught on quickly. After two hours of tuition he was methodically matching books to their delivery dockets, packing orders and sending stock down to the first floor where the longest serving staff dispatched the orders. And so it went each day for the next five weeks. Roy was pleased with his latest recruit. He liked the nature of the loner, a man who didn't waste time in idle chitchat with his fellow workers, a perfect employee really. Bossman occasionally saw him of a morning and they'd swap a pleasant greeting, but rarely more than that. There was work to be done and Lee got on with the job. Even at lunchtime he sat by himself, reading a book and sipping his Dr Pepper soda pop.

The morning of 22 November was like any other, a two-word greeting between the men then off to work. Roy noticed Lee once or twice at his sixth-floor workstation as he moved through the building attending to quality control. By noon the hum of the conveyor belts and clang of the noisy freight elevators on the north end of the building had hushed to silence as the depository stopped for lunch. Two of Roy's well-liked staff on the sixth floor, Charles Gibbens and Danny Arc, had downed tools just a few minutes earlier. They'd been laying new floorboards but thought they'd sneak off a little early to get a good spot outside to watch the motorcade. As the lift hit the ground floor and the rickety old timber doors opened, Charles realised he'd left his cigarettes upstairs. He ushered his mate onwards to secure their position and took the lift back up in search of his gaspers. As he placed them in his pocket he noticed Lee was standing at his usual workplace between the window and a stack of boxes. He was still holding his clipboard. In a friendly manner, Charles enquired if Lee was going to come down and join the others for the parade. Lee's answer was simply, 'No, Sir, when you get downstairs close the gates to the elevator.' Charles shrugged it off and ventured down to join the rest of his workmates and the Bossman.

Roy often ventured out for a stroll to a cafe with Mr Campbell, his second-in-charge. On this day he held back for a spell. Both men hung around the front steps of the depository on Elm Street where a mix of workers had assembled, waiting expectantly in the Texas winter sun. Mrs Reid, the company secretary, was there, along with a few of Roy's long-term employees, the 'coloured boys' Harold, James and Bonnie. Most of the staff were keen for a glimpse of the President of the United States. Roy smiled at the camaraderie of his employees as they waited for the motorcade to turn into Houston Street and approach them. It really was a perfect day.

James, who usually worked on the first floor, was particularly anxious to sight the President. Earlier that day he'd fielded a question from Lee, who had been keen to know the exact route the motorcade would take. The two had looked out the window and talked about Houston Street and the left-hand turn onto Elm. Bonnie, standing alongside James, nudged his workmate. He, too, was up for a parade and his face lit up at the sight of all the pretty women standing on the curb in their Sunday best. Bonnie had also been laying floorboards on the sixth floor during the previous week. Throughout the morning he'd noticed Lee stacking boxes near his workstation at the window of the sixth floor. Bonnie thought he was messing about. He rarely had anything to say to the quiet fellow and worked in silence until the lunchtime bell rang and he took the lift down to the bottom level. And now he was standing alongside his mate Harold and the Bossman. Harold also worked on the sixth floor and had noticed Lee fussing around a pile of cartons just before lunch. As a bit of a lark, when Harold and Bonnie took the two lifts down to the lower level, they left the lifts gate open, making it impossible to call the lifts back up. Apart from the stairs, Lee was stuck on the sixth floor, completely alone.

Just after 12.15pm Bonnie and his two mates James and Harold were starting to doubt the wisdom of their vantage point on the street. Their necks craned and stretched in the direction from which the motorcade was about to arrive. Glancing upwards, they made a hasty decision and sprinted to the lift, taking it back up to the fifth floor, settling on a position just under Lee Harvey Oswald's workstation. They believed Lee was still above, standing or sitting on the floorboards. All of a sudden the motorcade appeared on the horizon, on Houston Street, and heading straight for them. With the vehicles travelling at only ten or twelve miles per hour, the boys took in a grand view as the glistening limousines, shining, all chrome and black, turned into Elm Street. The President looked majestic, with his wife alongside and a carload of Secret Service suits following.

CHAPTER 5
THE BODYGUARD

Roy Kellerman was a special man, so it ran to rule that he was going to be a special agent. In charge of the White House detail to the President of the United States of America by 1963 at forty-eight years of age, he could glimpse early retirement in the foreseeable future, but he still loved the job, just as he loved his wife and two daughters. Since Kennedy's inauguration three years earlier he had spent the majority of his waking hours either up close and personal to JFK, or right on his heels. He was considered a Secret Service veteran and ran a tight crew. His detail worked in ten-man shifts around the clock, eight hours on and sixteen off, a fortnight straight. After twenty-three years Roy knew virtually no other way than that of an agent: it was his life. He did briefly put his toe in the water as a trooper for the Michigan State Police after leaving high school, but it was the allure of bodyguard to the President that drew him to Washington. As the man in charge, responsibility fell on his shoulders to select a crew, the types of vehicles that would transport the President, Vice President and dignitaries and the routes to be taken. Should the shit hit the fan, Roy was the go-to man, the fixer.

America in the 1960s was more innocent than in the racy decades to come. Terrorism, large-scale threats to public offices and security alerts were not yet day-to-day occurrences. Nonetheless, strategic planning was still a key element of Agent Kellerman's days. Thus far his team could boast never having lost a man. But times were changing, political climates warming and conflict over race, colour and creed was increasingly spilling over onto the streets of America. Always abreast of safety issues, the presidential motorcade had in recent times commissioned two styles of car for the main man: a convertible and a limousine with a bubble top made from armour-protective plastic glass. In parallel, the Secret Service implemented the use of a brand-new weapon, a state-of-the-art semi-automatic rifle in each detail; an AR-15 assault rifle was issued to one man per shift. The AR-15 was an efficient and lightweight rifle capable of inflicting devastating wounds. Plus, each agent carried a four-inch barrelled revolver, standard personal handgun of choice for an agent of the time. By today's standards, of course, the weaponry was conservative at best.

November 20, 1963, saw Kellerman and his posse head out of Washington towards Texas with the boss and Vice President Lyndon Baines Johnson on Air Force One. They were on a two-night whistle-stop tour, landing at San Antonio, then on to Houston, bedding down on the 21st at Fort Worth then on to Dallas. It was a bit more than just handshaking and baby kissing, there were heavyweight political issues hovering and some hardcore lobbying was required. The government of the day saw it as the ideal launchpad for the President in the upcoming re-election campaign. It was this fact that guaranteed the presence of the sophisticated first lady, Jackie Kennedy. Being such a rare occasion for the American public to see the wife of their leader, the media would be on hand to cover her every move and to discuss her hairstyle and wardrobe.

One of the things Kellerman enjoyed most about the Secret Service was that it was a man's world. There were no female agents, nor were there likely to be in the near future. Sure, women were attached to the agency, but they were in the administrative roles, clerks and secretaries. So when the detail went on the road, it was a team of ten men who worked together, socialised together and played up together. Southern hospitality being among the finest in the nation, the good people of Texas were mighty pleased to welcome the secretive men from Washington. By 11pm on Thursday night the detail had the President tucked in, getting some shut-eye at the Texas Hotel in Fort Worth. With eight hours to go before the Presidential business breakfast and the motorcade through Dallas, Kellerman said his men could knock off. A fresh crew could handle babysitting detail.

Kellerman's boys weren't due on till the next morning and they could see the flashing bar room lights from their hotel suites. Conscience fought yearning, reminding them that the 'use of intoxicating liquor of any kind, including beer or wine' was an absolute no-no while on duty or on tour with the President. The weighty Secret Service manual, Section Ten, Chapter Three, highlighted that misdemeanour very clearly. Any violation, even the slightest, was grounds for immediate removal of the agent from the elite group. A just clause, considering the responsibility of the position.

But as every agent knew, what happened on the road stayed on the road. So there was only one thing for the team to do: they went for a drink. Their first stop, a rendezvous organised by the Fort Worth Press Club, included reporters, White House staff and the socially curious. None of the Secret Service men had eaten during the day and with their rumbling stomachs they were to be disappointed as the Press Bar offered only drinks and off-the-record gossip. From midnight onwards, as many as eleven agents came and went, enjoying a run of beers, Scotch whiskeys and mixed drinks, but come 3am the publican had had enough. He had a home to go to; the agents didn't, so he pointed them down the road to a beatnik bar called the Cellar Door.

The proprietor, Dick Mackie, was quick to fling open his door, letting the loud music out and the secretive men in to be welcomed by his 'scantily clad girls who serve as waitresses and also entertain'. A local reporter for the *Star-Telegram* newspaper, Bob Schieffer, was also there. He recalled the waitresses doubled as strippers and wandered about in their underwear. Of some of the agents, he stated, '. . . we managed to see the dawn come up'.

In the liquor department, Mr Mackie's establishment was strictly bring-your-own. Guests were invited to enter with whatever drinks they desired and Mackie's girls were available to mix the brew and serve. Otherwise it was coffee, cola or fruit drinks on offer. The men settled on rounds of a concoction known as 'salty dick', of undisclosed ingredients, perhaps a wink to the cleverness of the proprietor who was not legally able to serve his own liquor. Such was the way in Texas at that time.

As the agents lounged around, listening to guitar music, gossip and recitals by beatnik poets, some of the bodyguards watching over the now-snoozing President broke from security protocols and popped in to join their workmates at the Cellar Door for a glass or two. And so it went, until 5.10am. As daylight started to sneak through the windows it was time for sleepy agents to try to catch twenty winks, literally. Among the shenanigans, an observer in the bar commented that someone within had become 'inebriated'. Not a fascinating observation for a bar perhaps, drunkenness is expected at times, but on this night it was newsworthy. Those being served were the men of the United States Secret Service. Like most slivers of news of its type that find their way into the clutches of the press, it pinged across the country from radio station to newscast, but fell under the radar of the momentous, history-making story, later that day.

Only one newspaper, far away on the west coast of the US, thought the story was solid enough to run, and they did.

CHAPTER 6
THE FULL CATASTROPHE

I had spent more than a couple of hundred nights reading text, studying and cross-referencing descriptions and comments to form a picture of the players in the Lee Harvey Oswald saga. Happy with the end result I settled in to tackle the Warren Commission volumes. Reading material such as this is often riddled with tedium; thousands of words are spoken and transcribed inside the courtroom each day. But every now and then a startling snippet of evidence will jump out and hit you and instantly the adrenalin pumps and the reading quickens. I read on . . . into the night, into another year. I wanted to document precisely the sequence of events on the fateful day, second by second. I wanted to join the factual dots into the full catastrophe . . .

Friday 22 November, 1963, arrived for most of the population of Dallas, Texas, as any other day would. There was a touch of drizzle, but the weather was expected to improve. For Kellerman's Secret Service contingent it arrived with bleary eyes and hangovers as they dragged themselves from their beds, braved a cold shower and settled up their hotel accounts. The tired were back on duty.

•

There had been many failed attempts to lure the charismatic President and his elegant wife to Texas; each time the pressures of running the number-one office had seen postponement and rescheduling. In mid-October, Jack, as he was affectionately known, took a call from Governor John Connally and the two men hatched a plan for a November visit to the southern state. The President was keen for the Governor to work up an itinerary that would see his entourage visit as many towns as possible. They would spend the Thursday night in Fort Worth, before a motorcade drive through Dallas on Friday, followed by a grand luncheon, to be jointly organised by the Governor's wife Nellie and her chosen committee, with a gala dinner in Austin, the Governor's home town, midway through the tour. Pomp and ceremony were coming to the desert as Air Force One touched down at Dallas's Love Field Airport on Friday morning.

The Governor took pride in guiding the stunningly beautiful Mrs Kennedy through the official welcoming committee on the edge of the tarmac. His wife, Nellie, who had whipped up excitement throughout the Women's Auxiliary in the past few weeks, was in raptures. And the public performance, handshakes and smiles from John F Kennedy didn't disappoint. The President stopped for spectators at every stride, against the sternest advice of his Secret Service, who had been hopeful of a swifter approach to the motorcade. But with an estimated 3000 people and the nation's TV cameras poised, the politically savvy leader saw great value in slowing the pace, just a tad. So once all were safely inside the convertible, Kellerman breathed a sigh of relief and the motorcade headed into town.

The Texan Governor soaked it up, observing the 'tremendous' response from the locals who were 'stacked from the curb line back against the shop fronts'. An estimated 250 000 people lined the streets. In among the sea of faces a pretty schoolgirl with a smile to win over a President held up her handmade sign requesting the motorcade stop. And they did. The children beamed as they met their hero. Moving on, JFK was touched by the sight of a Catholic nun herding in a small group of tiny toddlers. Again he called a stop for a chat before the motorcade travelled on.

Within the team of Secret Service agents trouble loomed. Agent Lawton from the follow-up team tailing the President's slow-moving limousine was out front, on foot, keeping his eye on JFK's back. Then all of a sudden he was recalled by his supervisor, ordered away from the President's car. The agent stopped, bewildered. As if to challenge the order he glanced at his superior, shrugged his shoulders a few times before doing as he was trained to do, obey instructions. Confusion simmered among the minders as the President's Lincoln moved on. Then a roar from the crowd changed the mood, the street was lined with adoration. The motorcade soaked up the sun and attention as cameras clicked and a nation of hands waved. Everything seemed to settle down as the motorcade snaked through the streets. Then only two turns to go and the accelerator would take the entourage out of the crowd, a couple of miles to a waiting ensemble of guests for a formal lunch.

The 'coloured boys' James, Bonnie and Harold had taken their window seat on the fifth floor of the Depository, and were being rewarded with the best view in town. Inside the Lincoln, Nellie leaned in to the President, 'Well Mr President, you can't say there aren't some people in Dallas who love you.' She beamed with pride, delighted at her town's response to the visit. JFK continued to wave simply replying, '. . . that is very obvious.'

Arnold Rowland, a young married man, was standing in Houston Street with his wife. They had been there a while, like everybody else, biding their time for a once-in-a-lifetime glimpse of America's 'royal couple'. Arnold would occasionally shoot a fleeting glance at the others in the crowd. He spied a man on the sixth floor of the Book Depository, a 'white man' of slender build, with dark hair and a light complexion. He guessed he was in his early thirties. He also noticed the faces of three 'coloured men' on the fifth floor, all eagerly watching, waiting. He found himself preoccupied with the man at the sixth-floor window. He was holding a rifle with a scope. Arnold thought he must be a Secret Service agent, part of the motorcade security. Just a short distance away a fifteen-year-old schoolboy, Amos Euins, was making the same deduction, as he watched.

Then the glossy black Lincoln Continental turned onto Houston Street and began a slow head-on approach towards the Texas School Book Depository. All eyes front and centre as distractions were cast aside in favour of seeing the nation's most loved statesman and his wife. As the car approached, the first dignitary in sight was Governor Connally, seated behind Agent Kellerman. The Governor sat on a jump seat, fifteen centimetres in front of the President. The jump seat was a removeable small seat behind the driver and in front of JFK and Jackie. It was only used when dignitaries were travelling with the President and was lower in height to the normal seats. On the other jump seat to the left sat the Governor's adoring wife Nellie. Both were proudly acknowledging their constituents. Behind Nellie, dressed in a fetching shocking pink Chanel suit and matching hat was the First Lady, the serene Jacqueline Kennedy. Both she and her husband waved and smiled at the spectators, playing to the crowd. They were in re-election mode.

For those gathered, the long wait offered a reward of a handful of seconds, for just as quickly as they appeared, they would surely pass by. As the City Hall clock moved towards 12.30pm, the Lincoln turned into Elm Street and the motorcade was out of the main part of the crowd and heading for lunch, driving past the Book Depository. The President acknowledged Roy Truly's workers as the big Lincoln straightened up and pointed southwards and big Jack Kennedy snapped one of his world-famous grins. Roy felt humbled, full of sentiment as he watched. A staff photographer for the local newspaper, Robert Jackson, was following behind the motorcade taking pictures. A student, Jim Worrell, had snared the perfect vantage position, immediately in front of the Depository. At that moment he glanced up and noticed something that worried him. A rifle was sticking out of a fifth- or sixth-floor window.

The motorcade moseyed along Elm Street as its driver waited for the signal, a call to lunch. The magic Texas formula was in play: sunshine, slowpoke ways and mighty fine company. Then, just as Roy Kellerman was about to nod to his driver to tap his accelerator and pick up the pace, a crack of noise shattered the calm. A bullet was fired. The relaxed remained unawakened, no one realised what was going on, what they were witnessing, as motorcade and confusion rolled on. Despite a crowd of more than one hundred milling along the section known as Dealey Plaza, only a trickle registered any reaction, some just raised an eyebrow, and scoffed it off as a firecracker; the dopey Secret Service also thought it was a 'firecracker'. Others believed it was just a back-firing exhaust. A few more astute onlookers thought it was a gunshot. Witnesses nearest to the limousine saw sparks on the road surface.

No one realised that Lee Harvey Oswald had come to work, and he wasn't packing boxes. He was wide awake and working on his aim.

Governor Connally, a man experienced with weapons, was positive it was a rifle shot. He turned intuitively, looking in the general vicinity of the Depository.

Then another shot rang out, as if to confirm the first suspicion of a bullet. Local resident Mary Rattan heard both shots and saw a rifle protruding from a window on either the fifth or sixth floor of the Depository. Nellie Connally also heard the first noise and the second noise, which she knew to be a shot. She turned towards JFK, seeing both his hands move upwards. The President stiffened. The shot had entered his upper back, penetrating his neck, and exiting his throat. His clenched fists rose to his neck, he leaned forward and left as a concerned Mrs Kennedy wrapped her arms around him. He then 'slumped over, no utterance'. The Governor was under no illusions; he believed at that moment an assassination attempt was underway.

Amos Euins, the schoolboy, saw the man at the window shoot twice and then step back behind some boxes. He saw that

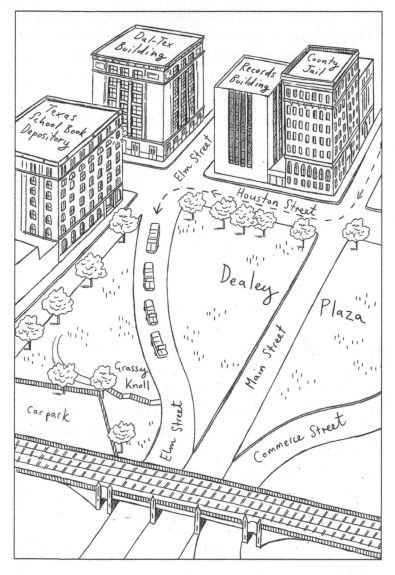

The route taken by the Presidental motorcade, showing the turn from
Houston Street into Elm Street and the orientation of the Texas School
Book Depository building

the shooter was a white man. Frightened, the boy ran off to find a policeman. Robert Jackson, the photographer, had looked up and saw 'negro men' staring from a window high up in the Depository. One floor above them, at a corresponding window, he had seen a rifle protruding. He could see boxes stacked up near that window, had heard the shots and observed the rifle being withdrawn back inside the building.

Howard Brennan, a forty-five-year-old construction worker, had snuck away from work to view the parade, taking a position opposite the Book Depository. He, too, saw a man at a window on the sixth floor, and watched him constantly. The same man, whom he described as slender, neat, five foot ten inches tall, fair complexion and in his early thirties, a white man, took aim with a rifle. Brennan didn't quite know what to think about who this was, he just kept watching, as well as watching the approaching motorcade. Then . . . he heard the shots. Brennan would identify Oswald in a police line-up later that day. The Governor, who heard the first shot, looked down at his chest; he was covered in blood. A bullet had passed through his body. Mrs Connally instinctively pulled her husband onto her lap, her loving action saving his life by stemming his blood loss. Roy Truly looked on in shock as the now dazed procession limped along Elm Street. He had heard the original shot, 'a noise like a cannon', and thought it came from the west, behind his building, behind him. 'Nothing seemed to happen on the first explosion, everything seemed frozen until after two more explosions.' He guessed it was a gun or a rifle, but was of the belief that the shots did not come from within the Depository. Roy continued to watch as the President's car swerved to the left. Bystanders had begun to scream, some fell to the ground,

The key positions within the Presidential motorcade on that fateful day in Dallas

others surged backwards into Truly as terror and panic started to take hold. Suddenly the crowd congealed around him, he was smothered and lost his bearings.

The Vice President's wife, who sat alongside her husband two cars back from the President, recalled, '. . . it all started off so beautifully . . . we were going to have the luncheon . . . there was a sharp loud report, a shot . . . then two more shots in rapid succession . . .'

The final explosion created a fist-sized hole in the right side of President Kennedy's head, covering the interior of the car and a nearby motorcycle officer with blood and brain tissue. There was a chunk of brain on the Governor's trousers and he was heard to say 'My God, they are going to kill us all'. Nellie held tight, reassuring her husband, saying '. . . you are going to be alright.' Later, Nellie Connally would observe, 'It was a car full of yellow roses, red roses and blood and it was all over us . . .' Nellie thought her husband was now dead. She was mistaken. He was very much alive, recalled the last shot and was adamant that the noise was from a high-powered automatic weapon. Later recalling the blast, he described 'a ring, kind of an echo to it, more of a metallic sound, a more penetrating sound'. He was just as adamant that no shots came from the expressway overpass (bridge) in front of him, the grassy knoll or any other location forward of the limousine. Each shot had come from behind.

The student, Jim Worrell, thought he heard four shots in all, but however many, he knew the sounds to be rifle shots. The 'coloured boys' on the fifth floor each recalled hearing three shots. James had plaster dust fall into his hair from the floorboards above, a reaction to someone upstairs moving about.

He also heard cartridges hitting the same floorboards in time with the action of a rifle bolt being engaged. A man with eight years' military service, James knew weapons and was convinced a person was above, working a rifle. Standing alongside him, Bonnie believed the shots came from inside the building and the second and third shots were 'real quick'. He, too, noticed the dust fall from above, landing on their heads. Harold, making up the trio, heard the shots and the sounds of shells hitting the floor above and the additional noise of shells being ejected from a rifle, believing it was a bolt-action weapon. He also observed the dust and dirt fall into his friend Bonnie's hair.

Kenneth O'Donnell, the special assistant to the President, had the task of representing the White House's interests in the organisation and smooth running of the motorcade. Seated in the left jump seat of the Secret Service vehicle immediately behind the President's limousine, he recalled 'two [shots] came almost instantaneously'. Mrs Kennedy, cradling her husband, who was now slumped near motionless, was heard to yell, '. . . they have killed my husband'. Oddly, the Secret Service man driving the President's limousine, Agent Greer, thought the shots were the 'backfire of a motorcycle'. He recalled three shots, the last two seeming to be 'just simultaneously, one behind the other'.

Secret Service agent Clint Hill leapt from his stance on the left running board of the follow-up vehicle and ran forward. His action was intended to save the First Lady, whom he saw as trying to escape the Lincoln convertible, climbing out. She was in fact instinctively reaching back, across the rear of the limousine, to gather a portion of her husband's brain that she had seen on the duco of the trunk. She retrieved what she was after.

Hill jumped onto the boot seconds after the last and undisputed fatal shot, and guided Mrs Kennedy back into the relative safety of her rear seat. He then grasped on tightly to the limousine himself. Apart from the jolting of the President's head, it would be Clint Hill's manoeuvre that caused the most animation at the scene. He felt the latter sound was like the shooting of a revolver into something hard, a different sound to the previous. Regarding the second and third shots, Agent Greer stated that he heard '. . . bang, bang, just right behind it almost. The last two seemed closer to me than the other . . .'

Similarly Agent Youngblood, in the Vice President's vehicle, believed that the shots rang out for a time of five seconds and the second and third shots were closer together.

Agent Kellerman, who had heard the three shots, believed the second and third '. . . came in all together. I'm going to say two [shots] and it was like a double bang, bang, instantaneous . . .' He was sure that the time between the first shot and the flurry of the last two was three to four seconds, no more. Kellerman instructed his driver to move, to head for the hospital. The vehicle exited Dealey Plaza and sped towards Parkland Memorial Hospital. A devastated cry from Mrs Kennedy announced, 'his brain is in my hand . . .'.

The immediate area of Elm Street became alive with panic. Police officers and spectators ran in all directions, including up the grassy area adjacent to the section of motorway the President's limousine had just passed. A myriad of spectators swarmed forth, some lying flat on the ground. Others moved about, shock starting to take effect as they sought out police, bombarding them with their breathless accounts.

Mary-Ann Mitchell, a clerk who worked nearby, was standing with her colleague Mr Campbell at the corner of Elm and Houston streets. She recalled 'the second and third [shots] being closer together than the first'. Mr Campbell recalled the three shots and with reference to the second and third shots offered that 'after the second shot it was followed very quickly by the third one'. Mr Campbell noticed boxes at the Depository's sixth-floor window and a glimpse of a nondescript person, a flash of something 'white coloured . . . a person having moved out of the window'.

Malcolm Couch, a news cameraman riding behind the motorcade, heard three shots close together and looked up at the sixth floor of the Depository to see a rifle being pulled back inside a window. His colleague Robert Jackson also saw the rifle; indeed, he was the one who had alerted Couch, by yelling and pointing at the weapon.

At the corner of Elm and Houston streets stood workmates Bob Edwards and Ronald Fischer, both auditors who had come to see the parade. Before the motorcade appeared, Fischer had nudged his friend and said, 'Look at that guy there, in that window', indicating a man sitting forward wearing a light-coloured open-necked shirt, a 'white man' of twenty-two to twenty-four years of age; he was possibly 'thin' in build. He was on the sixth floor of the Depository staring down onto Elm Street, towards the overpass, the end of the motorcade route. According to Ronald, the young man was surrounded by boxes and appeared, like them, to be waiting. Both men then turned to watch the approaching limousines. Ronald, a man of some experience with rifles, having used a long arm a few times, would recall four shots. At the second shot, the two men grew fearful and ran away before returning a short time later when the panic had died down.

Father and daughter Phillip and Linda Willis were following the motorcade on foot, having the perfect day out; dad was taking photographs. Phillip knew the Vice President and wanted a good picture, a souvenir he could cherish. Phillip and Linda ran towards Elm Street to gain a good position and take more pictures, and were among the closest to the President when he was shot. Phillip, an early retiree former army major, knew weapons; he was a deer hunter on weekends. He 'absolutely' heard three high-powered shots. 'It couldn't have been a firecracker . . .' His fifteen-year-old daughter heard three shots, the last 'two real fast bullets together'; they were 'too loud and too close together to be firecrackers'.

Officer Martin, a veteran of eleven years as a motorcycle cop, was following on the left side of the President's convertible as it moved along Elm Street towards the overpass. Martin had been instructed to stay close to Mrs Kennedy. His bike was less than two metres away. As he motored along, a southerly breeze hit his face, as it did the other police in the same location. The breeze was moving from the overpass towards the Depository building behind them. When the first shot rang out he turned instinctively to his right, towards the Depository. He then heard two more shots and his helmet and shirt became splattered with blood and human flesh.

In front of Officer Martin was Officer Hargis, another motorcycle patrolman who heard the same number of shots. He, too, was sprayed with blood and saw President Kennedy hit. As the motorcade raced towards the hospital, Hargis believed the shots had come from behind him. '[It] sounded like the shots were right next to me,' he would say as he tried to recall the events to the Commission. He searched the grassy area and Stemmons overpass before making his way back towards the Depository.

Riding on the right flank of the limousine was Officer Haywood, who heard three shots in succession, 'the last two were real close'. He abandoned his bike and helped search the area, also ending up at the Depository where, along with other uniformed police, he witnessed the finding of a rifle and spent rounds on the sixth floor, near the windows overlooking Elm Street.

Patrolman Craig, who was stationed very near to the overpass, believed the last two shots were 'rapid compared to the first', with the time between them 'not more than two seconds'. Craig offered an insight into the sound of each shot – an echo, caused by the overpass which was forward of the Presidential vehicle. 'There were actually two explosions with each one [shot].' Other police officers nearby also heard the echo, the doubling up of the gunshot blasts. Lee Bowers, the tower man at the neighbouring railway terminal, was certain that there were only three shots: he knew of the common occurrence of reverberations caused by the overpass. From the evidence and knowledge of key witnesses such as Mr Bowers, it appeared the Stemmons overpass acted as an echo chamber of sorts. This phenomenon became vital when assessing witness statements and accurately determining the number of shots fired – three or more than three. One witness standing by the overpass reported six shots; they may have added the sound of an echo with each shot.

Straight after the shots, Patrolman Craig ran towards Houston Street to investigate. Barbara Rowland, a young housewife who had been standing in the assembled crowd with her husband Arnold, stopped him to tell their story. While waiting for the motorcade's arrival, Arnold had looked up and seen a 'young white man' holding a rifle at the window on the sixth floor of the Depository. The young couple assumed he was a Secret Service agent as the motorcade approached. Barbara told Officer Craig that they had also noticed 'Negro men' on a lower floor. She also stated that the second and third shots 'were closer together than the first and second'.

Deputy Sheriff Luke Mooney had been watching the parade from the steps of the Dallas Criminal Court Building on Houston Street. In the company of several other officers, he followed the procession as it moved on to Houston Street. He recalled of the gun blasts, 'I can still hear them very distinctly; the second and third shot was pretty close together'. Mooney sprinted across the grassy area towards Elm Street with fellow officer Walters and Boone, who recalled a similar run of shots and spacing between each report. They ran towards the Book Depository and into the building, being among the first police officers within its confines.

Police Officer Weitzman, who was positioned near to the President's vehicle at the time of the shooting, recalled the 'second and third [shots] seemed to be simultaneously'. The officer also noticed 'something red on the street', which he later oversaw delivery to the laboratory as 'human bone'. It was a piece of the President's skull. Dallas Police Officer Stavis Ellis recounted his experience. He 'saw a bullet hit the pavement'.

Numerous witnesses saw a lone shooter fire a rifle from the sixth-floor window of the Texas School Book Depository. The critical mass of their statements offered the same description: youngish (twenty-three to early thirties), thin, short-haired, white, male – a description that matched Lee Harvey Oswald to a tee. Within minutes the Dallas police had the building shut down and sealed off. Their initial actions were excellent and crucial to understanding what happened. For mere patrolmen, used only in the roles of stationary or roving guards to the motorcade, they were thus far joining the dots perfectly. Each officer had played his part, kept an eye out, taken mental notes and watched the crowd. Reacting quickly and professionally to the shooting, those same officers ascertained the direction from which the shots were fired and the probable location of the shooter. Hence a wave of uniforms was converging on the area around the Texas School Book Depository.

Officer Baker, part of the official motorcade, manoeuvred his motorcycle as close as he could to the front of the Depository, then simply dropped it and stepped away, to save the time in having to park it up. A keen deer hunter when he was off-duty, he had no uncertainty over the sounds he had heard, adamant that there were three shots in total, 'bang, bang, bang . . . pretty well even (together)'. His experience led him to deduce that each shot was from a high-powered rifle. Although unsure of their exact origin, he surmised the general direction of their trajectory and the Depository seemed a good possibility. He'd observed flocks of pigeons scatter from the roofs of nearby buildings as he looked up at the time of the shooting. Clear of his bike, he sprinted towards the big red brick structure, up the steps and into the building. For now he was on duty and he was hunting an assassin.

As he ran he pushed anybody and everybody aside. Breaking free of the hordes, Roy Truly followed the big patrol officer as he entered the building. Close on his heels, Roy caught him in the lobby. The company director quickly saw that the policeman was unfamiliar with the floor plan. He was trying to get to the upper levels, asking for the stairwell. As they ran towards the first treads, Roy noticed that both the elevators were stuck on the fifth floor. The gates had been left open up there. Roy yelled up the void, 'turn loose the elevator' a couple of times but to no avail.

Roy Truly knew that if there was an assassin on the higher levels he couldn't exit the building using the lifts; he would be forced to use the stairs, the stairs he and the officer would be on. Still up he went, with the officer immediately behind. Their eyes scanned rooms cautiously as they moved. As they reached the first level the policeman was distracted by an image, a glimpse of movement heading away from the stairs towards the lunchroom. He branched off in that direction and confronted a lone man just shy of the lunchroom, but facing its doorway. With his hand gun pointed directly at the retreating figure, Officer Baker hollered 'come here'. Lee Harvey Oswald turned and walked straight back to him. The barrel of the gun was almost touching Oswald's body. The patrolman barked, 'This man work here?' to which the Bossman replied in the affirmative. Losing interest in the employee, Baker headed immediately for the higher floors, in search of an assassin. This was a mere minute and fifteen seconds after the last shot had been fired at the President.

Roy would not recall any obvious reaction or facial expression from Oswald other than that he might have been a little startled. The only other person to take any note of Lee in the lunchroom around the time was Mrs Reid. She had re-entered the building a little after Roy and Officer Baker, some two minutes later. Making her way to the lunchroom she had noticed that Lee was in there and had just purchased a bottle of Coke from the vending machine. He held onto it in his right hand.

Meanwhile, Roy and Officer Baker had made their way to the top floor and from there they were working their way back down the building, looking for the obvious, looking for an unknown gunman, but seeing no one. They followed the stairs down to the ground level where the building was rapidly filling with uniformed police and panic. Two of those arriving were Deputy Mooney and Deputy Boone. Both men had run from the grassy lawn area to the Depository and now headed straight for the stairs to the upper levels. Mooney, the senior of the two, was backing a hunch; he went for height and kept climbing. The rookie Boone puffed his way behind the older officer as they searched the sixth level. Mooney was rewarded for his quick assessment, discovering a row of boxes stacked high, close to the windows. Running up the stairs to lend a hand was Officer Weitzman, who had now handed over his piece of skull. Boone then located the most important exhibit of his short career thus far: a Carcano rifle with a scope lying abandoned between the boxes.

The three worked as a team, preserving the scene in textbook fashion. Their conscious concern fell to the possibility that fingerprints may be found on the exhibits before them.

One box, which sat alone at the actual window ledge, Mooney surmised could have acted as a resting place for the Carcano. The weapon was later proven to have been purchased by Lee Harvey Oswald, the same long arm in the treasured photograph kept in the suspect's family album. Beside the window were three spent cartridge cases from full metal jacket rounds, and nearby a heavy brown bag, possibly the brown bag Wesley had seen earlier that morning on the back seat of his car. A short distance away, near the stairwell and behind some other cartons, lay Oswald's discarded clipboard used to pack his orders, with three dockets still attached. Mooney leaned out of the window and hollered down into the street. He could see Captain Fritz, the city's number-one lawman, outside, trying to make sense of it all. The streets were alive with panic and bewilderment.

On the northern extension to Elm Street, was the landlady Mary Bledsoe, who had come to see the parade and was now heading home. She'd caught her usual bus on Elm Street and sat in her usual front seat, oblivious to the commotion behind her. Out of nowhere, just as the nearly full bus pulled away into the traffic, Lee Harvey Oswald jumped aboard. Mary recognised him instantly. That same man she never did like five weeks earlier and now he was standing only a few metres away. His shirt was dishevelled and dirty. She ignored him. While she chose not to talk to him she did eye him up and down, recalling that 'he looked like a maniac'.

Three or four stops later, the driver announced to the passengers that the President had been shot. Concerned gossip filled the bus. At the next stop, Lee hastily got off and flagged a ninety-five cent taxi that took him home, tipping his driver with a dollar note. Once at his rooming house he bounded inside. His landlady Earlene was preoccupied changing channels on the television set; the story was breaking and she was desperate to learn the details. She glanced up briefly at her lodger, whom she noticed was in an unusual hurry. But he headed to his room without comment, so she offered none and went back to her viewing. Three to four minutes later he appeared again, looking panicked, zipping his jacket to head out. Earlene offered conversation this time, stating, 'You sure are in a hurry.' The lodger left without reply, and was never again seen at the rooming house. What he left behind in his small room with its single bed included a holster for a .38 hand gun, a map of the city of Dallas with markings, an assortment of identity papers in the names of AJ Hidell and Lee Harvey Oswald and a notebook with scribbling in English and Russian. The very first thing detectives noticed when they entered the room were the neatly hung curtains and supporting curtain rods. There was no need for any other curtain rods.

In no time the Book Depository was swarming with cops taking stair treads two at a time to the trove of exhibits on the sixth floor. The captain was leading the way, dragging his crew of suits behind and shouting for the special assistance of Lieutenant Day, the Dallas police department's most experienced fingerprint expert.

Upon arrival, the lieutenant stood back and surveyed the crime scene and the exhibits before him. He passed an encouraging comment to his head of investigations that upon initial inspection there were fingerprints that seemed identifiable. Simultaneously, a sharp TV news cameraman arrived, documenting visually and independently the careful handling of the weapon. Subsequent tests on the 'resting place' boxes revealed that a fingerprint and one palm print found belonged to Lee Harvey Oswald. Similarly, a right palm print discovered on the weapon as well as a fingerprint and palm print on the scrunched-up brown bag wrapper that was strewn nearby also proved to be a match to Oswald. Two independent fingerprint experts, one from the FBI and one from the New York police department, would later examine the same exhibits and come up with the same findings. Lee Harvey Oswald's prints were on the vital exhibits.

Downstairs, questions were being asked, names demanded and workers accounted for, one by one. Fifteen minutes elapsed before it was realised that the only absentee from the employee list was the book packer from the now sealed off sixth floor, Lee Harvey Oswald. A fellow worker attested to having seen him fleeing the building only minutes after the shooting, and Roy Truly and patrolman Baker confirmed Oswald as the man they saw at the lunchroom. Bossman offered a full description of the suspect to the now adrenalin-pumped chief and a posse was formed. Men splintered off in all directions to hunt the man who had been elevated to the rank of chief suspect in the crime that was waking the world. Captain Fritz, preferring to allow the younger, keener detectives to chase the perpetrator, stayed back to observe the unglamorous but vital work of fingerprinting and photographing Lee Harvey Oswald's workstation. With the aid of Lieutenant Day, a live, fully jacketed round was ejected from the chamber of the Carcano rifle, falling to the floor before being pocketed by the big captain. With years of homicide experience the captain knew the shooter was a man who favoured military rounds.

Full metal jacket rounds came into play with the Hague Convention in the late-nineteenth century. Travelling at an accelerated velocity, they pass in and out of the body with minimal damage, allowing the victim a better chance of survival. They were and are designed principally for military purposes, the philosophy being that it's more humane to have soldiers wounded, repaired and returned to their loved ones than killed outright. These rounds are not designed to explode upon impact.

Within minutes an all-points bulletin of Oswald's description peppered the radio frequencies of every police vehicle. A short distance away, a sharp uniformed patrolman, Officer JD Tippit, was listening intently to the broadcast. He scanned footpaths, front lawns and shopfronts as he cruised the leafy suburban streets, hoping to get lucky. In an outstanding example of police response to the APB, the keen-eyed Tippit spotted a likely suspect moving quickly on foot. Oswald was walking along a sidewalk in the residential neighbourhood of Oak Cliff, near the shopping strip of Jefferson Street. Tippit pulled in to the curb and stepped from his police car. As he walked over to confront the stranger, Oswald pulled out a hand gun and shot three times at close range, killing the policeman instantly.

A local motor mechanic, Domingo Benevidis, was driving past on an errand, chasing a carburettor for a job. He saw the two and watched on alarmed and helpless as the murder took place. Stopping his own vehicle at a safe distance, he observed Oswald dumping spent shells from a hand gun as he walked, before reloading the weapon and hightailing it from the area. A shocked young housewife, Virginia Davis, had made the same observation, as did her friend Mrs Marksman and a passing taxi driver. The witnesses were stacking up and Oswald was on the move.

Succumbing to the pressure, a now desperate Oswald fled through the side streets and onto Jefferson. The uncharacteristic blasts in their normally quiet environ had neighbours telephoning for police assistance, intensifying the hunt in Oak Cliff. Domingo fixed the image of the assailant in his memory before stooping down to collect the spent rounds from where they had fallen. Hiding them in his cigarette packet to preserve the evidence, he began the short wait for police to arrive. Each of the witnesses to the brutal murder of the patrolman gave near enough to identical descriptions of Oswald. The Dallas police department started scouring the streets for anyone who fitted the description; with such an intense manhunt something had to give, and soon.

A young shoe store manager, John Brewer, was fussing about his store on Jefferson Street, a few blocks away, when a man popped up in his front door alcove. He thought he'd seen him once before, perhaps a customer, so he took a closer inspection. The man was seriously dishevelled. His hair was 'messed up'. He '. . . looked as if he'd been running, scared. He looked funny . . .' Mr. Brewer could hear the sirens wailing in the distance and continued to spy surreptitiously on the fellow. Oswald was pretending to look in the window when he was actually looking at nothing. He glanced around once or twice, his eyes darting in the direction of the sirens before he took off down the street in a hurry. The manager watched him disappear into the Texas Theatre without purchasing a ticket, so he headed that way. He was onto him. A good friend of Mr Brewer was an usher at the movie house, so he pulled him aside and filled him in on the situation. The two men left the ticket girl to call the police and stepped into the dark cinema in search of a fugitive. Brewer and his usher friend were quick to check the two rear exits and discovered the doors had not been released. Obviously the man was still inside.

It was now well over an hour since the assassination. Oswald had taken a seat towards the back of the stalls. The place was near empty, with only fifteen to twenty others viewing the daytime matinee. Dallas police had again responded without delay. A flood of uniforms streamed in the front door of the theatre, meeting the two friends who passed on their tale as they turned the house lights up and illuminated a lone gunman, who all of a sudden had company. He was completely surrounded. The twenty-four-year-old Oswald, who had wreaked havoc on the streets of Dallas with a display of violence unequalled in Presidential history, simply stood calmly, as if someone had interrupted his movie. Then he pulled out a gun and pointed it at his captors. George Applin was seated in the audience. The commotion diverted his attention away from his B-grade Audie Murphy movie to watch the real-life crime thriller unfolding behind him. He witnessed Oswald holding a hand gun, pointing it menacingly, and heard the snap of the hammer over and over, as it dry fired; the bullets were obviously faulty.

The other theatre patrons, police reinforcements and several sticky-nosed citizens all later recalled the unforgettable sound of the Smith & Wesson pistol being fired. Less successful in this shootout, Oswald was dragged to the ground. With the numbers now overwhelmingly in favour of good, Lee was arrested and taken from the scene, yelling 'I am not resisting arrest, I demand my rights'. His only further comment was made while in a patrol car on the way to headquarters: 'I had a pistol and that's all I've done, just carry a pistol.' Otherwise there remained an eerie calm about the man suspected of killing the 35th President of the United States. Subsequent tests on Oswald's .38 Smith & Wesson proved a match to the spent cartridges gathered up by the quick-thinking motor mechanic after the tragic murder of Officer Tippit.

As the handcuffed captive stepped from the rear of the squad car, he declined an offer to shield his face from the TV cameras. He seemed to embrace his moment in the spotlight, as the photographers' bulbs flashed away. The world news was focusing on an unusually cool, calm young man from Dallas who showed no signs of having committed the crime that had stopped a nation in its tracks. Walking with ease along the corridors and between floors of police HQ, Oswald was guided through a process he was neither familiar with nor flabbergasted by. In his back pocket, tucked in his billfold, police discovered an assortment of identification papers in the name of A Hidell and Lee Harvey Oswald. The first detective to face Oswald was Guy Rose from the homicide division, who had just come on duty. It was the biggest collar of his career. Receiving the prisoner, he asked for his name, to which Oswald replied 'Hidell'. The detective, looking at both sets of identification, quizzed which one was correct, to which Oswald replied, '. . . you find out.'

CHAPTER 7

THE PATRIOT & THE LAWMAN

Like every other newshound on the day of the assassination, columnist Dorothy Kilgallen was flat out writing copy, hoping to get an angle to fill her space for the *New York Journal*. She was to file many stories about that one day in Texas, but none was more poignant than her first. She sensed early on that the world would spend 'whole lifetimes trying to analyse the drama of this week and this scene'. And in her prophetic opinion, 'What it all comes down to – after the assassination of a president, the wounding of a governor, the slaying of a policeman, and the killing of a man nobody really knew . . . is little Jack Ruby.'

•

For a short, stout, rugged type, Jack Ruby was certainly handy with prose when required. His self-description was that of a man with 'a spotty background, one that ran burlesque houses in Dallas'. A tabloid reporter might have labelled him a loner, a thug, and the proprietor of sleazy clubs, but even in that he wasn't alone. Dallas was full of gin joints back in the early sixties, saloons and nightclubs that dispensed cocktails till the wee hours to a clientele of knockabouts, off-duty cops, tired barmaids and empty-pocket drunks. A practising Jew on the wrong side of middle age, the impeccably dressed Ruby could also be portrayed as an often failed and always struggling businessman, an entrepreneur before the word itself had entered the vernacular. In a nutshell, Jack Ruby was a man who made his living from the simple, over-priced virtues of vice: fleshy strippers, imported booze and trendy Marlboro tailor-made cigarettes.

One of eight siblings, young Jacob Rubenstein grew up in rough and tough Chicago in the 1930s, working rodeos and sporting events. He sold refreshments, soda pop and popcorn and dabbled in scalping entrance tickets on the side. He was often in the shadows, staring at the bright lights. In his early twenties he moved on to California to flog tip sheets at racetracks by day and by night sold hand-painted turtles, an oddity that pulled a crowd at the fairground and wallets from their trouser pockets. It was moving towards the end of the 1930s and Jack was moving and shaking his way up in the world. He returned to Chicago, gave up his flimflam ways and took a job as secretary to the unlikely sounding Scrap Iron and Junk Handlers' Union. A world of hard men, where sleight of hand could get you killed. Within two years Ruby was on the move again, heading out of town as fast as possible. His union boss, a genuine thug with a reputation that could slow a train, had been shot and killed. All of a sudden life for the not-so-tough Jack Ruby was a bit too scary. He joined his brothers as they scampered to the east coast and tried their luck at selling lucky dip punchboards. Not long afterwards, Jack signed up for the army, which in turn bequeathed him a touch of discipline. Enough at least to avoid the obvious, as despite having amassed a succession of debts, Ruby somehow managed to stay shy of the long arm of the law.

At the end of World War Two, a rebirthed, street-wise Ruby arrived in Texas, land of opportunity. With a thirsty returned serviceman on every street corner, at last Jack felt he was home. In the heady days of capitalism that followed, the lone star state of America grew in prosperity as the jumping-off point for tourists, gamblers and sun-seekers headed south of the border for Mexico and Havana. Racketeers followed in the path of the early American hotel groups buying into Cuban nightclubs, casinos and the vast profits. Jack watched the play and licked his lips, hoping for some of the spoils. He didn't have to wait too long. Early in 1959 he received an invitation from a friend to take a short break at his Cuban gaming house. At a time when Fidel Castro was still more of a headline than a dictator and everyone was talking of fortunes made, Jack jumped onto a jet airliner.

His seven nights on the troubled island were to be his only trip to a foreign land and the only period that could in any way be considered intriguing in the world of Jack Ruby thus far. The non-gambler, who was bored by roulette wheels and blackjack, remained virtually housebound at his mate's 'Tropicana' casino, feasting on complimentary dinners and flirting with local girls. He even caught a glimpse of the beautiful Ava Gardner who was in town enjoying the sights. While unpersuaded by the lure of the cards and chips, he did turn his hand to talking up potential buyers of consumer goods among his contacts, but nobody was listening. So Ruby returned home with a poor opinion of Cuba and a fresh longing to improve his lot. Six months later, whatever attraction the island of gaming might have held for other Americans, it all ended with Castro's coup.

Dallas was the making of Jack. Running his late-night bars he soon became a popular part of the big town's low life. The well-known owner of the Carousel Club and the less frequented Vegas Club, he had, in his earlier days, run a string of even seedier venues with names like the Silver Spur. His strip joints allowed him to befriend news reporters, journalists, detectives, even district attorney staff and the occasional judge. It was as if the brush of respectability had touched him. And the more free grog he let hit his bar top, the more friends he made. Even some of Dallas's finest (cops) worked for Ruby in the early days of their police careers. Yet, as far as local punters were concerned, Jack was just a mug bar owner, a big-timer, and known to carry a gun in 'stick 'em up' Texas, due to the amount of cash he carried. The life of the bar owner plodded along quietly enough, year after year, as long as the gratuities kept coming. After seventeen years of rolling out empty beer barrels, Jack could realistically consider himself popular, particularly among law enforcement circles, yet in real life he preferred the company of dogs. His latest was a dachshund, his constant companion, often seen in his arms as he fussed about town.

The intended visit of the 35th President of the United States in 1963 was a highlight for the fifty-two-year-old big shot. Jack referred to John Fitzgerald Kennedy as his 'beloved President'. He was a staunch supporter of Kennedy and even Roosevelt in earlier days and had been known to eject people from his club who criticised either man. Strangely, for all his loyalty, it wasn't on his schedule to watch the passing motorcade. On the Friday of JFK's arrival, Ruby was busying himself in the classified ad section of the *Dallas Morning News* building, placing his regular trading notifications. It was late morning by the time he had penned the week's variations on the words he wrote fifty-two times a year: names of bands, hours of opening and a general invitation for all to attend. He was predicting a full house, a weekend of gossip and hordes of thirsty drinkers. At least he hoped so, for he was carrying an extraordinary level of debt. The IOUs were starting to be called in quicker than he could count his greenbacks.

It was his decidedly unhealthy current account deficit that kept Jack's mind juggling new ideas. While at the news building he chatted with fellow publicans about his latest brainwave: the introduction of automatic car washing machines that ran on tokens. Never put off by the occasional scoffing, he was also working up another clever concept: a 'twist' board. The overweight purchaser stood on a circular timber disk held up by a ball bearing and twisted the night away, just like Chubby Checker. Ruby spent a week in early November selling and demonstrating his boards at the Texas Trade Fair, with a couple of strippers to do his twisting. He liked the invention and was always up for a demonstration. His plump body wobbled and his calves tightened as he gave it a run for the audience. Even the affable guffaws of his associates didn't seem to slow him. Truth be told, Ruby was more than a little unfortunate not to have made a killing with either of his ideas. His timing was bad, not his inventiveness. Both went on to be profitable ventures in the hands of other, more astute businesspeople.

At 12.30pm the atmosphere of frivolity was well and truly interrupted when a colleague bounded frantically into the advertising section. There'd been a shooting downtown. The initial scuttlebutt was that a Secret Service agent had been hit. The story then took a turn, suggesting it was Governor Connally who had taken the bullet. The phones rang madly. In the back office images flickered on a black and white television. Jack could spy a streetscape he knew well and the looks of frightened kids and a scattering crowd. Within half an hour he had learnt the truth. His 'beloved President' was the one shot, the one dead. Jack Ruby started to cry. The gregarious bar owner withdrew into himself, becoming aimless and morose. Heading immediately back to the Carousel Club, he sought out his rouseabout, Andy, a man he called his 'coloured boy', and gave a brief instruction to call everybody associated with his venues. Jack had lost all interest in his debts and the drinking habits of his customers. He had decided to close his clubs for the weekend, out of respect for the deceased President.

Struggling with a dark mood, Jack left the club to seek consolation. His destination was the apartment of his sister and business partner Eva. As he drove, his appetite gnawed at him; he craved a tangible distraction from his sorrow, food. The man who was always on a diet threw caution to the wind and his diet pills aside. His travels took him past the Ritz delicatessen, one of his favourite eating-houses, a place he normally worked hard at avoiding. This time he stopped, stepped inside and emptied his wallet to buy bags of delicacies.

At Eva's, Jack became even more despondent. He settled in, surrounded by his feast and spent much of his time eating. Between mouthfuls he took to the telephone, calling friends, discussing the shooting. He spoke briefly to a newspaper journalist who had latched onto the possibility of bars closing out of respect. Jack offered a comment then went back to his tasty kosher tidbits. By early evening, with his appetite sated, his mind turned to his faith. Collecting his small dog under one arm, Ruby stepped into his car, and went in search of a synagogue offering prayer and a service dedicated to JFK. After a short detour home for a shower and shave he drove around and around the streets of his neighbourhood, from synagogue to bar room, until it was time to do it all again as he scouted for yet more food.

It disappointed Jack to see people drinking, mingling and enjoying sporadic bursts of laughter, seeing it as a slight against his 'beloved President'. He decided to call on as many clubs as he could to see who was closed and who wasn't. Who really was a patriot and who was not? As he drove, he listened to his car radio for updates on the assassination. A constant stream of updates, more conjecture, more fact, more speculation, Jack listened to it all. Along with the food it became his fuel. He realised that the police were putting in extraordinarily long hours in pursuit of the solution to the crime, an atrocity he considered the most despicable in history. He sought out a favourite delicatessen and ordered a dozen mixed sandwiches for his mates from police headquarters, his mates in blue, currently keeping company with an assassin. Pastrami and rye bread seemed to offer Jack purpose. He would head downtown to lend a hand, to offer nourishment to the 'best [police department] in the whole world'. He made a brief call to a detective while the sandwich boy buttered the bread. As the mayo hit the top layer, he pondered again the hard work being undertaken by the homicide squad detectives.

Inside headquarters, Chief Curry was fussing about in the 'total confusion'. The biggest day of his career was now a sorry nightmare. Normally a man who delegated, this time was no different. Chief Curry had quickly handed the whole sordid affair to his head of homicide, Captain Fritz, the city's so-called finest lawman, hoping like billy-o he would make it turn out right.

Like a sheriff from a bygone era the captain in the ten-gallon hat was now staring down the killer, working up another notch on his gun. He just needed a confession to secure this latest scalp. Trouble was, since early afternoon the world's media had begun arriving on his doorstep, and each and every reporter wanted answers, comments, a scoop. It was as if someone had opened the floodgates at the front door of HQ, and nobody was shutting them. So swamped was the captain that he had been forced to post a few of his better men outside the interrogation room, just to stem the flow of pesky reporters. At least a hundred with cameras and microphones were jammed in the hallway already; another hundred outside the building were scouring surrounding streets for yarns, and the numbers weren't looking like dwindling. Small-town Dallas was being overrun and the police department didn't have a media section; heck, they didn't even have a television set.

Squashed inside the interview room on the homicide squad level was yet another army. This one was a sweaty-palmed group of cops, playing musical chairs with the only three seats in the tiny room, a room normally reserved for one good cop, one bad cop and a crook. But that, too, had changed with the inevitable fuss over this shooting. Now the room held two FBI agents, two Secret Servicemen, a ranger, two homicide detectives and a strangely calm Lee Harvey Oswald. Cops were swapping seats with other cops, dependent on who wanted to get in on the action, squeeze into the room, into the body odour. None of the suits realised they were facing a man who had fantasised himself responsible for a high-profile killing for two years. No one comprehended they had a man who had ached to be centre stage, to hold a place in the spotlight, for the skinny clean-skin Lee Harvey was proving a hard nut to crack. The law watched as he lifted his chin and smirked a lot. No longer would he need to hand out measly pro-Castro leaflets, nor would he have to stand alone on his windy street corner and suffer the turning of heads from disinterested passers-by. He had landed smack-bang in the middle of a massive scandal. And he was, at last, very, very important.

Presiding over the motley ensemble in the interview room was the captain. He, too, was very, very important, but he was the one looking dazed. An ageing lawman with nothing more than a basic education and no specialist detective training, Fritz had worked his way to the top in an era when promotion came more readily to those who woke early. And the chief rose each day at 6am. Joining the Dallas Police Department forty years earlier it was longevity that had ultimately pushed him upwards. He didn't care for the fancy ways of big-city detectives, like those from New York City and Los Angeles, with their university degrees and law courses. The captain was old school, where a guilty look at a murder scene was as good as a weapon. He had been in charge of the homicide division for almost thirty years, at a time when confessions came easily and there was a hanging every second week. But now he was looking down the barrel of far too many TV cameras and he didn't care for such hullabaloo.

Normally big Fritz cut a familiar figure in his city, with his pale-coloured suits and dour look. And of course there was always the hat. If a shot rang out in town every face turned to their captain; like Wyatt Earp, he'd take care of it. He was an advocate of the adage that to get anything done properly you had to do it yourself. So he held each enquiry tightly with both fists and not one of his men would dare offer an independent thought without the full sanction of their captain. But 1960s America was changing. New procedures and principles were being introduced into the complex world of investigation, and Fritz had started thinking of retiring, sometime soon. It was only that morning he had talked about a patch of dirt that would take a few head of cattle. Then the ruckus came and the thoughts of a more simple life were pushed aside.

By late afternoon the captain sensed he was in strife. His tried and true investigative ways were abandoned as he watched a new phenomenon take hold, something rarely seen in Texas: celebrity mayhem. As he observed his world being turned upside-down he began to long for his normally quiet interrogation room, where suspects sat pensively and signed their admissions. Where was the note-taking, the jotting down of words that fell from suspects' lips? Where was the slow and methodical questioning? What happened to only one or two police in an interview room, an environment conducive to fairness and frankness? The captain's room was so crowded, so disorganised. He found himself stuck somewhere between a rock and inadmissible evidence in a law enforcement nightmare. He was charged with supervising an environment that was 'against all principles of good interrogation practice'. Even outside the interrogation room, confusion reigned. Chief Curry anxiously paced the corridors. Still, the interview of the prime suspect, the only suspect, persisted, as did the media. Instead of overseeing the show and keeping the circus at bay the big captain seized the role of chief interrogator. No one else would have that trophy! Yet, oddly, Fritz often abandoned Oswald's interview to dash about the building watching over line-ups, listening to raid briefings, reading media memos and helping gather evidence. Not a man to delegate, the captain was frantically multi-tasking while a cocky Lee Harvey was left to sit twiddling his thumbs and ogle the other cops and hangers-on left sandwiched in the room. On one occasion Fritz personally sought out a bottle of ammonia for a witness who had been overcome with emotion and fainted, leaving his team bewildered. In trying to keep charge of everything, Fritz was creating a catastrophic investigative mess. Like a pressure-cooker the mayhem bubbled as the clock ticked, hour-by-hour. He pushed through the hordes from interview room to muster room, from one chore to another, praying that all the balls would somehow drop into the right holes as his men sat idle. But what he got was more of the same. As for his suspect, all Lee Harvey gave was a run of blanket denials. Mr Oswald had the captain's mettle.

As the big man kept throwing questions, the little man's answers kept bobbing back. Oswald first denied the evidence of a network of 'Hidell' identifications linked to a maze of PO boxes across Dallas and New Orleans, and then he suddenly agreed with the identities, before finally scoffing them off as irrelevant. He refuted the existence of the photograph taken by his wife earlier that year at his home showing him proudly holding his Carcano rifle with a revolver on his hip. And he denied living at the address where Marina took the image. Somebody must have created the image, he protested. Still no admission. He denied the existence of the rifle, usually stored in Ruth's garage, and would have nothing of the proof of purchase of the weapons from Klein's Sporting Goods store. The only thing the Dallas Police Department had going for them were the line-ups, as both the taxi driver and the housewife positively identified Lee Harvey Oswald for the killing of Officer Tippit.

Luckily, Dallas had a highly competent district attorney in Henry Wade. A former FBI agent, Wade was used to filing murder charges. Prosecuting criminals was his career, and he was very good at it. When he first learnt of the shooting of the President at 3pm that afternoon, he visited the Sheriff's office where he was informed that a suspect had been arrested and was good for the crime. Conscious of protocols, the DA knew he had no place in the investigation at that point so he headed home for dinner. Dropping into police headquarters on the way home, he had a quick word with Chief Curry and Captain Fritz. Ultimately, whatever charges were to be laid would end up the responsibility of DA Wade to prosecute, so his visit was not only part of his role, but appropriate, especially as the case concerned the President of the United States.

Privately Wade had little regard for Fritz, a man he believed was a poor gatherer of evidence, a detective prone to secrets, withholding information and notorious for running a one-man operation. He was a dinosaur in a modern world. At best the two men tolerated each other; at worst they never spoke. On this November afternoon, however, both managed to overlook their differences. The DA finished his meeting and then literally had to fight his way out of the building against the current of the slow-moving media stampede.

At 10pm, at his home, with a good meal underway, Wade heard talk on his radio of a charge of 'international conspiracy to murder' being filed on Lee Harvey Oswald. Chief Curry was preparing an arraignment and Henry almost choked on his roast chicken. Protocols or not, the district attorney knew it was time to step in. He jumped in his car and headed back to police headquarters, riddled with angst in his knowledge that there was no such crime. It was either murder or nothing. He instigated a hasty meeting with the chief and the captain and together they battled through the evidence.

Principally, Wade learnt there was a sound belief that Lee had taken his Carcano rifle to the Book Depository that morning hidden in the brown paper sack in which it was originally purchased. No curtain rods were located. Fingerprint experts had identified Oswald's palm print as that found on the underside of the suspected murder weapon abandoned on the sixth floor along with three spent rounds from fully jacketed ammunition. Oswald had been seen rushing from the Depository shortly after the shooting and three co-workers placed him on the sixth floor at lunchtime. Furthermore, in the time between fleeing the Book Depository and his subsequent arrest Oswald had admitted to catching a bus and taxi home to change his clothes and collect his hand gun. He also admitted carrying his gun into the Texas Theatre and struggling with arresting officers. With the witnesses' positive identification of Oswald as the killer of Officer Tippit, the case was looking good. One of the five witnesses at Tippit's shooting was an ex-marine who not only saw Oswald but spoke to him. Some witnesses watched Oswald run from the scene, dump the spent rounds and reload his weapon, yelling that the policeman was dead. The taxi driver collected the spent bullets and they proved a match to Oswald's hand gun. The investigation was gaining witnesses by the hour.

Fattening out the prosecutor's briefcase was a marked-up map of Dallas with the intended motorcade route of the President, found by police at Oswald's apartment. Add to that the presence of paraffin on Oswald's hand, an indicator that a weapon had been fired from that hand. There was also evidence of a false alibi, Oswald claiming he had lunched with his co-worker James Jarman. Jarman, in turn, vehemently denied this, stating he was eating with his friends on the fifth floor and ceiling dust had fallen into his hair as he heard shots being fired, sensing spent cartridges hitting the floorboards above him.

Wade gave the instruction to cease the nonsense of an international conspiracy, as he had not seen a skerrick of evidence to link the suspect to any other person. A charge of murder was drafted. DA Wade breathed a deep sigh of relief and directed that Lee Harvey Oswald be despatched immediately to the County Jail, for reasons of security. Fritz looked up at the wall clock; midnight was looming. Exhausted, he nonetheless disallowed the instruction, citing the need for further questioning of Oswald. All the while the media squawked in the background, demanding a look at the assassin.

Across town Jack Ruby had his bags of sandwiches packed and ready to go. But he was disappointed; from his telephone call he had learnt that many of the detectives had just knocked off; the pastrami sustenance was not required. Undeterred, he mulled over the next most worthy to benefit from his good deed. He would take his gift to the news reporters at the local radio station: men working around the clock, 'the best disc jockeys in the whole world'. Ruby's rationale was twisting with his melancholy. He dialled the stations after-hours telephone number. A little girl announced that her father was busy elsewhere, reporting. She had nothing more to offer Jack other than that her mother had already taken care of business in the sandwich department. Everybody, it seemed, had eaten. Jack couldn't give his sandwiches away.

With an increasingly desperate need to be close to the action, Jack pointed his 1960 Oldsmobile sedan towards police headquarters and drove with a determination that was consuming him. Benevolence was becoming a burden. His back muscles ached and his heavy frame stooped. The patriot left his car and the sandwiches at the front of headquarters, counting himself lucky for a car space as the building was surrounded by dozens of news crew vehicles. It was as if the circus had come to town and the main tent was police headquarters. Ruby entered the building, elbowing his way through the smoky room. For more than an hour he mingled among the 300 law enforcement officers, one for every media man. The world wanted to see an assassin and Jack had a free pass to the action. He walked, unchecked, from floor to floor, free to push and shove through the stench. At every stride were faces he knew, thirsts he'd served and the occasional nod, even from a passing judge. So many regulars from the Carousel Club were seeking to attach themselves to the investigation. Jack requested a PA page message to a police contact over the loudspeaker. The operator obliged, sending out Ruby's call. As Jack waited he noticed Fritz step out of his office with Lee Harvey Oswald in tow. Apparently the captain was hoping to parade the assassin before the media but the location was wrong, so they disappeared again.

In the corridor Ruby continued to mingle from one police contact to another, reminding them of past good times at his bar. He would rub shoulders with the swamped Captain Fritz and Chief Curry as they flitted in and out of rooms. Fritz had taken to pacing a lot, but he wasn't after exercise, he was walking off anxiety, awaiting the autopsy results from the team of pathologists. Like an expectant father, he waited and waited; he knew the case would hinge on the autopsy reports.

Jack Ruby was pacing off just as much anxiety, but he was finally on the inside, within the inner sanctum of those investigating the death of his beloved President. He hoped to talk to District Attorney Henry Wade. He thought of all those years dispensing free drinks; perhaps now he would reap his reward. Then, a gift presented itself in the form of an impromptu press conference. The world was about to see the killer and Jack had a front-row seat that he made good use of by standing on it, turning it into a platform. He watched the learned district attorney attempt to silence the press, who were demanding a look at the killer. Reporters poised their pens over spiral notepads and television cameras zoomed in on grey-suited men with etched frowns and hard words. DA Wade prepared to make the most significant address in his thirteen-year career.

One of the first people the DA noticed in the sea of faces was that of Jack Ruby, standing on a chair looking wild-eyed and clutching a notebook. Alongside, reporters, too, were on top of chairs, on top of tables, on top of each other. It was a mob scene and they were all firing questions. Ruby listened intently as Henry Wade began to speak. He had heard during earlier news broadcasts that Oswald had been a member of the Play Fair for Cuba Committee. When the DA got the name of the committee wrong, Jack leapt in to correct him. The cameras rolled on and Henry, Jack thought, seemed almost appreciative of his interjection. Both men had seen each other only two or three days prior. Ruby had been lounging around in the DA's office in the company of half a dozen Dallas police, discussing a pornography case under prosecution. DA Wade knew the owner of the Carousel Club as 'a man about town'. Ruby radiated pride as the main event, Lee Harvey Oswald, appeared, his thought processes spinning into delusion, believing he had now been deputised as a reporter. All of a sudden meaning and purpose pumped through his veins. He took mental note of a shiner that Oswald sported over his right eye, the handiwork of one of his police mates, he surmised. Ruby stared at the now most hated man in America, studying his face, his build and his overall persona. He listened to Oswald's comment suggesting he was being set up, that he was a 'patsy'. The throwaway line was more befitting a street-smart thug than a twenty-four-year-old assassin. As Ruby watched, hatred festered within him. Then the rapid-fire questions from the press jolted him back into the here and now. A moment later the circus was over and newsmen scurried in all directions.

Ruby used a telephone in the assembly room to call a radio station and make it known where he was and whose company he was keeping, offering to broker an introduction for the radio disc jockey with DA Wade. He was now feeling mighty important. The district attorney noticed that the chunky little man was still running about everywhere, huffing and puffing.

Wade had an odd feeling about Mr Jack Ruby. He thought him a glory seeker, a champion type, a man on the edge. As the assembly room emptied, Ruby helped out another anxious reporter looking for the ear of the DA. As he left, Wade gave him another thought, but couldn't quite put his finger on his worry. As he watched Ruby disappear down a corridor, the feeling nudged him again. Then it was time to get back to his work.

At the radio station, Ruby and his sandwiches were warmly welcomed. For more than an hour he ate with the newsmen, discussing the assassination from every angle. He espoused the need for brave men in the community. Then it was time to head home. His sombre mood had started biting again; it really was the worst day of his life.

As hard as Jack tried his car never quite reached that homeward destination. He drove around thinking, worrying, obsessing; his mind covered the same territory, the killing dominating his thoughts. On his back seat was a copy of a book that encouraged people to take matters into their own hands, to act like a hero. Jack let the idea run a lap or two of his troubled mind. Then he spotted a bar room mate from the Carousel Club, an off-duty cop named Harry Olsen. Harry was cocooned in a car with Kathy Kay, one of Jack's strippers. They were in the throes of a steamy affair but today they were only crying on each other's shoulders. Jack stopped to lend a tear. He boasted of being up close and personal to the assassin and described him as 'a little rat . . . real sneaky like'.

The police officer was glowing in his remarks towards Ruby, calling him 'the greatest guy in the world' for his generosity and his willingness to help. It was a few other words that really resonated with Jack, though. Words of how Oswald should be cut down, inch by inch, into ribbons for the atrocity he had caused. This cocktail of bittersweet oratory on the one hand and high praise on the other found a home in the bar owner's mind, tucked away among all that had gone before him that day. For well over an hour the crying game continued until Jack broke free and headed for the news building. He needed to change his advertisement to declare closure of his clubs in a show of respect for the fallen President. Cursing many of his competitors for continuing to trade at this solemn time, he selected an appropriate in-mourning border for the copy.

Oddly, Jack's mood broke long enough for him to demonstrate his twister board to the rollicking laughter of others placing late-night ads, but his twist was buckled and his rhythm gone. Then the darkness crept back in as his thoughts returned to the tragedy that had befallen his President's wife. Surely someone owed it to poor Jackie that she shouldn't have to return to Dallas to witness a trial for the heinous murder? The more he thought of it, the more discomfort he felt. Then a 'solution' gripped him, held on tight and eventually took him to bed, into a deep and restless sleep.

On Saturday morning, Jack once again went seeking answers from his religion. The words of Rabbi Seligman that 'a man [President Kennedy] that fought in every battle, went to every country and had to come back to our own country to be shot in the back' gave strength to his growing conviction. Jack was completely overcome by emotion. In his words, he was 'carried away for the rest of the day', depressed and stormy of mood. Later that morning the distraught man visited the site where his 'idol the President' was assassinated. He sat for an hour as if reliving the atrocity and spoke at length to Officer Channey, a uniformed policeman he knew. He continued to brood throughout the afternoon.

A feeling of downheartedness hit DA Wade that same morning. He had been up early and in at the office conferring with his colleagues, the Dallas police and Chief Curry. The DA was disappointed that the chief of police seemed not to have a handle on the situation. The media were getting seriously out of hand, demanding a quote by the minute, a news conference on the hour. With Lee Harvey Oswald now charged with the murder by malice of the President, the carriage of the prosecution lay with Wade. And he made it abundantly clear that a complete lockdown on information needed to occur, now. Confidentiality was the key; the rest would be up to a jury in good time.

Wade returned home by early afternoon to sift through the evidence from the dozens of enquiries and police raids, as well as the information seized via search warrant from Oswald's two residences: the home Marina shared with Ruth, and the rooming house. At the latter address, investigators had located the documentation revealing the purchase of the Carcano rifle by mail order, from Klein's Sporting Goods store, under the pseudonym 'A Hidell'. The cost of the rifle was a mere $19.95, a cheap weapon. A secondhand clunky rifle that said much about the assassin.

Apart from providing a twisted inspiration for an alias, 'Hidell' being a play on the Christian name 'Fidel' (Castro), Wade came to the conclusion that any other connection to communist activities was exaggerated, amounting to only a few pamphlets and a couple of letters. Both matters, in his opinion, were irrelevant to the charge at hand. Furthermore, he found absolutely no evidence of anyone else being involved in the assassination. Wade wanted his own powder to be bone dry in the area of accomplices and co-offenders so he studied the available evidence thoroughly. He firmly believed that Oswald had acted alone.

Putting his paperwork aside, he turned on his television set to relax a spell. Confronted with an image of Chief Curry at a news conference showing off Lee Harvey's Carcano rifle, the DA was livid. Police were doling out all the evidence to the media! Included, word for word, were critical comments made by Oswald, remarks on what he did and what he didn't do, all evidence for a future trial. Wade started to brood a different strain of misery, for surely here were the good guys happily creating an insurmountable bias for any future jury.

When night fell Ruby called a friend, a former member of the Dallas police department with whom he discussed the assassination in detail before again venturing out into his city. He tried a drink at a bar but could only manage a Coca-Cola. Unlike the night before, large numbers of people were out partying, enjoying dancing and having a good time, not at all grief-stricken as he was. He left his soft drink unfinished and hung his head in mourning as he exited the club. A news service he caught on his drive home reinforced his misgiving that it would be Mrs Kennedy who would suffer the most. The cogs in Jack's mind clicked over and over, 'Someone owed a debt to our beloved President . . .'. His television screen at home flashed images of a grief-stricken Bobby Kennedy and the President's children, stirring within him an overwhelming sense of duty.

Meanwhile, inside police headquarters, Captain Fritz was still hard at it, wading through his own quagmire. The media weren't going home and neither was he as the battle played on. Although he did wish the noise, the push, the shove and the wretched world would just go away so he could sit quietly with the young assassin and extract 'more facts from him, if we could just talk quietly'. As conscious as he was of the claustrophobic pressure, Fritz did not once attempt to shift or alter it. He was way out of his depth but elected to sweat it out. He had taken no notes of the events of the past two days; not a single piece of paper would contemporaneously record the questions, the answers or the chronology of the most important murder investigation in American history. Commonsense had become an equal casualty to investigative incompetence, yet somehow the evidence still trickled out. Fortuitously DA Wade was there to catch what affidavits, statements and depositions became available.

On Sunday morning Mrs Kennedy's face re-entered the mind of the patriot. He saw her sadness, the horrible pain and wretched agony. For Jack Ruby it became 'the Jackie factor'. The man with the 'spotty background' was deeply angered that a cold-blooded murderer was sitting in a jail cell downtown surrounded by police, Jack's mates. Jack owed it to his President to rid the world of the murderer. If the opportunity presented itself he was going to kill the man, the man who killed his President. He was going to save the First Lady from an ordeal. He was going to right a wrong.

Due to the closure of the Carousel Club over the weekend, Karen Bennett, the stripper known as Little Lynn, requested Ruby wire her owed wages. Jack agreed, not necessarily out of a need to see the young woman paid but because the task of wiring her a twenty-five dollar money order would give him the perfect excuse to head down to the Western Union office, across the street from police headquarters. He dressed in his best brown suit and tie. By the time he and his pet dog had settled into the front seat of his car, his plan was well on its way to becoming a mission. One pocket was full of money – he was carrying more than a thousand dollars in cash – and the other pocket was full of ammunition and a snub-nosed hand gun. Although Jack didn't have a permit for his pistol he carried it daily, what with all the cash generated by his strip clubs. His police mates knew he was always armed but no one cared. All Jack needed to do was get close to the assassin one more time. No problem, he thought, he had an all seasons pass to the most televised fortress in America. He became aware from radio broadcasts that his quarry would be relocated from police headquarters late that morning. With the Western Union transfer of funds made smack on 10.17am, Jack wandered across the street which was laden with wreaths and mourners. He cried to himself as he moved down a ramp and into a very familiar police building. His clammy palm massaged the barrel of his handgun, safely in his right hip pocket.

In his usual manner the debt-ridden entrepreneur bar owner wandered unchecked through police headquarters, saying howdy to his various cop mates, keeping his ear to the ground and his eyes focused. He followed news cameras and reporters to the basement, where emotions overheated in his head. Lee Harvey Oswald was being marched along a corridor by Captain Fritz and an army of detectives in matching ten-gallon hats for the entire world to see.

The captain was against the plan Chief Curry had conjured to transfer Oswald via wagon to the county jail. Cameras moved in and the media went into scoop mode. Over the microphone leads and between clearing throats of the commentators stepped Ruby, a patriot on a mission to save a First Lady. He raised his weapon and uttered the last six words he would ever say as a free man, '. . . you killed my President, you rat!', then his trigger finger found its home and with one shot the patriot felled the assassin.

'I'm Jack Ruby, you all know me!' he yelled as he was grounded by his mates from the Dallas Police Department. Jack had sacrificed himself for 'the few moments of saving Mrs Kennedy the discomfiture of coming back to trial'. As he was dragged away by two police officers he was heard to say, 'I hope I killed the son of a bitch . . .'

Within minutes the news had bounced around every radio station in the city of Dallas, in the country and around the globe. DA Wade was walking away from his church congregation; a fine service had been overshadowed by his lone thoughts and worry about the Oswald case; he feared more of the same, more damage to the prosecution of his case, as he walked his family to their motor car. When he started his car to commence the short journey home, he decided to turn on the radio. His foot would find the brake pedal as he listened to the breaking news announcement that a 'businessman' had killed Lee Harvey Oswald. Wade's hands gripped the steering wheel as the news sank in, his knuckles whitening. Shocked, dazed and full of uncertainty, the first thought that came to him was, who could have done such a thing? Within a split second the wild eyes of Jack Ruby came into his mind's eye. He carefully selected a gear and slowly moved forward.

CHAPTER 8

THE CONSPIRACY THEORIES

From virtually the moment the fatal bullet found its target, the truth behind the assassination of JFK has been shrouded in theories. I have studied many of them. Some are interesting for their sheer creativity; others are clever at joining the dots; some have far too many dots, so many players that the script becomes illogical; others are just scandalous and make no sense at all. To comprehend fully how these theories came into being is to delve into events a few years preceding the tragedy, to the cusp of 1960s America and the commencement of an introspective social and political identity crisis.

The rigours of World War Two were a generation past. Fast food was on the table and a nouveau nation was trying to pull away from the suburbia so fabulously depicted in Norman Mailer and Richard Yates's writings of the preceding decade. A brash, self-confident country was emerging where chiffon, porkpie hats and pencil-thin neck ties were being challenged by Levi's dungarees, black shirts and duffle coats. No longer were white-bread citizens suspicious of one another, neighbours, their boss or the local ethnic motor mechanic down the street. The 1950s McCarthy period had inferred that communists lay in wait under beds. Such propaganda had gripped the nation and paranoia during this time was at risk of strangling America. Popular culture identities had been outed for the slimmest association with any individual who didn't share the *Revolutionary Road* dream of a house, two kids, a car and a mortgage. It had been a time when the weekly visit to the supermarket and a helping of 'Leave it to Beaver' happy family television was the required antidote to avoid being publicly hung out to dry by the McCarthy hearings. Decent people were being blacklisted. Careers were ruined. Communities became polarised. The politics of communism had been well and truly galvanised as evil. There were only two choices: West or East, democracy or ruin.

By the early 1960s, the horrors of McCarthyism were waved an overdue farewell, banished to the outfield along with their namesake. The hollers of a nation of freethinking critics resounded; the wounded picked themselves up and dusted off their integrity. Life slowly went back to normal and the sounds now blossoming were those of cool jazz, hip poets and avant-garde artists. A toll, however, had been exacted on the minds of a smart people; suspicion had crept into their psyche. It was as if they had been programmed to suspect the worst, fear everything and believe little; the perfect footing for storytellers to step off, the ideal gestation for conspiracy theorists.

Enter the 35th President of the United States, delivering to his people a new, youthful administration with a very different mindset. The youngest man to hold the top job in US history,

'Jack' was unlike any of his predecessors. A friend to movie stars, he invited sporting icons to the White House, spoke with a verse that captivated, and came from a family that was the nearest thing to American royalty. And he was so charismatic. His new broom approach had a slim mandate to improve the economy and bolster the country's military outpostings. His constituents, along with the rest of the democratic world, breathed a sigh of relief and watched and waited.

The global political stage at this time was like no other period in history. It was the peak of the Cold War. And JFK was a cold warrior, intrigued by the intrigue. He dropped his sights from the homeland spying game and threw his vision abroad. Standing firm on 470-year-old American soil, he faced off his off-shore opponents not with arms, but with intelligent intelligence. He was a CIA man.

Across the Atlantic Ocean the political climate was frosty. The Berlin Wall was under construction, keeping a people in and socialism alive. Further east and Russia was flexing her muscle, gathering in the weaker states of Eastern Europe, ensuring communism remained a viable option. It was as if the pieces to a new game of chess were being marshalled, a game that required only two players but many pawns. From behind his White House desk, Kennedy studied his opponent. In Khrushchev he saw a formidable adversary; Russians had always been masters at playing chess. Striding forward to take up a position on the board was Fidel Castro. The two statesmen of the left linked arms and swapped private telephone numbers. All of a sudden politics became the stuff of Ian Fleming novels, with a new breed of soldier, the type who wore no uniform and carried no Tommy gun. The game of spying required only a bottomless expense account and a trenchcoat. Cloak-and-dagger secret agents, double agents, British MI6 intelligence officers, Israel's Mossad operatives, Russian KGB moles, East Germany's Stasi and the CIA followed no rules, just each other. And the USSR and USA excelled.

The resultant skulduggery saw a string of defections. Each side lost valued academics, strategists and political figures. Curiosity and unrest bred the swapping of allegiances as unsure patriots studied the form and imagined greener grasses. The superpower play that followed filled magazines, inspired screenwriters and sired the exposé documentary. A new style of entertainment found a haven in America's loungerooms: espionage. Wild stories of truth serum confessions, cyanide pills and chloral hydrate, government hitmen and nuclear scientists who disappear at the flick of an audio button on a listening device recorder, and governments under threat from recalcitrant Dr Strangelove types.

And in among it all, the domestic journalist hungrily fed the nation's growing appetite. Newspaper front pages offered readers a writing style and colour previously unused. Before long there were as many correspondents travelling the globe phoning in copy as there were spies sending dossiers to clandestine rendezvous points.

On the doorstep of Texas, only a rowboat away, sat Cuba, now an angry little cub to the Russian bear. With Fidel Castro's version of communism firmly stamped on this once capitalist island society, his northern neighbour began to get a little fidgety. Too close to home, the US thought. World dominance was a serious agenda and from Cuba you could see the feathers of the big eagle. Many recalled a few years earlier when Fidel had literally tossed out US entrepreneurs and mobsters, shut down the casinos and nightclubs and seized countless bank accounts. Long memories, most owned by racketeers and mafia bosses, vowed to get even with the khaki-clad maverick with bad taste in facial hair. Being mates with Castro was not a feasible strategy. The President's intelligence was telling him to invade the rebel: restrain the cub or face attack. And he believed it. The result was an ill-conceived invasion of Cuba's Bay of Pigs and the inevitable retreat came at the cost of the condemnation of the world media and the snarl of the Ruskies. It was time for the eagle to lie low for a while and lick her feathers. A second election year was also looming.

That same year art would imitate life and life would imitate art as the political landscape started to blur for the handsome young President. As a retaliatory manoeuvre for the attempted invasion of Cuba, Russian ships delivered an urgent despatch to their cub: nuclear missiles, to be pointed directly at the US mainland. The tussle over arms proliferation and the threat of nuclear warfare escalated to a dangerous height. Russia was taking on America, black spy was facing white spy and only one could survive. The stand-off, written in history as the 'Missiles of October' saga, may have led to the destruction of the superpowers. The global press ran wild and quiet Middle America took to huddling behind the venetian blinds in their front rooms, glimpsing, reading and waiting. Like McCarthyism once more, everyone was nervous, everyone was peeping through the blinds.

That same month saw the premiere of what would become the most popular movie series in history, the ultimate spy film that inspired many: Agent 007, James Bond in *Dr No*. The first in the string of films was set in the Caribbean Sea, on the island of Jamaica, involving a CIA agent, nuclear rocket launches in Texas and the risk to national security of the US. Sound familiar?

Back in the real world, a stand-off between Cuba and America was to play out over two weeks of the most tense days of the twentieth century. At the height of the Cold War, Russia's Chairman Khrushchev sent a fleet of Navy destroyers towards Cuba, who the US suspected of hiding Russian warhead missiles, pointing at mainland America. A resilient President Kennedy held firm, ordering the missiles be withdrawn from the Caribbean. Tensions got within a wink of war, until commonsense prevailed, both sides compromised and Russia sent their death rockets home. But Khrushchev still had one big gun, in Cuba. Castro, who was walking taller for the experience, waved the hardware away and the keen young bear went back to once again lie in his tropical sun.

A few months later saw the release of one of the most critically acclaimed films of the year, *The Manchurian Candidate*. A blackish Cold War thriller about brainwashing and conspiracy, the plot centred on an assassination attempt by an ex-US army man who was in fact a Soviet sleeper/mole agent programmed to kill. October 1963 saw the latest James Bond epic hit the world screens: *From Russia With Love*. A tale with a touch more pepper than the last offering, as the writers had been inspired by real-life events. This time a defector from the West was handed the task of plotting an assassination. There was a pretty Soviet femme fatale involved and state-held secrets. But of course the defector was a double agent. In real time one month later the 35th President of the United States was fatally gunned down.

Seriously bruised by the shooting, the American people were ready for the conspiracy theorists.

A simple explanation to the shocking crimes set in motion on 22 November, 1963 – the shooting of a governor, assassination of a president, murder of a policeman and killing of a killer – would not satisfy an American public, its journalists, commentators, or the television anchormen who stared a nation down each night at 6pm. Nor would it satisfy a new breed of amateur sleuths, fuelled by the wiles of the CIA, the KGB and the Cold War. These aficionados of intrigue were transformed overnight into conspiracy theorists and by the end of 1963 they were like overripe mangoes ready to fall from trees. And they did; it was a bumper harvest. The amateur sleuths plied stories that would match it with the best, even Ian Fleming, focusing on the disgruntled and confused ex-US marine Lee Harvey Oswald, who had three years previously defected to the Soviet Union and sidled up to his own pretty Russian. A man of many secrets who fostered both violence and vendetta, Oswald had defected back to America and carried out an assassination. The parallels between art and life can be uncanny, especially when you are prepared to hide facts and witnesses. But as everyone started to really look at lazy, sunny Texas, home of the gun and a gunman, they realised matters weren't quite as they seemed. Television coverage highlighted the ineptitude of the Dallas Police Department and confused Americans started to wonder if the conspiracy theorists might just be right. Overnight, the theorists became the experts.

For those with wild imaginations, President John Fitzgerald Kennedy had no business dying an explainable death. So the Olivetti typewriters came out and authors constructed words that fell into the laps of many. Joining the dots had arrived, forever changing the way in which celebrity deaths would be reported. Indeed, a new style of writing was born out of the death of the 35th President: 'crackpot journalism', the reporting of irresponsible, unsubstantiated and uncorroborated scuttlebutt. Preferring to believe in espionage, conspiracy and communism, a perfect support cast was assembled to explain the murder. Truth was forced to hide behind a nonsensical forest of trees and intrigues were ripe for the picking. In no time the thinking of a nation of intellects started to cloud. Suspicious minds were fuelled by links, connections, invented facts, hearsay, real evidence and documents, witness accounts and hunches, all blended into highly readable stories of this most shocking crime. Anything and everything was proffered as the storytellers licked their pencils and wrote.

The scenarios and theories put forward to explain the reasons behind the assassination would be wide and varied, and at times just plain absurd. The person or persons labelled as responsible included, apart from Lee Harvey Oswald: Cuban President Fidel Castro, the anti-Castro Cuban community, a Jack Ruby and mafia joint venture, a Jack Ruby and Castro joint venture, Vice President Johnson, the mafia, the office of the FBI, the CIA, Russian Soviets, a Russian/Lee Harvey Oswald collaboration, a Clay Shaw and David Ferrie coupling, New Orleans mobsters, pro-Castro Cubans, and on it went, and still does. In the following pages I will explore them in great detail.

Lawyer and minor-league politician Mark Lane became the granddaddy of this fancy. Scribbling bestselling works on the subject, including *Rush for Justice* and *A Citizen's Dissent*, misquoting witnesses, omitting evidence, embellishing information and massaging the facts to suit his version of the truth, Lane created a tale full of riddles and low on evidence, an embarrassment to the principles of sound investigation. And he did the American people no favours as he spun his tales. He wasted hours of the Commission's time waxing eloquent about an alleged mix-up with the Carcano rifle owned by Oswald, how JFK was really shot in the throat, and how there had to be two shooters involved, one from the front and the other from the rear. Lane was the man who coined the phrase 'the grassy knoll', labouring on the 'fact' that four to six rounds were shot, evidenced by what others heard near the grassy area under the overpass. What Lane failed to take into account was the 'echo effect' experienced by some witnesses and later explained by workers at the railyard who often heard echos near the overpass. Lane questioned the civil rights of Oswald, quoted the opinions of people who weren't even at the crime scene, and badgered many of those who were. He did nothing more than cloud the opening days of the hearing, lighting the spark to fire up a succession of theorists. Fourteen years later, Lane also inveigled himself into the murky Jonestown tragedy, in which 918 brainwashed (mostly) Americans became caught up in a bizarre murder suicide pact. Lane had some wild theories for that mess, too. Why he was allowed to give evidence at the Warren Commission is beyond comprehension; he wasn't at the crime scene in Dallas, he played no role in the formal investigation and he offered nothing more than unsubstantiated stories to bolster later sales of his many books on the death of JFK. That he was allowed to raise the Bible and give sworn evidence about his wild conspiracy theories is a shock. Mark

Lane planted the seed of conspiracy, which helped confuse the masses.

Of all the yarns to jostle for air space, the one known as the 'Garrison theory', put forward by New Orleans Parish District Attorney Jim Garrison, was possibly the most ridiculous. He attempted to link Lee Harvey Oswald to David Ferrie, a pilot from Louisiana. Claiming that the New Orleans police had received a tip-off alluding to a role played by Ferrie in the assassination, he further alleged that Ferrie made a mysterious trip to Texas immediately after the assassination. His premise was that Ferrie had gone to debrief Lee Harvey Oswald, but he was never able to substantiate any connection. Four days after the assassination Ferrie himself died of a brain haemorrhage, a fact that would frustrate both Garrison and his theory. In a classic 'attack is the best form of defence' manoeuvre, Garrison cited another conspiracy as being behind the death of Ferrie, and on it went.

As his hypothesis faltered, Garrison added prominent New Orleans businessman Clay Shaw to his hit list, and a search warrant was taken out on Shaw's home address. The vigilante DA made fast work of the private and personal equipment uncovered during the search, used by Shaw in his homosexual lifestyle. Reading the sordid list of love toys on the front page of their newspapers horrified the sexually unliberated American public and the name Clay Shaw was blackened. Not to be deterred by his lack of pertinent evidence, in 1967 the megalomaniac prosecutor charged Shaw with conspiracy to murder. His smoking gun was a series of coded numbers, linked to his suspects. The decoding method Garrison put forward was so complex that it would take a classroom full of

Mensa students to unravel. Inevitably, due to an abysmal lack of evidence, the matter was thrown out of court. Despite being publicly ridiculed the media-obsessed Garrison would go down yelling connections with Castro's Cuba, mafia families and the CIA, still desperately grasping for evidentiary straws.

Shortly after his last outburst he resigned, his credibility completely shot. While Garrison shrank back into society, he left behind an unfortunate legacy, a stain on how the American public perceived the death of their President. His nonsense had permeated the mentality of a people starved for answers to the death of a much-loved man. As the saying goes, mud sticks; if you hear something long enough you start to believe that at least part of it is possibly true. Enter filmmaker Oliver Stone. The focus of his 1992 blockbuster, the Academy Award-winning film *JFK*, was the Garrison theory, spiced with a handful of other co-conspirators, mafia, corrupt political figures, a touch of the James Bond, gun-runners and magic bullets. But that's Hollywood entertainment, and understanding the death of the 35th President of America is not.

The world has become so accustomed to the idea of a conspiracy being behind the assassination of John F Kennedy that opinion polls still regularly show the vast majority believe a conspiracy was behind his death. The question is, which one? It is said there are more conspiracy theorists linked to the death of the President than there are detectives in the Dallas Police Department. And these people have their own union, their own network, their own 'home': cyberspace. Online they continue to discuss the facts and autopsy the theories. They meet annually in Dealey Plaza and debate the most mundane aspects of the crime, latching onto the meaningless. They hang

off the 'fact' that Jack Ruby visited Cuba three times, steadfast
in their attestations that he was a gun-runner, had an audience
with Fidel Castro, and it was Castro who funded the hit. No
such evidence has ever existed. The same theorists forget to
mention that Jack Ruby underwent six hours of polygraph
lie-detecting tests during the Warren Commission. A table
of distinguished counsellors watched on as the polygraph
technician, Agent Herdon, asked Ruby hundreds of scripted
questions and monitored his comprehensive responses. Agent
Herdon covered Ruby's movements and associations leading up
to the assassination and his subsequent killing of Lee Harvey
Oswald. The questions were not only thorough but also at
times repetitive, covering the crucial details, such as previous
associations with criminals, any history with Lee Harvey Oswald
and reasons for shooting Oswald. The technician stated under
oath that '. . . there was no physiological response to the stimulus
of the questions.' Simply put, Ruby showed no stress and no
strain; the needle hardly wavered and his heart rate remained
a consistent sixty-six to seventy-two beats per minute. Agent
Herdon, a veteran of thousands of polygraph examinations and
arguably the nation's most experienced lie-detector technician,
would sum up by stating of Ruby that there was 'no indication
of deception'.

Not to be silenced, the conspiracy theorists grasped onto
the issue that southern fried chicken bones (the leftover lunch
of a co-worker of Oswald) were located on the sixth floor of
the Texas School Book Depository when the crime scene was
being searched. Somehow the presence of the bones (apparently)
provided proof that a second shooter lay in wait. Surely they
weren't suggesting an assassination team would take their

own lunch with them! Theorists still postulate, pontificate and ponder such a no-brainer, displaying great difficulty in differentiating between fact and obvious fantasy. But, then again, it's all to do with the jigsaw puzzle approach to a solution: find a piece that fits and if it doesn't then force it in or toss it aside. There's a table full of pieces.

In contemplating the scene at Dealey Plaza, with all its intrigue and skulduggery, it's worth noting that in the half a century that has elapsed since, not one trace of solid evidence has been uncovered to support or elevate any conspiracy theory to a level above tabloid splash. This, despite the efforts of hundreds of investigators, the probing of the Warren Commission, the printing of countless theses and papers, as well as the publication of countless books on the subject. And let's not forget the dozens of JFK conspiracy theory websites, most proffering a point of view, many holding out their morsel to show their 'proof' of a conspiracy. More importantly, not a single witness has been able to offer any credible evidence of another assassin at the scene, other than Lee Harvey Oswald. Even Oswald's mother, who would not accept any fault or blame of her son, could only offer sensationalised ramblings and unspecific finger-pointing at scapegoats such as the CIA and the FBI. In short, the conspiracy theories amount to nothing more than idle gossip.

The always-controversial J Edgar Hoover, head of the FBI for longer than most people care to remember, sums up all that needs to be said on the subject. He assigned dozens of staff, investigators, experts and agents to the task and stated under oath at the Warren Commission that the resources of the bureau were 'unable to find any scintilla of evidence showing any foreign conspiracy or domestic conspiracy that culminated in the assassination of President Kennedy'. No doubt a conspiracy theorist would put forward the argument that Edgar himself was part of the plot to rid the American public of their President, and so it goes.

This author agrees with Hoover's final analysis.

My reading of the pages of the Warren Commission documents and the Assassination Records Review Board transcripts failed to find a skerrick of evidence to hold up a proposition of conspiracy to kill JFK, Governor Connally, Officer Tippit or Lee Harvey Oswald.

CHAPTER 9

TWO CLEVER MEN

Four years after the shootings, the American people remained sceptical. A CBS television crew attempted a re-enactment of the shooting. Using live rounds of ammunition they employed an identical model Carcano bolt-action rifle with the same Optics Ordinance 'Made in Japan' cheap four-point telescopic scope. Interestingly the telescope seized at the crime scene was set slightly off-centre, which would result in its shooter missing the target unless he compensated for it, or corrected his alignment. The scope used in the CBS crew's controlled experiment was set in the same manner.

The re-enactment was performed under the professional supervision of the White Ballistics Laboratory in Maryland, considered one of the most prestigious independent ballistics laboratories in America. Since the day of the shootings the question of whether a lone gunman could fire three rounds so quickly had troubled many. So the question posed was simply,

Is it physically possible to fire three rounds from this weapon in 5.6 seconds or less?

The time derived (5.6 seconds) was taken from a study of the famous home movie footage taken by Abraham Zapruder as President Kennedy's motorcade travelled along Elm Street. This fascinating footage runs for 26.6 seconds before, during and immediately following the assassination. Mr Zapruder, who also heard echoes from the shots due to his position in relation to the overpass, was not the only witness to have photographed at least part of the assassination. Indeed, an assortment of amateur movies and still photographs from a total of thirty-two 'photographers' were later seized by law enforcement officers. Some were never to fall under public scrutiny, locked away at the conclusion of the Warren Commission under the secrecy provisions that shrouded the entire saga. The most telling amateur films taken on the day are from bystanders Robert Hughes, Tina Towner and Orville Nix. Robert Hughes's footage shows the motorcade turning into Houston Street and approaching the Texas School Book Depository. Then there is a few seconds of footage from thirteen-year-old Tina Towner as the President's car turns into Elm Street, along with that of Orville Nix, whose vision is from across the Dealey Plaza, showing the President's car moving towards the overpass, and the moment the shots find their target.

All dramatic stuff. But none of the footage is as graphic as the Zapruder film. Abraham Zapruder was in the ideal position to capture what has become accepted as the most important piece of amateur film ever taken. His images were comprehensive, with the focus at the critical point being on the President, his wife Jackie, and their limousine.

Eleven elite marksmen were each invited to fire three rounds over distances that matched studies from the crime scene analysis. Each shooter was in the same position, replicating the position of Lee Harvey Oswald, a purpose-built high tower taking the role of the Book Depository. The exercise was conducted in weather conditions similar to those on the fateful day. Each of the marksmen complained that the Carcano rifle was 'clunky' insofar as the bolt had to be slammed hard into place after each round was fed into the chamber. Not the ideal assassin's weapon compared with the myriad of sophisticated options on the market at the time.

Candidates scored varying results; some fielded well, others failed. Some were fast, others slow. Despite the accuracy of each of the highly skilled candidates, only one man scored three hits in a time of 5.2 seconds. That man was Howard Donahue, a gunsmith and ballistic expert. A well-credentialled firearm marksman, forty-seven-year-old Howard actually achieved three bullseye headshots. A clever man. In fact, he achieved the result despite his Carcano rifle jamming and playing up. Until this time, Howard had no real opinion of the veracity of the Warren Commission outcome into the death of JFK. He had fallen into line with the general consensus that Oswald was responsible and had acted alone. Although he knew of all the conspiracy theories, he had no thoughts one way or the other. Donahue left the experiment happy for the involvement but for the first time questioning the findings of the Warren Commission. No one was better than Howard with a long arm, least of all Oswald, and certainly not with a 'clunky' Carcano bolt-action rifle. So, he thought, something is missing in the Warren Commission explanation into the death . . . but what?

From 1967, this question gnawed at him and led to what would become a twenty-five-year study on the findings of the Commission and a search for the real answers behind the shooting. His home laboratory, occupying most of the cellar to the family home, was the base for his work, and among his tools, lathes, files and ballistics textbooks he lost himself to research for months on end. The story of his dogged pursuit was documented in a small-time book by Bonar Menninger entitled *Mortal Error*, released by St Martin's Press in 1992. This exceptional book, a study and outcome unrivalled in the growing true crime genre, hardly made a noise in the literary world, fading away after its first print run. Overcome with sheer disappointment and a great sense of frustration and anti-climax, Howard was never to realise the outstanding contribution he made in unravelling the mystery surrounding the shooting of JFK. He worked tirelessly for more than 20 years trying to solve the case, but gave up after a threat of a lawsuit from the Secret Service.

Donahue's first accomplishment in the early days of his ballistic study was to settle once and for all the issue of the Warren Commission's 'magic bullet'. The 'magic bullet' theory relates to the second shot of the day, which hit JFK on the back of the neck. The same bullet hit Governor Connally. The media suggested the bullet was 'magic' insofar as it must have been turned and twisted along its path as it travelled through JFK and Connally. Few believed a bullet could take such an extraordinary path. All that was needed was an explanation, and Donahue found it. That one single bullet that had supposedly entered the neck of the President, exited through his throat then turned sharply ninety degrees to the right, then again sharply ninety degrees to the left and shot Governor Connally (sitting in front of the President) through the shoulder, before finally exiting through the Governor's right wrist – a very magical bullet indeed! Donahue analysed all the available photographic evidence of the limousine, including a view of the interior and the position of its occupants. He noted that the jump seats (where the Governor sat alongside his wife) were closer to the centre of the vehicle than the President's rear seated position. Governor Connally's right shoulder was nearly in line with the President's head. When the correct positioning of the Governor's seat was taken into consideration the bullet was hardly magical – it simply passed in a straight line through the President and into Connally. This inexcusable oversight by the Commission explained the nonsense of the 'magic bullet' theory. Donahue was indeed, a very clever man.

As the years marched on, Donahue's work intensified. His next goal was to determine exactly how many shots were fired, three or four. All he could learn from the Warren Commission Report was that they believed Oswald had fired three rounds and that the bullets were full metal jacket copper casings, the type of rounds that are designed to stay intact and pass cleanly through the body of the victim. This type of ammunition was designed to comply with the nineteenth-century Hague Convention, and the 1923 Geneva Convention, which demand that wartime rounds pass cleanly through a body, thereby offering the soldier some expectation of survival. Up until the time of the JFK shooting most warring nations were committed to using full metal jacket rounds. The bullets were not designed to fracture or explode on impact. This well-known ballistic fact teased Donahue as the last and fatal round to hit the President, clearly evident when viewing the Zapruder and Nix films, had resulted in the right side of JFK's skull being blown violently into the air, an impossible outcome with a full metal jacket round. Yet the round that passed through the President and into Connally went cleanly through both bodies.

As Donahue read more of the Warren Commission's report it became clear that there had never been any ballistics tracking. The use of rods and string lines to determine the actual course of a bullet, in simple terms the path it took from firearm to victim and beyond, is a commonplace course of action in the world of ballistics. Donahue set about reconstructing tracking lines by using all available mentions of angles, distances, photographs and the Zapruder film images. It would take weeks, but the result was conclusive; the Warren Commission Report was seriously flawed in its 'one shooter' finding. Another shooter had to have been in play.

In an attempt to allay the fears of an increasingly suspicious American public during this period, the government had commissioned an independent analysis of President Kennedy's skull. The expectation was that independent scrutiny would give credence to the Warren Commission's findings that two full metal jacket rounds from Lee Harvey Oswald's Carcano rifle had penetrated the President. A six-man team of pathologists was to perform the tests. One of America's most pre-eminent pathologists in the field of gunshot injury was selected as its chief. Dr Russell Fisher had in fact performed over 1000 autopsies involving this type of wound. He was at the top of his field.

It was more or less at this moment in time that fate stepped in to the investigation of the death of President Kennedy. Through an innocent set of circumstances the distinguished ballistics expert Howard Donahue met the equally highly regarded State Medical Examiner, Dr Russell Fisher. After their introduction by a mutual friend, the two men enjoyed a very interesting lunch. The entrée was bullet fragments, the main course brains and the dessert would be a healthy serving of doubt that both men would carry for the rest of their lives. They talked, two clever men, about their thoughts on the case.

The research carried out by Fisher and his team documented that the fatal shot had entered at the rear of the President's skull and exploded once inside his head, causing a massive wound (about the size of a tightly clenched fist). Such a wound was completely at odds with the damage normally inflicted by a full metal jacket round. The doctor and Donahue both knew, as would any experienced homicide detective, that such a wound was more typical of a frangible round, such as a hollow point or soft point round. A round designed to explode upon impact.

The bullet that hit the President's head disintegrated completely, scattering fragments throughout the brain tissue and embedding them in the interior wall of the skull. The President's car also yielded fragments on the floor mat. This is a classic consequence of a hollow point or soft point round disintegrating. Intriguingly, back in the 1960s, this type of round was used almost exclusively by law enforcement agencies, bodyguards and Secret Service agents. Designed to cause as much internal damage as possible to the victim, such rounds are, in short, intended to stop an offender or villain dead in their tracks. In the world of policing and presidential security, the officer is concerned only with ending the run of an armed offender, should they be approaching with felonious intent.

These rounds are both devastating upon impact and tell-tale by the tiny fragments into which they explosively disintegrate.

As a result of this extraordinary find, Fisher requested a viewing of the President's brain matter, slides taken of the brain, or brain tissue samples. All that had been supplied to him at this point of his investigation was autopsy photos and X-rays, the President's clothing, bystander photographs and the Zapruder film footage. It was the X-rays that confirmed the presence of fragments throughout the brain and the skull. Examination of the actual brain or tissue samples, Fisher reasoned, would irrefutably determine the existence of a frangible round, such as a hollow point or soft point round. When his request was refused, the eminent medico discovered that the brain of President Kennedy had, in fact, gone missing. Such a discovery was unimaginable in the field of forensic science.

In the back volumes of the Warren Commission I discovered some fascinating comments by Kellerman, the agent in charge on that day, who stated under cross-examination that immediately after the autopsy, '. . . all the X-rays that were taken we viewed them all together . . . people who were in the morgue at the time, the two bureau agents, myself . . . looking for pieces of fragmentation of this bullet . . .' Kellerman was being cross-examined by Counsel Specter, who later posed a telling question and received an even more telling answer. 'Did you observe during the course of the autopsy bullet fragments which you might describe as little stars?' Kellerman replied, 'Yes . . . of the skull and head . . . when you placed the X-ray up against the light the whole head looked like a little mass of stars, there must have been thirty, forty lights where these pieces were so minute that they couldn't be reached . . .'

One has to question the obvious. What on earth was an agent doing in a pathologist's domain looking at X-rays, and why was he interested in fragments when Lee Harvey Oswald fired full metal jacket rounds that don't fragment?

I delved deeper into the testimony, wading through the evidence of Agent Greer, driver of the President's car, one of the very few agents along with Kellerman to raise the Bible and give sworn evidence. He outlined his movements after the assassination. He admitted being in the company of agents Kellerman and Hill while the autopsy was being performed. He also mentioned looking at the X-rays and seeing '. . . very little small specks on the X-rays . . .' and that there was a discussion between the men about 'little specks of lead'. This is the classic description of the residual of a hollow point bullet, having exploded as designed, into minute fragments.

Undaunted, Fisher persevered with the material on hand. His subsequent analysis of the photographs located a fragment of metal about the size of a small child's fingernail embedded on the outside surface of the President's skull near the point of entry of the fatal bullet. This metal fragment had not been mentioned in the Warren Commission Report. Further study by Donahue suggested that the fragment was a 'ricochet piece' from the first full metal jacket round fired by Lee Harvey Oswald, which missed the motorcade, hitting the roadway. So, what's it doing attached to the President's skull? The Warren Commission testimonies locked onto the evidence of salesman James Tague, who while standing off-side of the motorcade was hit by a ricochet fragment, causing a small wound to his face. He described the shots as 'a loud cannon type sound'. This incident was witnessed and substantiated by two police officers.

Scrutiny of the metal fragment found in the back of the President's head may well have confirmed that it originated from a full metal jacket round, but what was it doing stuck to JFK's skull, and how had it survived the later shot to the head, the panicked embraces of Jackie Kennedy, the rush to hospital, the attempts to revive him at Parkland Hospital, the journey to the airport via a makeshift coffin, the flight to Washington, followed by the police escort to the Bethesda Naval Hospital and autopsy room, on the tenth floor? This piece of bullet was becoming more magical than the famed magic bullet. However, all subsequent requests by both Fisher and Donahue to have it analysed were met with rejection. Refusal of such a request, especially from a man as eminently qualified as Dr Fisher, smacked of a cover-up. At the very least it was suspicious. One must ask, as Fisher and Donahue obviously did, why the authorities ignored the evidence of a missed bullet. And, more importantly, the questioning of two men at the top of their professions concerning the veracity of the ricochet round that hit the back of the President's head.

•

Fisher and Donahue were looking for anything to advance their endeavour, anything that would explain the glaring issue related to the rear head wound. They knew that shortly after JFK's assassination the FBI had undertaken spectrographic tests on some of the ballistic exhibits and also on the bullet pulled from the window of Oswald's earlier target, General Walker. All that could be said about these bullet compounds was that they were 'similar'. A less than satisfactory link; indeed, by forensic standards not a link at all.

After further enquiries it came to their attention that the Warren Commission had undertaken testing of fragments found within JFK's brain. These included the fragment on the skull. The outcomes were never reported publically and subsequent freedom of information requests were flatly declined for reasons of 'national security'. It is fair to assume that had the results favoured the lone gunman theory, the FBI would have rushed to disseminate the information to all and sundry.

Some ten years after the death of JFK, a secret report from J Edgar Hoover to the Warren Commission accidentally surfaced via a media release indicating that the FBI had undertaken sophisticated metal fragment testing during the time of the hearing in 1964. Known as 'neutron activation analysis' (NAA), this type of test had become popular after the end of World War Two, and was commonplace by the early 1960s. It was used to determine the composition and concentration of elements in a particular sample, thereby allowing scientists to compare samples with a high degree of accuracy. Interestingly, this secret report found 'minor variations' in the metal fragments located inside the limousine when compared with those taken from the President's skull. No further details were mentioned, nor were the 'minor variations' or the report itself tabled in the Warren Commission. Both Fisher and Donahue had issue with the results of the secret testing. They queried the definition of 'minor variations', as does this author. An exact breakdown is necessary for a proper assessment of the tests and results. To simply claim 'minor variations' is unscientific.

Dr Fisher later learned of similar NAA tests undertaken by Professor Vincent Guinn of the University of California for the 1978 House Select Committee into the assassination. Guinn had access to the 1964 FBI data on neutron activation analysis, but admitted to the Committee that he couldn't make sense of it. Guinn stated that of the five samples he analysed, three had an antimony content of around 600 parts per million (ppm), and the other two samples had an antimony content of around 800 ppm. As part of his explanation Guinn had divided the five samples into two groups – the 600 ppm group and the 800 ppm group – and stated in his evidence that both groups were so close in the number of parts per million that they could be considered the same. He argued that the difference was in line with the acceptable 'minor variances' cited by the original FBI tests, going on to explain that he believed only two rounds were in play, and that both bullets were from the same batch of bullets and therefore from the same weapon. Guinn concluded with an extraordinary comment: 'I think that is their most likely origin, yes'. Surely the HSCA hearing would expect a stronger opinion than that? Yet, they went for it and reinforced their belief in the lone gunman theory. Guinn neglected to tell the hearing that the same composition of alloy used to manufacture the rounds used by Lee Harvey Oswald was also used to manufacture other rounds of that period.

Donahue took issue with the description of the metal fragments tested. Their weight sizes were different to those logged by the FBI agents O'Neill and Sibert at the time of the autopsy. In addition, the tests focused on lead content, ignoring copper content, which is also a feature of full metal jacket rounds. It is worth mentioning that a full metal jacket round is a lead slug cased in a copper skin. The copper casing is designed to pierce the target neatly and pass cleanly through, remaining intact. A frangible round is a copper encased projectile, with a hollow pointed lead cap, or soft nose or thin-skinned tip that is designed to explode upon impact, shattering and fragmenting. Some frangible rounds have a very thin casing, almost like a tissue of copper. Such rounds cause devastating internal wounds.

When Dr Fisher conducted his own enquiries on full metal jacket bullets he discovered a significant difference in copper content to the copper found in hollow point rounds. And Donahue knew that lead is a nonhomogeneous compound and open to variation between samples, as is the analysis and expert opinion on the subject.

Herein lies the problem with science. It is often contradictory. Since Guinn's findings, scientists from across America have analysed and attempted to explain the compound breakdown of the various fragments and the 'pristine' bullet (the 'magic bullet' taken from Governor Connally) that made up the ammunition used on 22 November, 1963. As recently as 2006 the *Journal of Forensic Science* labelled Guinn's outcome as '. . . [having] no justification for concluding that two, and only two, bullets were represented by the evidence . . .' Even the respected journal *Science Daily* published an article about the five bullet fragments that formed the basis of Guinn's tests. The journal reminded the reader that the three fragments attributed to JFK's head wound, and from within JFK's own car, had no copper jackets, and so couldn't be matched ballistically to the other two samples, commonly accepted as having come from the wounds to JFK's neck and to Governor Connally.

I have studied research papers on neutron activation analysis by some of the most qualified scientists in the US, only to find an ongoing squabble between great minds who not only differed in their outcomes but at times were scathing towards each other and of the standards and testing regimes employed.

My study of Guinn's antimony tests found a worrying generalisation. Of the five samples, the lowest parts per million reading was 602 ppm, and the highest was 833 ppm. The poles were getting further apart and certainly didn't seem to me to be minor in variation. The numbers represented a 35 per cent-plus variance. I consulted data contained in the publication 'Forensic Analysis Weighing Bullet Lead Evidence' by the esteemed US National Research Council and read a massive, comprehensive outline of more than 200 pages dealing with analysing lead content in bullets. The paper acts as a guide on how to assess the lead content and the veracity required in testing as well as determining content and variances in content. Less than 5 per cent variance is acceptable when identical tests are done on two different bullets. The paper cited an example where seven bullets were tested together. (In the case of JFK, there were five fragments tested.) The paper then stated, '. . . if the data suggests that the mean chemical concentrations are the same, the bullets or fragments are assessed as "analytically indistinguishable" . . . if the concentrations are "far" from those . . . the data would be deemed more consistent with the hypothesis of no match.' Using this standard, the results of the tests undertaken by the FBI and later by Professor Guinn were clearly evidence of a 'no match.' But, then again, I am far from being a scientist, merely a retired detective.

Regarding the overall opinion of Guinn's analysis, I firmly believe that it proves two very different rounds were in play on the day. One round (800 ppm) is tested to have been from the pristine bullet on Connally's hospital trolley and also matched to the wound on Connally's wrist. I don't believe there is anyone who doubts this finding. The other three samples, each of 600 ppm, were fragments found in the President's skull, on the floor of his car and on the rug, which was near the President and used for the comfort of JFK and his wife during the motorcade. Obviously, the '600' group bullet, by way of neutron activation analysis, had caused the shot to JFK's head and landed, fragmented, throughout the motor car. Such fragmentation is classic behaviour of a hollow point round that explodes upon impact. And let's not forget, the neutron activation analysis failed to locate any copper on those three samples, more in line with a frangible round where the copper casing peels back upon impact, leaving the inside lead to fragment, splinter off and fly in all directions to cause its damage.

So, as the two clever men well knew and I was starting to understand, even science comes down to interpretation. For all its worth, it has become riddled with debate as professors with more initials after their name than the alphabet go tit for tat against fellow professors as they argue tests and results. In the end this important kernel of evidence is lost to academia. How can the laws of physics be, in the end, completely meaningless, leaving much of the original early evidence into the shooting as inconclusive and open to a myriad of interpretations? That's why I value the words of a real-life, there-at-the-time witness, who saw what happened, kept a clear memory and had the guts to step up and tell their story.

Back in the relatively sane world of ballistics, expert Howard Donahue continued to advance the subject of who killed JFK. He explained the anomaly of the three spent full metal jacket casings found alongside the Carcano rifle at the window of the sixth floor of the Book Depository, juxtaposed with the three shots fired at the time of the shooting.

According to the lone shooter theory, the position of the Warren Commission, Lee Harvey Oswald shot each of the three rounds on the day of the killing. However, the disintegrating final shot to JFK's head contradicts this theory. Donahue was quick to highlight a solution. It is not an uncommon practice for some shooters to leave a spent casing in the chamber of their weapon. A practice used by hunters, it stops dust and grit getting into the chamber and barrel. I am also aware of this practice being employed by soldiers carrying weapons in wet terrain. Some shooters forget to clear the final round, unwittingly leaving it in place until the next occasion the weapon is used. After many years spent investigating dozens of shootings and gun-related crime, many years of searching criminals' homes, confiscating weapons, looking into gun chambers and at bullets seized, I am also aware of the anomaly. Again, of the countless number of illegal weapons I seized during my law enforcement days, it was not unusual to find a gangster's weapon with 'one up the spout': a spent cartridge in the chamber. Bear in mind that Oswald used his rifle to take practice shots at Love Field Airport before the assassination attempt, and also to take a shot at General Walker some months prior, after which he had hidden the weapon outside, in the countryside. He even claimed to have buried the rifle, which would certainly have exposed the weapon to dirt, grit and moisture. Any reasonable hunter or firearm hobbyist would never consider doing this with their weapon. The Carcano rifle was certainly in considerable use, so a spent casing in the chamber is conceivable. Oswald would have needed to clear the spent casing at the time of his assassination attempt on 22 November. Hence, his first spent cartridge may have been an old spent casing.

The first police officer on the scene at the Texas School Book Depository located three spent casings. Two of the casings were lying grouped close together, only centimetres apart. The third casing was dented and some distance away, on the floor on the other side of Oswald's workstation. Did he eject the already spent dented casing as he was setting up, getting ready to take aim? Certainly the dents in the casing made it likely that it could not have been fired and ejected properly. Remember too, he had to mount his sights as well, and take a position he was comfortable with, behind the cardboard cartons. It is feasible that Oswald quietly cleared his weapon before taking position. The location of the casings noted during the police crime scene search supports this scenario.

Donahue would also discover that ballistic tests were carried out on behalf of the FBI. The actual tests conducted worried him enough to encourage him to persevere with his research; he knew he was on to something. The tests were on gelatin mock-up blocks, sometimes used to track the performance of bullets. Using gelatin blocks, gelatin mass having a close similarity to flesh and brain matter, and from a distance that replicated the crime scene on Elm Street, several rounds of ammunition were fired and the results documented. As anticipated, the 6.65mm rounds used passed cleanly through the blocks. The findings were logged. Nothing extraordinary here, really, merely confirmation of the thoughts of open-minded investigators. But were they? Donohue learnt of additional tests done on that same day, wherein the scientist who undertook the full metal jacket (6.65mm rounds) tests repeated the test, this time using .223

rounds, bullets used in an AR-15 weapon. Why on earth? The
only .223 rounds anywhere near Elm Street that day belonged
to the AR-15 assault weapon carried by the Secret Service
agents. Their brand-new weapon. The results, predictably, were
devastating. Each round blew the gelatin block to smithereens,
typical of the design and purpose of those rounds. The .223
rounds are frangible bullets, designed to explode upon impact
and cause the maximum amount of internal damage to the
victim. They are high velocity bullets. The Carcano rounds
were low velocity.

Oddly, these gelatin block test results were never made
public, another instance of secrecy. And the photographs of
the gelatin results of the full metal jacket rounds were on
file, but photographs of the devastating .223 rounds were
missing. It is worth recalling Fisher's comment when pressed for
further information or evidence during his revealing lunchtime
conversation with his new likeminded chum, Donahue, that the
government to whom he was reporting displayed some 'strange
antics'. Dr Fisher made another fascinating discovery, to do
with the width of a Carcano full metal jacket round and that
of a .223 round that suits an AR-15 rifle. The Carcano round
is 6.65mm wide, hence it is referred to as a 6.65 calibre round.
When shot, it will leave an entry hole larger than 6.65mm
wide in the wound. Due to the natural elasticity of skin and
(in the case of JFK's rear head wound) skull bone, the entry
wound would be around 7mm wide. Whereas the .223 round
is a 5.56mm wide projectile. Such a bullet would leave an entry
wound 6mm wide.

The entry hole width to JFK's skull wound measured 6mm
in width. A stunning fact!

This means Lee Harvey Oswald never fired the third and final shot, the shot that hit the back of the President's head and exploded, as he was only using ammunition 6.65mm in width. Yet the Warren Commission failed to grasp the importance of this irrefutable piece of evidence. Such a telling fact to any investigator or courtroom proceeding, one would think. Still, unbelievably, the American public was not served a full explanation on this key information that negated the involvement of Lee Harvey Oswald with the fatal head shot.

I checked the sworn ARRB testimonies from the autopsy pathologists and located that of Dr Boswell, who stated that the measurement across the entrance wound hole was '6mm'. Dr Humes, the head pathologist, agreed the hole was 6mm wide when giving sworn evidence to the Warren Commission. Dr Boswell would also mention the 6mm hole to the House Select Committee into Assassinations in 1978, so there was no doubt of the width of the entrance wound hole to JFK's skull. Unfortunately the two clever men, with their fusion of forensic scientific expertise and medical science know-how, didn't have unimpeded access to the historical testimonies, and the ARRB hearings were twenty years later. This author took over one year to read the entire twenty-six back volumes of the Warren Commission report via PDF; it is unimaginable that Donahue and Fisher could have access to the same volumes of information. Had they done so, the story of the death of JFK may well have been put to bed then. The 8124 pages of the volumes had me concurring with Donahue and Fisher's conclusions, completely and with absolute certainty. I, too, was convinced that there was more than one gun in play that afternoon and, furthermore, that there were two distinctly different types of ammunition flying around the Dealey Plaza. However, thus far I had only one gunman.

I wasn't about to lose my head to Soviet spies, Fidel Castro or James Bond. I was looking for the facts and what I found over the next two years would shock me to the bone.

CHAPTER 10
THE SECRET SERVICE SECRET

In the Secret Service lead car, two vehicles in front of JFK's limousine, was Agent Lawson. Prior to joining the President's minders, he had served in the US Army in counterintelligence. He had been given the task of organising security for the President's tour of Dallas, all the preliminary arrangements and liaisons with other agencies. He thought, like most of the witnesses on that day, that 'the second two [shots] were closer together than the first . . . two reports closer together'. He explained, '[shots] two and three were closer together than one and two'. At the time of the second and third shots he was looking back at the approaching motorcade and '. . . noticed right after the reports [shots] an agent standing up with an automatic weapon in his hand, and the first thing that flashed through my mind was, this was the only weapon I had seen, was that he had fired, because this was the only weapon I had seen to that time.'

Mother of two Jean Hill had decided to stand away from most of the congestion and had taken up a position at the south

end of Elm Street, near the overpass. There were few other
bystanders around and the view was unimpeded. Accompanied
by her best friend, Mary Moorman, and a camera, Jean had
been standing in her long red coat for nearly an hour and a
half when the motorcade finally arrived. With Mary acting as
photographer, Jean jumped forward and looked at the President;
she was unusually close to the main man. She yelled out, making
a request of him, 'Hey, we want to take your picture!' Both
JFK and Jackie seemed preoccupied, focused on a bouquet of
red roses on the centre of their seat, not noticing the woman's
plea for a picture. The President momentarily lifted his head,
his attention then diverting to Jean. Since the crowd was thin,
Jean was able to nudge forward, to get right up close, looking
'right at his face' as the first shot rang out.

Mary quickly snapped a shot of Jean with the President
and Mrs Kennedy behind, just before he fell backwards. Jean
froze, she '. . . just stood there and gawked around'. Mary was
close enough to see Governor Connally slump onto his wife's
lap, shot, and also the President slump forward. She grabbed
Jean by the slacks and pulled her to the ground, where they
lay together, terrified. While unsure of the number of shots,
possibly '. . . four or as many as six . . .' Jean firmly believed
there were two rifles in play that afternoon. The first shots
she thought were from a bolt-action rifle and the last from
an automatic rifle. She believed the shots were 'rather rapidly
fired' and that the Secret Service was returning fire, '. . . they
are shooting back . . . I did think there was more than one
person shooting . . . I thought, well, they are getting him and
shooting back . . . oh goodness the Secret Service are shooting
back'. Later that day Jean made a sworn statement to the

Sheriff's department, stating, 'I thought I saw some men in plain clothes shooting back . . .'

Mr Sam Holland, a local railway signalman with twenty-five years' service behind him, was on the Elm Street overpass, looking out for the approaching Presidential cars. He noticed Jean and Mary taking pictures and observed Jackie Kennedy looking towards them. Standing with a crowd of 'between fourteen to eighteen people', he heard the shots and watched, horrified, as the President slumped forward. '. . . After the first shot the Secret Service man raised up from the seat with a machine gun and then dropped back down in the seat . . . and immediately sped off . . .' With reference to the shots, Mr Holland stated, '. . . two of them was rather close together though', and after the last shot he noticed smoke two to three metres in the air, above the road surface, under the line of trees.

Another person in the crowd, electrician Frank Reilly, thought the shots came from the trees on Elm Street.

Patrolman Earle Brown was on duty. He had been allocated the south end of Elm Street and was standing with the crowd. He could see along Elm Street to Houston Street and, like the rest of those gathered, he watched with anticipation as the motorcade approached. His vantage point would prove the ideal location to see the tragedy unfold, looking straight down at the convoy of vehicles. He heard three shots and observed the President's limousine momentarily slow down before rapidly speeding up, '. . . then I smelled this gunpowder . . . at least it smelled like it to me'. As the motorcade drew near, he noticed a Secret Service agent in the follow-up car. 'He had this gun and was swinging it around, looked like a machine gun, and the President was all sprawled out . . .'

Alongside the patrolman stood two co-workers, mail clerks Royce Skelton and Austin Miller. Royce heard the first two shots as the President's car was travelling towards him. 'I thought that they were dumballs [sic] that they throw at the cement because I could see smoke coming up from the cement . . .' Austin Miller believed the shot or shots '. . . sounded like it came from the, I would say from right there in the car . . .' Miller also said he '. . . saw something which [he] thought was smoke or steam . . .'

Railway switchman Walter Winborn was also standing on the Elm Street overpass. He saw smoke, '. . . it looked like a little haze . . . but it was a haze there . . . at least ten feet long and about two or three feet wide . . .'

Motorcycle cop Bobby Hargis, who was riding alongside the President's car, said '. . . I was staying pretty well right up with the car,' which puts the police officer among the closest persons to the President at the time of the assassination attempt. Hargis believed the shots had come from 'behind' him, '. . . sounded like the shots were right next to me . . .'

Officer Martin, on motorcycle duty on the left side of the President's convertible, was close to Mrs Kennedy. He recalled, '. . . you could smell the gunpowder . . . you knew he wasn't that far away. When you're that close you can smell the powder burning . . . . Why, you can smell the gunpowder . . . right there in the street.'

Patrolman Joe Smith also smelled gunpowder, '. . . a distinctive smell of gunsmoke cordite,' as he moved along Elm Street towards the grassy section of Dealey Plaza.

In my investigator's brain, alarm bells had started to ring. As I trawled through the many hundreds of pages related to the witnesses' observations from the overpass and on the street closest to the President's vehicle I could sense a pattern forming, and detectives love finding evidence of similar facts. Not only is it corroboration, but it helps to understand exactly what happened at a crime scene. Here was sworn testimony from a supervisor, several police officers and two mail clerks telling me, the reader, that smoke or gunpowder was on the street in or around the President's vehicle. Extraordinary! I delved deeper and kept reading, remembering the old adage, where there's smoke, there's fire.

The next testimony I studied was that of bookkeeper Virgie Rachley, who had been standing on Elm Street enjoying the passing parade. As the President's car rolled by and the shots rang out she recalled smelling 'gunsmoke'.

Clemen Johnson, a machinist at the railway yard, also witnessed the catastrophe. He saw 'white smoke' near to where the motorcade had passed. Fellow railwaymen Nolan Potter and James Simmons also witnessed the 'smoke'.

Press photographer and keen hunter Tom Dillard was travelling as part of the motorcade, in the press car, an open-top Chevrolet convertible. His car followed the long convoy of press men and woman and political figures, all eager to be part of the big day. Dillard, an astute photographer who was hoping for some unique images, had taken some fine shots back at Love Field Airport, but was under pressure from his newspaper to bring back as many worthy photographs as possible. As his car approached the Texas School Book Depository he heard three shots. Jumping from his vehicle at the first shot, he ran towards the Depository building, clicking photos as he ran. His focus was the sixth-floor window, and in all he took twelve negatives. As he stood near the path of the motorcade he smelt gunpowder. As an experienced hunter, he had a great deal of expertise in handling high-powered weaponry, and stated that 'I very definitely smelled gunpowder . . . I very definitely smelled it . . .' Dillard later told of discussing the smell of gunpowder with fellow journalist Robert Jackson, also in the convertible. Jackson agreed with Dillard's observations.

The value of Dillard's photographic work would not come into play until some years later, when he handed his twelve negatives over to the HSCA enquiry into the shooting of JFK. The idea was to enhance the negatives to allow a better view of the window and imagery inside the window in the hope that they might show if Lee Harvey Oswald was standing in the window frame at the various times of each bullet being fired. Apparently in some shots, an image was vaguely visible; however, enhancement would confirm one way or the other. From an investigative perspective the twelve 'cleaned-up' negatives would determine who shot the third and fatal round. It would be easy enough to work out the time and chronology of each image, and compare the sequence with the timing of each shot and where everyone was. If Oswald was not at the window, or if his rifle was not protruding from the window at the time of the third and fatal shot, then it stood to reason that he could not have fired the final bullet. The obvious question would then be, who else had a rifle at the immediate location?

All twelve negatives were irreversibly destroyed during the enhancement process, a process that did not involve Tom Dillard. Not only did Dillard never get asked to explain his gunpowder observation to the original Warren Commission hearing, his now destroyed negatives denied him, and anyone trying to unravel the death of JFK, an opportunity to see if there was a picture that might have told a thousand words. Tom's disappointment was followed by his comment on the entire affair: 'a nauseating boondoggle'.

Despite Dillard's disastrous experience, others also told of smoke at the street level area. Ed Johnson, a reporter for the *Fort Worth Star-Telegram* newspaper, '. . . saw little puffs of white smoke that seemed to hit the grassy area in the esplanade that divides Dallas' main downtown streets.'

From her third-floor office window, clerk Patsy Paschall saw 'smoke' near the motorcade as it travelled down Elm Street and past the grassy knoll.

Thomas Murphy, a railway foreman saw 'smoke' near the motorcade.

All of a sudden I had more people smelling gunpowder or seeing smoke at street level. As detectives say, the evidence was getting fatter. I kept delving.

Senator Ralph Yarborough, who was a veteran in the field of infantry and marines training and combat with more than fifty years' firearms experience, was an impressive man and a compelling witness. He was riding immediately behind the follow-up car in a Lincoln open-top convertible with the Vice President. Yarborough recalled three shots and estimated that there was 'only one and a half seconds between second and third shot'. It worried him that 'all the Secret Service men seemed to me to respond very slowly . . . I'm amazed at the lack of spontaneous response by the Secret Service.' Yarborough also recalled, '. . . one of the Secret Service men sitting down in the car in front of us [in the follow-up car] pulled out an automatic rifle or weapon and looked backwards . . .' Some time later in an interview on the subject with a journalist, Yarborough recalled 'smelling gunpowder' and that 'it clung to the car throughout the race to Parkland Hospital'.

Travelling in the fourth open-top convertible with a clear view to the front were Dallas Mayor Earle Cabell and his wife, Elizabeth. Elizabeth was thrilled to be involved in the parade and had been enviously admiring Jackie's glamorous outfit. Her husband was enjoying the company of Congressman Ray Roberts, the only other VIP in their car, and they were all eagerly anticipating the Presidential luncheon at the end of the motorcade. After the first shot Mayor Cabell recalled, 'from out of nowhere appeared one Secret Service man with a submachine gun' in the follow-up vehicle. After the third shot rang out Elizabeth was 'acutely aware of the odour of gunpowder . . . there was no question about that'. Later she spoke of it with Congressman Roberts and he agreed that there had been a smell of gunpowder as their convertible passed the location where the follow-up car had been at the time of the shooting.

The chief postal investigator (the person who investigates suspicious packages and postal items for the postal service) for Dallas, Harry Holmes, was also watching the motorcade from his fifth-floor office building overlooking the Dealey Plaza. With a face-on view of the Texas School Book Depository, he observed the motorcade turn onto Houston Street then left onto Elm Street. From there, he had a side view of the motorcade as each vehicle crawled along. Harry was suspicious by nature, a self-titled 'suspicioneur', the perfect postal investigator. He spied the President's car through a set of binoculars, not taking his eyes from JFK and the First Lady. Then he heard shots and saw the car dodging, almost stopping. He '. . . did see dust fly up like a firecracker had burst, up in the air'. His vision took in the lead car, then the Presidential vehicle behind, then the follow-up car. The plume of 'dust' was in line with the Presidential car. He thought the time between the second and the third shot was less than between the first and second, and that the shots came from within the crowd on the street near to the motorcade.

Secret Service Agent Youngblood noticed 'a greyish blur in the air above the right side of the President's car' right after the third shot.

It didn't bother me at this point whether smoke was seen or smelt at the rear of the President's vehicle, or to the left or right side of the vehicle, or indeed in front of it. It was of no consequence, nor should it be to any investigator at this point of discovery. What was important was that smoke or gunpowder was evident at street level in the immediate or general vicinity of the motorcade. The presence was all that mattered. That's the gold, the diamonds, to any detective.

Characteristically, gunpowder or gunshot residue will linger within a two- to three-metre radius of the weapon, for a time of up to a minute after a shooting, sometimes longer, dependent on the wind and other factors. There are plenty of examples in crime scene records where gunshot residue has lingered for an extraordinary length of time and wafted over a greater distance than initially thought. This wafting is known as a plume of residue, and it omits a distinct smell of gunpowder. The plume of residue has been used many times in homicide and shooting investigations worldwide to determine whether a suspect was involved in the firing of a gun.

Of the prevailing breeze on the day of the shooting, Officer Martin, on motorcycle duty, said 'it was blowing out of the south-west'. Photographs taken by bystanders clearly show the breeze was strong enough to blow the dresses and coats of the women in the crowd in a direction away from the overpass towards the Book Depository. It was a south-westerly breeze blowing to the north-east. Weather records from the Love Field Airport from around midday state that the wind was approximately thirteen knots, increasing to seventeen knots by 1pm. In lay terms this means the wind was gusty and noticeable. For witnesses to have smelled gunpowder on the street in close proximity to the motorcade can only suggest (due to the wind factor and the forensic maxim of plume of residue) that a firearm was discharged in the immediate vicinity of the motorcade. But who discharged a firearm so close to the scene as to cause the odour of gunpowder? Certainly gunpowder from Lee Harvey Oswald's weapon would not be evident at street level with him secreted eighty metres away from the motorcade, on the sixth floor of a building, behind a window, crouched down and wedged between boxes of books. If the gunpowder from Oswald's weapon was able to waft or drift it would either have been contained within the building or, if it drifted through Oswald's window, would have dissipated in the opposite direction to the travelling motorcade, into the atmosphere.

Like Governor Connally did on the day, I (figuratively) turned my head and looked behind, in the direction from where the witnesses said the shots were coming. Sure, up high there's an old-world red-brick building, the Texas School Book Depository. But immediately behind my mind's-eye position was the looming presence of the follow-up vehicle, another convertible bulging with Secret Service bodyguards, the protectors of the President of the United States. And one man, it seems, was armed with a high-powered automatic weapon.

Like the Presidential limousine, the follow-up car was without its roof. It was a 1955 Cadillac with two front seats, two centre jump seats and two rear seats. With the exception of the two jump seats, which were occupied by the Presidential staffers Dave Powers and Kenneth O'Donnell, the four other seats were given over to Secret Service agents. Additionally, there were two agents standing on the left-side running board and two agents on the right-side running board, making a total of eight agents. Each of these agents was armed with a hand gun. The only person with a long arm rifle was George Hickey, who was seated high on the left rear seat. He was actually crouched on the seat, his backside was elevated towards the rear seat head rest, a strange and surely unsteady position. He was on sniper duty with a Colt AR-15 semi-automatic assault weapon, a lethal high-velocity weapon made from aluminium alloys and synthetic materials, capable of being stowed easily and prepared for use without fuss with its simple rotating lock bolt. A new weapon to the agency's arsenal, it had only been in use since that morning.

Hickey, the newest member of the team, was normally attached to the garage unit as a driver and chauffeur, yet today he was detailed to the AR-15 assault weapon. In case of an attack on the President, the most important role. His overall experience was zero compared with the task he was given as the lone sniper. By choice of the Secret Service, rounds issued for the weapon Hickey was handling were .223 frangible bullets designed to explode on impact. As I have mentioned, these rounds have a dramatic effect on a target. They kill. They pierce the body then explode and fragment violently ensuring death is quick yet horrific. Understandably, they are the chosen round for law enforcement officers. It stands to reason that should a crazed gunman come running at a policeman, the officer needs to drop him dead, instantly. There are no second chances, plus the lives of innocent civilians may also be at risk.

Hickey had the perfect line of sight to the back of the President's head, which was slightly to his right and coincided with the fatal entry and exit wounds. Hickey's position also coincided with the 1967 'bullet tracking lines' that ballistics expert Howard Donahue projected in his home laboratory.

Senior Agent Clint Hill was personally responsible for the safety of Mrs Kennedy. He was stationed at the front of the left-side running board and clarified the distance between the front of the follow-up car and the rear of the Presidential vehicle as five feet. He recalled George Hickey being in possession of the AR-15 assault weapon and reported that the first noise he heard 'seemed to be a firecracker'. He added that their vehicle had been travelling at approximately twelve to fifteen miles per hour, when it 'lurched forward' and Hickey lost his footing. Hill believed that the second shot 'had almost a double sound'. Hill's recollection of the sound could only mean the shots were heard almost simultaneously.

On the rear of the left-side running board was Agent McIntyre. Immediately after the fatal head shot he recalled seeing most of his fellow agents 'had drawn their weapons and Hickey was handling the AR-15'. He recalled the three shots were over within five seconds. McIntyre's recollection of the time makes it impossible for the three shots to have come from

Oswald's rifle, as proven by the subsequent White Ballistics Laboratory tests.

Opposite McIntyre, on the rear of the right-side running board, was Agent Landis. He heard 'what sounded like the report of a high powered rifle from behind me.' Landis, who was less than a metre in front of Hickey, referred to the final shot as being like 'shooting a high powered bullet into a drum or melon'. Landis had dropped his sunglasses and fumbled. Agent Bennet, the person closest to Landis, assisted him by retrieving the glasses. Bennet was seated alongside Hickey in the rear of the car. He declared, at the time the third shot hit the President's head that he '. . . reached for the AR-15 located on the floor of the rear seat. Hickey had already picked up the AR-15 . . . I had drawn my revolver when I saw Hickey had the AR-15 . . .' The observation of Bennet places the AR-15 assault weapon in the hands of Hickey prior to the final and fatal shot, at a time when another agent had fumbled and bent down to gather his sunglasses.

Remember Agent Lawson? He was overseeing the proceedings from the lead car, looking back towards the President's vehicle and the follow-up car. He noticed Hickey standing up in the follow-up car with the automatic weapon and his first thought was that he had fired at someone. Why did Lawson think this? Did he see Hickey's AR-15 fire a shot? Did he see gunsmoke or a plume of residue? No one quizzed him as to why he thought the agent had used his gun. Indeed, Lawson's observation was not dealt with by the Warren Commission in any inquisitorial way. Why not? It's an observation that would normally have an astute lawyer labouring in cross-examination for a long, long time.

In the front passenger seat of the follow-up car was Senior Agent Emory Roberts, who was in charge of planning and had allocated the AR-15 assault weapon to George Hickey. Interestingly, he '. . . turned around a couple of times just after the shooting and saw that some of the agents had their guns drawn. I know I drew mine and saw Hickey in the rear seat with the AR-15 and asked him to be careful with it . . .' The fact that Agent Roberts directed this comment to a fellow agent is fascinating. Roberts was obviously worried about Hickey, normally a driver and not a sniper, and his handling of the high-powered weapon. What had Hickey done with the AR-15 assault weapon to make Roberts ask him to 'be careful with it'? Remember, Agent Roberts is in the front right-hand seat, Hickey is in the back left-hand seat. There are two men seated between them, in the middle jump seats. Roberts would have had to yell it, over the men in the middle. Roberts's comment should have received rigorous cross-examination before the Commission, but didn't.

Like his fellow agents, Hickey claimed to have heard the shots and confirmed the distance between the vehicles. He professed that during the shooting he 'reached to the bottom of the car and picked up the AR-15 rifle, cocked and loaded it and turned to the rear . . .' Hickey later made an amendment to his first statement, declaring that he actually '. . . reached down picked up the AR-15, cocked and loaded it and stood part way up in the car and looked about . . .' Here we have an inexperienced United States Secret Service agent saying that, at the frontline security of the world's most powerful individual, he first needs to find, then cock, then load his weapon in the case of strife. This situation seemed completely absurd, so I delved deeper into the Warren Commission transcripts of evidence, in particular to the sworn testimony of Hickey's supervisor, Agent Kellerman, who was in charge of the detail. He stated in relation to the AR-15 assault weapon in the follow-up car that '. . . this is a rifle and it is on all movements . . . it is out of its case, it won't be shown, it could be laying flat on the floor, but she is ready to go.' 'Ready to go' doesn't mean it needs to be found, cocked and loaded. 'Ready to go' means it can be fired in a split-second. 'Ready to go' means all the instinctive training of the agent will come into play, should an attempt be made on the life of their President. 'Ready to go' means the finger is on the trigger. So, who is wrong here, Kellerman, or the newest member of the team, George Hickey? And why wasn't Hickey ever placed in the witness box to answer this inconsistency?

In a black and white photograph of the follow-up car taken by a bystander, Mr Willis, just before the shooting, Hickey is seen raised up from his earlier seated position, head and shoulders above others still seated in the car. Hickey is also turning inward, facing the centre of the follow-up car. The AR-15 is unsighted, as are Hickey's hands. If what Kellerman states is in line with correct weapon protocol, sniper protocol, the weapon would in all likelihood be in Hickey's hands, '. . . on all movements . . . it is out of its case, it won't be shown . . . it is ready to go . . .'

Following this section of Kellerman's testimony he recalled Mrs Kennedy saying, just after the flurry of shots and in reference to her now dying husband, '. . . what are they doing to you . . .' The Presidential car then raced off towards Parkland Hospital.

Secret Service Chief James Rowley's report details the procedural arrangements, itemises each car and lists the agents on duty. Oddly, it does not address in any detail the issue of who was carrying what weaponry. Rowley offers a brief summary of the actions of each agent, listing George Hickey last. He states that Hickey mentioned a 'disturbance' in the follow-up car at the time of the fatal shot. But Rowley offers nothing more, and Hickey didn't ever see the witness box. We are left to wonder what 'disturbance' played on the inexperienced George Hickey. By observing Hickey in the Zapruder footage and the still photographs of those crucial seconds before the head shot to JFK, we see Hickey turn 250 degrees. From looking to his immediate left to turning quickly to look sharply to his right, to look back at the Book Depository. Then he turns again towards the direction of the President, grabbing the 'ready to go' AR-15 rifle. He then stumbles backwards, just before the fatal shot. All this within a second or two, and at the same time his supervisor Agent Roberts yells at him to 'be careful' with that rifle.

Behind the follow-up car the Secret Service agents riding with the Vice President reacted efficiently and immediately after the first shot to preserve the lives of their charges. Agent Youngblood describes how he 'stepped over into the back seat and sat on top of the Vice President. I sat in a crouched position and issued orders . . . I heard two more explosion noises and observed Hickey in the Presidential follow-up car poised on the car with the AR-15 rifle . . .' This means that, according to Agent Youngblood, after the final and fatal shot, Hickey was poised with his weapon, a position consistent with the weapon potentially about to be fired, or possibly having been fired. Youngblood's observation seems to match that of Agent Kivett, the other secret service man in the Vice President's vehicle, who looked up to witness '. . . the follow-up car with some agent holding the AR-15 pointed in the air . . .'

Amateur cameraman Robert Hughes, who was filming along Houston Street, zoomed in on the motorcade. Hickey is seen squatting high on his seat, head and shoulders above the other seated agents. For Hickey to be in that position, his feet would be on the rear car seat, his backside resting on the rear seat head roll. As the motorcade turns into Elm Street, Abraham Zapruder films the Presidential car and follow-up car. Hickey is seen still head and shoulders above the other agents, still squatting on the rear seat head roll. Zapruder captures the agent gazing to his left, as if looking at a little girl in red knickerbockers. At this point, a second or two from the shot that hits the President in the back then passes through Connally, the Texas School Book Depository is immediately behind Hickey. This is the time of the first shot, the shot that startled everyone but was impotent. The building would be up to 250 degrees to Hickey's right. If he was to be startled by the first shot he would need to turn his body up to 250 degrees to look to his right. All the agents said they turned to their right, to look up at the Book Depository. Indeed, Hickey states that he looked to the rear (up to 250 degrees). This is the crucial aspect of Hickey's evidence, bearing in mind his precarious seated position for a sniper. We know that Hickey is the newest and least experienced member of the team. He is seated in a moving car in an unstable squat position, hauling a 'ready to go' AR-15 assault weapon. A shot has been fired from high above to his rear. As the man on sniper duty he has to react quickly, yet the way he was sitting could only hinder any kind of efficient action. Hickey is not braced, therefore has no support to be able to accurately work a high-powered weapon from a moving car and turn to his right up to 250 degrees at the same time. Lee Harvey Oswald's shots continue. At this time Zapruder zooms in on JFK and Jackie and the agent's follow-up car is lost, out of frame. Abraham Zapruder's simple act of focusing on his beloved President unwittingly allowed thousands of shooting theories to flourish.

Photographer James Altgens from the Associated Press in Dallas was in front of the motorcade taking pictures. He snapped his famous 'first shot' picture, one single frame, which showed Hickey turned right around to look to the rear, towards the Book Depository. He is still head and shoulders above the other agents, turning, looking, and reacting in this awkward, squatting position as the car continues to move forward. This is the sum total of images of Hickey before the shot to JFK's head. He is then seen by other agents and witnesses to fall backwards.

Seconds later, in the Zapruder film, the two fatal shots are captured in all their devastation. The head of the President explodes. Immediately after the shooting, a photographer takes two telling photographs of Hickey pointing his AR-15 assault weapon aloft in the air as the follow-up car and the Presidential vehicle race beneath the overpass towards Parkland Hospital.

The abovementioned excerpts from sworn testimony and/or agents' affidavits are a snapshot of events regarding Hickey and his handling of the AR-15 assault weapon. There is no doubt that the rifle was in his hand at some point immediately after the first round left Lee Harvey Oswald's weapon, the round that ricocheted off the roadway. By the end of my research of the entire 10,000 pages of documents I found six Secret Service agents placed the AR-15 rifle in Hickey's hands, as well as two dignitaries on the motorcade and one policeman and five bystanders who saw a Secret Service agent with a rifle. A total of fourteen individuals. When using the words of Hickey's co-workers, remembering they are all trained and proficient experts in the duties of close personal protection and the use of firearms, and the witnesses watching from nearby, a compilation of their observations could read as follows . . .

> *'After the first shot we turned and saw Hickey handling the AR-15 assault weapon. He was poised, standing up with the rifle pointed in the air as the vehicle lurched forward; he stumbled, he fell backwards. We heard more shots; we thought he had fired at someone. An agent near to him told him to be careful with the rifle.'*

Each agent in and around the motorcade prepared a statement late on the day of the shooting or on subsequent days. Remarkably, few reported hearing or seeing anything of consequence. An extraordinary imbalance became evident when weighing up the sworn evidence of witnesses against the scant statements of the agents. More than twenty agents had supposedly been scanning the crowd and surrounding buildings and not one saw a lone Lee Harvey Oswald at the sixth-floor window leaning out with his firearm or retreating after the shots. Yet men and women in the street did. Some of the agents in the motorcade appeared confused, shrugging shoulders, dropping sunglasses, falling backwards. Four agents in the follow-up car had defined duties, part of standard operational procedures in the case of trouble – they were to descend on the President's car. Yet only Agent Hill ran forward to assist his charge, the First Lady. The other three had lead feet. Those same four men had been up to the wee hours of the morning and had admitted to drinking scotch and beer at the Fort Worth Press Club and later at the Cellar Door, where scantily clad strippers dispensed 'salty dick' drinks. Those same men were now on duty guarding the President and most of them were wearing dark-lens sunglasses, hardly the best eyewear for scanning crowds and buildings, or sniper duty; more the kind of equipment to hide behind if you have a hangover.

After analysing the agents' affidavits together it is alarmingly clear that the wording of their statements regarding the gunshots is near identical. It is almost as if they sat together and wrote up a 'joint' account of what happened. Today this practice is taboo in evidence gathering, yet it was often the way things occurred in the days before investigations became more professional. Almost all the agents mention that the first round (the ricochet shot) sounded like a 'firecracker', not a high-powered full metal jacket round smacking into the roadway and splintering off to hit the body of the limousine. One could be forgiven for wondering how trained experts like Secret Service agents thought the round a firecracker when many of the general public who were nearby thought it a gunshot. And the more qualified citizens in the area of weaponry, like Senator Yarborough, had no doubt it was a gunshot. Governor Connally 'recognized the first noise as a rifle shot and [it] immediately crossed [his] mind that it was an assassination attempt.'

None of the Secret Service agents in the follow-up car, in particular Hickey and Landis, were subject to cross-examination by the attorneys assisting the Warren Commission. Why? And who kept them off the witness list? The omission of vital evidence from the agents in the follow-up car smacks of a cover-up by the executive level of the Secret Service.

Just after 1pm, only moments after the President had been pronounced dead, Agent Hill telephoned a mortuary, requesting they 'bring the best casket immediately available'. The Secret Service was on the move; their request was fulfilled by 1.40pm, barely seventy minutes after the shooting. Hill assisted Kellerman, both men rushing the body of the President to the airport. It was Agent Hill again who, just after the assassination, clearly recounted the guttural cry of Jacqueline Kennedy: '. . . they've shot his head off . . .'.

To whom was Mrs Kennedy referring when she said '*they*'?

CHAPTER 11
LET'S GET OUT OF TOWN!

One of the few Secret Service agents to take the stand before the Warren Commission was Agent Sorrels, from the Dallas office. On the day of the shooting he had been seated in the lead car, looking back at the President. As he said himself, it was his job 'to observe the people and buildings as we drove along the motorcade.' He knew his city well, all the streets, the high-rise buildings and the vantage points, and had been placed there for that express purpose. With regard to the Texas School Book Depository, Agent Sorrels '. . . saw that there were some windows open, and that there were some people looking from the windows. I remember distinctly there were a couple of coloured men that were in windows . . . two floors down from the top. There may have been one or two other persons that I may have seen there.'

People lining the motorcade route also saw the open windows of the Book Depository. Newly married Arnold Rowland, fifteen-year-old schoolboy Amos Euins, local resident Mary Rattan and forty-five-year-old construction worker Howard Brennan among them, all noted the 'coloured men' and the lone person a floor above. Trouble was, the lone man held a rifle. These witnesses saw the rifle and the man leaning over the windowsill, aiming the rifle. Their observations were remarkably clear and frank. As witnesses go, they were as good as it gets. And their observations appear to have been made at the same time, heads looking up as the motorcade approached. Yet, trained Secret Service Agent Sorrels saw nothing but a sunny Texas afternoon.

These same witnesses would, in a line-up, identify Oswald as the shooter.

One can't help but speculate a very different outcome to that sunny Dallas morning of 22 November, 1963, had Sorrels observed what these bystanders had. There was a man with a gun pointing directly at the motorcade. If Sorrels had alerted his fellow minders, as was his job to do, the chain of events leading to the President's tragic death may have been halted before it began. Here we have a sixty-three-year-old agent appointed to the role of observer. Was this a wise choice? How did Sorrels fare at his last agency eye test? Perhaps this crucial security task would have been better suited to a man with younger eyes and less of a penchant for late-night socialising?

Having missed his chance to be a hero from his position in the lead car, Sorrels should still have been able to state, apart from the obvious, what the President or Governor Connally did when the shots rang out and, just as crucially, what the Secret Service agents in the follow-up car did, or didn't do. He should have seen George Hickey stand with his automatic weapon and then fall back to his seat. Had Hickey fired a shot, accidentally or not, Sorrels would have been in the ideal position to observe the action, to see the fall, to witness the error.

He did remember bits and pieces. He was adamant there were 'three shots'; there was no doubt in his mind, he said; he heard the sound of a 'firecracker' and shots. From then on, however, his memory was remarkable only for its lack of detail. He offered the odd comment of 'a bit of movement', a phrase begging for hardline cross examination, but sadly not one of the attorneys assisting the Warren Commission took up the challenge or probed further. So when Sorrels left the witness box, the world was no closer to filling in the gaps.

As a group, back in 1963, the Secret Service did not interview suspects or manage crime scenes; their duties were confined to the personal protection of the President, the First Lady and associated dignitaries. Yet they were to play a major role in the forthcoming investigation when, in fact, they should have been considered witnesses only. And while Agent Sorrels was an expert in the President's security, he was not trained to take charge of an investigation of the magnitude of the assassination of a US President. This is a role that requires a seasoned detective at the very least, yet Sorrels chose to put himself in the middle of this one. On the afternoon of the shooting it was Agent Sorrels who spoke with witnesses who had taken photographs at the time of the shooting.

Jean Hill had a story to tell him, one that any investigator would surely seize upon. Jean claimed to know of at least one telling photograph, snapped at the instant of the gunfire by her best friend Mary. She offered up the camera and photographs to the agent. Before the sun set over Dallas that day, the same fate would befall many cameras and rolls of film, all confiscated by the Secret Service or other law enforcement officers working alongside.

In the hours after the shooting, Agent Sorrels trudged from one end of Dallas to the other in search of leads. He received word from an old contact, a reporter from the *Dallas Morning News* who was scouting for leads himself back at the Texas School Book Depository. The reporter chirped 'I've a man over here that got pictures of the whole thing.' Sorrels dropped everything and rushed over. The nervous bystander, clutching his movie camera tightly, offered, '. . . my God I saw the whole thing. I saw the man's brains come out of his head.' This was an extraordinary revelation and one that required action. Agent Sorrels noted the man's photographic equipment and promptly steered him towards the nearby Kodak processing factory.

In the interim, Lee Harvey Oswald had been arrested by Dallas police officers and was sequestered at station headquarters. Captain Fritz sent out a call to Sorrels, who remembered '. . . [it] would be fairly close to 2 o'clock, I imagine.' Sorrels was desperate to speak with Oswald and the big Dallas detective obliged, inviting the agent to his office. Disconnecting the call, Agent Sorrels made one of the most significant decisions of his career. He chose to leave the bystander with another witness who had also headed for the Kodak building with his own film for development. A lucky twist of fate for those on the side of the truth, as Agent Sorrels had just abandoned Abraham Zapruder, the man who had filmed what is still considered some of the most important few moments of moving pictures in cinematographic history. So Mr Zapruder sat and waited patiently for his film to be processed while Agent Sorrels hurried downtown.

Police headquarters was awash with TV cameras, tripods and newshounds, so Sorrels had to elbow his way along the corridors towards the interrogation room. Somehow a few newspaper reporters had managed to talk their way into restricted areas. Sorrels described the station as a 'deplorable' working environment, with detectives and uniformed officers literally tripping over each other. It was in this melting pot of law enforcement and media, less than an hour after the arrest of Lee Harvey Oswald in what could only be called a fishing expedition, that Sorrels was heard to pose a range of questions about Oswald's background. He admitted asking Oswald '. . . whether or not he had ever been in a foreign country, and he said that he had travelled in Europe, but more time had been spent in the Soviet Union, as I recall . . .' It was during this Q&A session and two others, held on Saturday and Sunday mornings, that Sorrels learnt of Oswald's past domesticity in Russia, his obsession with Marxism, his views on communism, his visit to Mexico and his attempts to reach Cuba. After the first meeting Sorrels would state, 'Of course I contacted the chief's office when I got that information as to who he was, and gave that information to them.' He was referring to Chief Rowley at the Secret Service head office in Washington, who had now become aware of Oswald's communist Russian history. Sorrels's interviews with Oswald garnered a treasure trove of information from the man in a tight corner, notions that on face value sounded more like a script of a James Bond movie. Was this the welcome deflection the Secret Service needed from the growing uncertainty over how many shots were actually fired and, more so, by whom?

The interview room must have lit up with the revelations. Captain Fritz was listening open-eared to Sorrels's orchestration and Oswald's diatribe. Analysis of the testimony and statements reveals that the more Sorrels discovered of Oswald's communist connections, the more he tailored his interview. Oswald should have been interviewed by the lead investigator and/or his partner. He seemed to be interviewed by all and sundry, many of them with no experience in interrogation. The interview should have focused on the assassination, a murder, not Soviet migration or fascination – that should have been held back for another time and forum. The most pressing issue would be to gain background information that might establish the facts of the shooting, the ownership of the rifle and spent rounds, Oswald's history with weapons, the reasons for selecting JFK as his target; Agent Sorrels conducted himself in total contradiction to accepted methods of professional questioning of a man in custody. One of the key ingredients to the success of any investigation is for the lead investigators to keep an open mind, but in this interview room it wasn't long before Captain Fritz also began to lose himself to fantastic theories of international conspiracy and communism.

Another privy to Sorrels's interview was the Dallas postal inspector, Harry Holmes, who was instrumental in linking the network of postal boxes to Oswald and his alias of 'Hidell', proving the mail order purchase of the Carcano rifle and .38 Smith & Wesson revolver. Suspicioneur Holmes had no trouble with his memory before the Warren Commission; he recalled clearly the topics under discussion and also the slapdash method of interrogation. 'There was no formality to the interrogation. One man would question Oswald. Another would interrupt with a different trend of thought or something . . . it was sort of an informal questioning . . .'

Curiously, it was soon after the unorthodox Sorrels/Oswald interview that the seeds of communist intrigue and Russian agent hi-jinks found their way into the public arena. Certainly, it was from that point forward that 'leaked' revelations spawned innumerable conspiracy theories, some of which would prevail for fifty years. Did Sorrels turn the communist ramblings of the lone gunman into a clever throw-off, cunningly shifting the heat of investigation onto Oswald and his communist connections and opening a Pandora's Box for the world media? Strangely, Sorrels's subsequent half-page affidavit to the Warren Commission detailing his discussions with Oswald made no mention of the communist connections. Why the omission?

Soon after Fritz bought the story and journalistic hell had broken loose with the media frantically feeding the rumour monster, District Attorney Wade was forced to step in. Wade could see matters were getting out of hand; he had no time for the Russian/Cuban hypotheses. Moving to hose down Captain Fritz's international conspiracy theories, Wade struggled unsuccessfully to steer the investigation back on track. Back to the facts on hand: a lone gunman and a single rifle pointing from the Texas School Book Depository. Unfortunately for Wade, much of the valuable evidence that may have been captured via still and moving pictures had disappeared, and no one seemed all that concerned.

Any federal agent would know that misinformation and deflection from the truth is fundamental to a propaganda strategy. But a good propaganda strategy also needs a concerted campaign to keep reinforcing the story. In the following days,

Above: Oswald distributing 'Hands Off Cuba' flyers in New Orleans. This photo was used in the investigation.

Below: Oswald holding his Carcano rifle, with a six-shot revolver on his hip.

Above: This photograph of Marina Oswald was found in the wallet of her husband, Lee Harvey Oswald, after his arrest on the day JFK was shot.

Below: Marina and Lee Harvey Oswald with their daughter, June Lee, in Minsk in what was then the USSR.

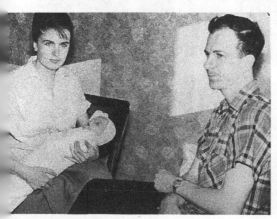

Above: President John F Kennedy (*left*), Governor John Connally (*centre*) and Jackie Kennedy being greeted on arrival at Dallas Love Field airport on 22 November 1963.

Below: During the Dallas motorcade on that fateful day. The Presidential limousine had been flown in from Washington, DC. The plastic bubble top was removed and the bulletproof windows were down because the weather was beautiful. This was how the President preferred to ride.

Above: The President was relaxed and happy as he looked out at the crowd, totally unaware of what was about to happen.

Below: The President's convertible on Elm Street, with the Book Depository behind, to the left. The car behind is the Secret Service follow-up vehicle full of agents, some standing on the running boards. Two agents look back after the first shot, the other agents and crowd seem oblivious to a rifle being fired. Agent George Hickey is seen raised up, in the back seat, seconds before he grabs the AR-15 assault rifle (*see arrow*).

Jacqueline Kennedy leans over her dying husband to gather his brain matter. Secret Service Agent Clint Hill is seen jumping on the rear of the limousine to get to the President and help the First Lady. At this point, no one knows if more shots will follow.

Her clothing splattered with her husband's blood, Jacqueline Kennedy watches as the President's body is placed in an ambulance on arrival at Andrews Air Force Base. From there, it was taken to Bethesda Naval Hospital for the autopsy.

A Dallas police officer holding up the Carcano rifle allegedly used to kill President John F Kennedy. It was the same rifle Marina Oswald had photographed her husband holding.

Lee Harvey Oswald's hiding place, and the window he fired from, on the sixth floor of the Texas School Book Depository building.

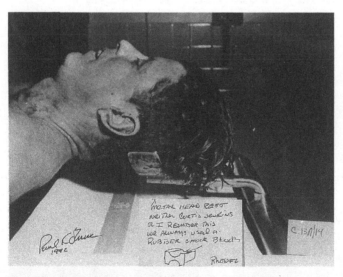

The official autopsy photo of John F Kennedy. The autopsy summary notes concluded that the President died from 'gunshot wounds inflicted by high velocity projectiles fired by a person'.

Above: Twenty-four-year-old Lee Harvey Oswald flanked by officers of the Dallas Police Department after his capture. Oswald received a cut on his forehead and a blackened left eye during his arrest.

Below: Jack Ruby, the man who shot and killed Lee Harvey Oswald, is photographed here surrounded by three women from his burlesque club.

Left: Homicide chief, Captain Will Fritz, was in charge of the investigation of Lee Harvey Oswald. In his mind, 'this man killed President John F Kennedy'. By the end of Oswald's first day in custody Captain Fritz had lost his thinking to an 'international conspiracy'.

Below left: An unfired 6.65mm round-nose full metal jacket cartridge from Lee Harvey Oswald's Carcano rifle, designed to pass cleanly through a victim's body. Alongside it (*below right*), the .223 hollow point round, a 5.56mm high-velocity round designed to explode upon impact and leave metal fragments within the wound zone.

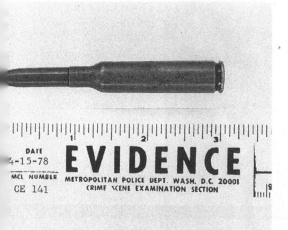

John F Kennedy's widow, Jacqueline (*centre*), during the President's funeral procession. Her brothers-in-law, Bobby Kennedy (*left*) and Teddy Kennedy (*right*) are with her. A fresh team of Secret Service agents, on high alert, surround the three of them.

Chief Justice Earl Warren (*centre*) hands over to President Lyndon Johnson his report (the first of twenty-six volumes, 8124 pages) on John F Kennedy's assassination. *The Warren Report*, submitted to the President on 24 September 1964, was composed by a seven-member committee who investigated the murder.

weeks and months, the Secret Service furnished hardworking FBI agents with report after report of 'Cuban connections', 'communist connections', 'mafia connections', 'involvement with the Teamster union', 'opium trafficking', 'counterfeiting rackets', and 'relationships with Fidel Castro', concerning either Lee Harvey Oswald and/or Jack Ruby. They even wrote a memo of an alleged 'homosexual relationship' between Ruby and Oswald. All of the 'information reports' proved completely baseless. However, the months of detective work to clear those reports would seriously erode the mettle of the dozens of FBI agents on the case.

A veteran bodyguard, Secret Service Agent Kellerman was another of the few agents to raise the Bible and offer sworn evidence at the Warren Commission. Due to Kellerman's role as detail leader he was the one to receive the bulk of the Commission questions and bat the hard balls. From the instant the President was shot, Kellerman had stepped up and taken absolute charge, throwing orders and navigating those in the motorcade through the crucial first two hours. He was the architect of the series of hasty manoeuvres that saw the dead President, his wife, the Vice President, his wife and the Secret Service exit Dallas in record time. And through it all, he had never left JFK's side, remaining with the body until it was embalmed in Washington the following morning, some fifteen hours later.

Moments after 1pm, when President Kennedy had been pronounced dead, Kellerman ordered Agent Hill to organise a casket to be brought immediately to the hospital; the entourage was heading to Washington and Kellerman was taking the corpse of JFK with him. The dogged agent slashed through the medical red tape in his quest to get everyone out of town. Two Dallas health department representatives insisted that the body not be removed from the city. Under Texan law it was mandatory for any murder victim to undergo an autopsy. Kellerman snubbed the law. City bureaucrats made frantic telephone calls as the determined agent summoned an ambulance to take the casket. A judge attempted to block the hospital exit, only to be blocked himself. This agent was in one hell of a hurry.

Dr Charles Crenshaw, the resident physician of Parkland Hospital trauma team, painted a bleak picture of the Secret Service's abuse of authority and total disregard for procedural correctness in his sensational memoir, *Trauma Room One*, published in 2001. '. . . We opened the door and rushed into the emergency room. There is always a commotion around trauma, but what I saw was sheer bedlam . . . I looked to my left and saw a man in a suit running. To my amazement, another man in a suit jumped in his path and smashed a Thompson submachine gun across his chest and face. The first man's eyes immediately turned glassy and he fell against a grey tile wall and slithered to the floor unconscious. When I heard that gun slam against his face, I just knew the man's jaw was broken . . . I was to learn later that the man with the gun was a Secret Service agent, and the one who had been hit was an FBI agent . . .'

This is an explosive observation by Crenshaw, one that demanded a better understanding. First of all why would a Secret Service agent smash a 'Thompson submachine gun' across the chest and face of an FBI agent? Police from neighbouring agencies tend to work closely together; it's all about the fraternity. Certainly the FBI and Secret Service were close during the lead-up arrangements for the JFK motorcade. Now moments after the fatally wounded JFK enters the ICU rooms of Parkland Hospital a Secret Service agent is beating on an FBI agent with a long arm weapon.

The only long arm in play that day was the AR-15 rifle, which has a distinct look; to a novice it looks like a machine gun. Was the FBI agent trying to seize the AR-15? Was the extraordinary struggle in the emergency room all about a diligent FBI agent who suspected the President had been accidentally shot by a Secret Service agent and had gone into investigative mode, attempting to secure the weapon as an exhibit? A standard crime scene principle that the FBI would automatically fall back on.

Interestingly, George Hickey and the AR-15 were both despatched to Love Field Airport, along with JFK's limousine, a short time later, the gun never seen again.

Dr Earl Forrest Rose was the Dallas County Medical Examiner – in other words, the coroner, the man charged with investigating death by unnatural causes or, in this case, by a criminal act. The role of the coroner is among the most powerful individual roles in any jurisdiction. It has to be. With homicide being a capital offence, the most brazen of all crimes, the office of the coroner should not be hindered in its search for causation and explanation. To hamper a coroner's work is to risk suffering the full weight of the law. Dr Rose quoted chapter and verse of state procedure to Kellerman, telling him, 'you can't break the chain of evidence . . .'. Rose knew the importance of this valued maxim in criminal investigations. His words fell on deaf ears, however, as Kellerman ignored protocols and laws, ordering the body be placed in the casket and taken to the waiting ambulance. A game of body chess ensued; one heavyweight after another stepped in to debate the issue. Texan Judge Brown spelt out the law and reinforced the importance of undertaking an autopsy at Parkland Memorial Hospital. This was countered by JFK's own physician, Dr Burkley, who backed the Secret Service's desire to transport the body to Washington. The squabble turned to rigorous argument; even the President's aide and best friend, Dave Powers, sided with the need to flee. Kellerman, with his allies standing alongside, kept repeating, 'This is the body of the President of the United States and we are going to take it back to Washington'. Eventually Kellerman's demands were accompanied by an increase in brute force.

As Dr Charles Crenshaw recalled in his memoir, '. . . a phalanx of guards poured into Trauma Room 1 just as the coffin was being rolled out. They looked like a swarm of locusts descending upon a cornfield. Without any discussion, they encircled the casket and began escorting the President's body down the hall towards the emergency exit. A man in a suit, leading the group, holding a submachine gun, left little doubt in my mind who was in charge . . . Dr Earl Rose, chief of forensic pathology, confronted the men in suits. Roy Kellerman, the man leading the group, looked sternly at Dr Rose and continued, "My friend, this is the body of the President of the United States and we are going to take it back to Washington." Dr Rose said with equal poignancy, "The body stays." The Secret Service managers and White House staffers offered no logic or rationale with their demands. Eventually Kellerman took an erect stance and brought his firearm into a ready position. The other men in suits followed course by draping their coattails behind the butts of their holstered pistols . . .' Dr Crenshaw also detailed in his emotional memoir the tit-for-tat struggle and verbal battle between Dr Rose and others. He recalled the end of the tussle with the comments of some of the agents: '"Goddammit, get your ass out of the way before you get hurt . . ." screamed another one of the men in suits. Another snapped, "We're taking the body now." Strange, I thought; this President is getting more protection dead than when he was alive. Had Dr Rose not stepped aside I'm sure that those thugs would have shot him. They would have killed me and anyone else who got in their way . . .'

Ambulance driver Aubrey Reich would recall, 'There was a lot of pushing, shoving, cursing. We were trying to roll the casket out. Someone would grab it and try to roll it back towards the trauma room. This went on for quite a while. It was a push and shove type thing. Quite a bit of, like I say, obscene language . . . I was scared to death. I was really frightened.'

The doctors and assorted lawyers looked on helplessly as the body was taken away. Whatever excusable blunders or poor judgement the Secret Service had exercised in Dealey Plaza prior to this point, nothing could justify the removal of the President's body from the Parkland Memorial Hospital; at least nothing in law or within the rules of crime scene principles and procedures.

Under the globally accepted forensic science principle of 'every contact leaves its trace', a body found in suspicious circumstances should not be moved until the crime scene procedures are completed. This principle is fundamental to sound management of a crime scene and subsequent criminal investigation. No police department anywhere would dare interfere with this most important principle in crime scene management. The President was in a moving car when he was shot. The decision to transport him immediately to the nearby

Parkland Hospital for emergency treatment was just. Medical assistance is the only exception to the rule. Upon the declaration of death, however, Parkland Hospital is where his body should have remained. Under lock and key. Not just for the autopsy, but also for any forensic testing required. Relocating the body (clothing and remains) means a loss of fibre, fragments or vital evidence and contamination of that same material. It is inexcusable. To move the body a few thousand kilometres is an insult to forensic science procedures, let alone the autopsy laws of the state of Texas.

The logical solution would have been to guard the body at Parkland Hospital and arrange a thorough forensic autopsy. President Kennedy's personal physician, George Burkley, was there in the emergency room watching the attempts to revive the now doomed President. He saw the tracheotomy wound placed in the bullet exit hole to the throat; he saw the whole bloodied mess. He could have been the independent doctor, the one to watch over the autopsy and verify the standards. All of a sudden the reasons to get out of town were looking illogical. Something was telling the Secret Service to go, and go quickly, something bigger than an autopsy and a guarantee of the proper chain of custody of evidence.

Perhaps a hint of what was festering within the Secret Service lay in the two telephone calls the agents made to Washington once JFK had been pronounced dead. Kellerman told agent Clint Hill to make the calls, one to the head of their secret service unit and the other to the Attorney General, Bobby Kennedy. Once a line to the White House was open Kellerman grabbed the phone and stated to his superior, '. . . there has been an incident . . .' An underwhelming way to describe an assassination attempt. Kellerman then handed the phone to Clint Hill who would go on to speak to Bobby Kennedy. In the limited evidence that Agent Hill gave to the Warren Commission it is impossible to comprehend the full extent of his conversation. It is possible, however, to glean that he was instructed to keep open the lines of communication to the White House. He did, so it stands to reason that much was discussed; conversations to which the Warren Commission was not privy, as they failed to probe deeply.

During my research I found a fascinating recollection of these telephone calls in *The Day Kennedy was Shot*, the 1968 publication of highly respected investigative political journalist and renowned US author Jim Bishop. Mr Bishop had a distinguished career as the biographer of several presidents. He had previously met and interviewed both John and Jackie and kept a well-clipped ticket to the inner circle. Bishop had the ear of the men and women on the ground, in the White House and around Dealey Plaza on 22 November, 1963.

On page 225 of what was one of the finest books I read in my research phase, Bishop recounts undoubtedly the most difficult call in the life of any Secret Service agent: that made by Agent Hill to Robert Kennedy. With reference to Robert's brother being shot Bishop states that Hill used the phrase, '. . . There has been an accident.'

Those five words gripped me. I must have read them over and over. I scoured the sources listed at the back of Bishop's book but was unable to locate the primary, the person who passed him the comment. I spent days sitting in the reading room at the Melbourne library trying to take the 'accident' sentence further, but to no avail. In the end I was left with five words that on face value opened the doors to a massive story. If correct, were they telling? Unquestionably. Were they legitimate? I couldn't conclude one way or the other. All I had was the impeccable reputation of Jim Bishop and a sentence that had sat unchallenged through the many reprints of his book over 45 years. What did it mean to my investigation? Certainly Lee Harvey Oswald wasn't on any 'accidental' path that day – he was out to kill the President.

Something along the lines of 'We've been hit', 'The boss is dead', 'There's been an assassination attempt', might have been a more apt way to report on the killing of the President. In context of the tragedy, to use the word 'accident' was to shift the horror of the event to something very different, something far more troublesome. '. . . There has been an accident . . .' I was to carry those words of Agent Hill's with me for the remainder of my cold case study.

With complete disregard for forensic science, Agent Kellerman pushed on and arranged to have the deceased JFK's body placed inside a casket. Ritual and presidential protocols were now lost to haste. With one of their agents as a driver, the Secret Service sped the deceased across town to the waiting presidential aircraft, where the casket was urgently loaded. After the mandatory few minutes' delay for the swearing in of the Vice President as the caretaker leader, Kellerman pushed on. Dr Rose made one last-ditch effort to demand the body undergo an autopsy as Kellerman closed the aircraft doors. The Secret Service crew, JFK's physician and their dead leader were airborne a mere two hours after the first shot was fired, leaving in their wake a host of unanswered questions and the lingering stench of a cover-up.

CHAPTER 12
BEHIND CLOSED DOORS

By mid-2011 my reading glasses were telling me loudly and clearly, no more! I had scoured each page of the Warren Commission volumes many times over as I checked and cross-checked. I was becoming a tad like Howard Donahue. I had loads of smoke but I was missing the fire. I needed icing on my cake, or 'the potatoes', as detectives say. I thought I had read it all until I discovered the Assassination Records Review Board (ARRB) records. The ARRB was established after the proclamation of the JFK Act, which allowed the review board to demand all records associated with the assassination of John F Kennedy. Such records included the autopsy notes, testimony, affidavits, photos and the like, which took place at the US Navy Bethesda Hospital on the night of the assassination. The board took evidence and listened to testimony between the years 1995 and 1998, thirty-five years after the assassination. These hearings would uncover some of the most dynamic and telling evidence ever presented on the death of JFK. In a word, they were a revelation. Sadly, however, the facts it uncovered came at a time when the American public had largely forgotten about finding the truth behind the death; a new generation was more focused on their own sensations. Nonetheless, if what I had read in the ARRB hearings was true, then the autopsy provided crucial information about JFK's death. All of a sudden I felt rejuvenated, a bit like Captain Fritz on the night of the killing, awaiting the results of the autopsy. I, too, started to pace around my office like an anxious father-to-be. Suddenly my aching back stopped having writer's chair spasms and the view through my reading glasses started to look crisper. I renewed my gym membership, set up a research schedule that would give me another six months and sat back down . . . and read some more . . .

●

Back in Washington, at the Andrews airbase, an escort was waiting. Agent Kellerman and his Secret Service entourage were finally working efficiently. Their head, Chief Rowley, was on the tarmac with a motorcade and the streets were clear for a beeline to Bethesda Naval Hospital. It was familiar territory for the Secret Service, a safe haven, a military hospital, the finest of its kind with a hefty Whitehouse budget. While Air Force One was in flight, J Edgar Hoover appointed two FBI agents to meet the body and remain with it until the embalmment. This investigation needed the FBI up front giving its all; it needed forensics, pathologists and experienced detectives. FBI agents James Sibert and Francis O'Neill were veterans of many sensitive cases and Sibert had met the President on numerous occasions; indeed, he had seen JFK off on the fatal visit to

Dallas, and here he was now waiting for the President's final homecoming. Along with his partner, O'Neill, Sibert was to play a crucial role as official witness to the autopsy and handler of exhibits. Sibert and O'Neill filled the gap that Dr Rose at the Parkland Memorial Hospital was so concerned about – chain of custody that would ensure a conviction against the perpetrator of the crime.

But on the ground, as the casket was unloaded, the Secret Service continued to stamp its authority. The FBI agents were relegated to the bleachers, to the third car behind the President's hearse. Chief Rowley was taking charge and his Secret Service men were running to rule, running the show. The escort took the laden casket to the hospital basement and up to the seventeenth floor of Bethesda, where a team of White House-appointed pathologists were being mustered by Dr George Burkley, the head of the hospital and JFK's personal physician. He and Roy Kellerman would stick together for the next half a dozen hours. Dr Burkley knew as much as most about the shooting – he had been in the Presidential motorcade (four cars back) when President Kennedy sustained his fatal gunshot wounds. He had stood by Mrs Kennedy and watched over the emergency treatment of her husband in the trauma room at Parkland. After the official pronouncement of the President's death Burkley had remained with the body all the way to Bethesda. There he arranged for the head pathologist, Dr James Humes, to meet the casket, along with members of Humes's team.

There was an air of expectation among those selected to perform the autopsy, overshadowing the deep sadness of the occasion. Having heard that a man was in custody in Dallas for the shooting and that a weapon and spent cartridges had been seized, the participants knew the outcome of the autopsy would be paramount to any court proceeding. A wrong needed to be righted by a thorough examination of the body and determination of death. The American justice system was on show, its mettle exposed for the world to see. Dr Humes's team breathed in the sense of the responsibility that lay before them.

The autopsy suite was a newly designed facility, state of the art and with enough room for a team to work through their tasks. Typically, a team for such a procedure could consist of a chief autopsy pathologist, his immediate second, perhaps a third specialist, X-ray technician, medical photographer, an orderly-cum-note-taker and an independent law enforcement witness to handle the chain of evidence, continuity and physical exhibits. A team of six, or eight at a stretch, could work for four to eight hours methodically determining the causation, the type of bullets used in the killing and the path of the projectiles, as well as any peculiarities or contributing factors. The appointed FBI agents would then back up the autopsy effort with a thorough logging of all forensic samples and establish a sound chain of custody of the exhibits to assist the prosecution case.

When the President's body was brought in it was noted that one of the casket's handles was broken. Obviously it had been a rough journey. Agent Kellerman must have breathed a sigh of relief as the body was delivered and the last man stepped into the room. They were finally behind closed doors. And not one member of the American public would hear what went on in that autopsy suite until the ARRB hearings took place thirty-five years later.

From the moment of arrival it was apparent to Dr Humes that the Secret Service was going to continue to exert an iron-fisted control over matters. He recalled access being allowed to men from the Army, Navy, the President's aides, FBI and Secret Service. By the time he was ready to begin the autopsy Dr Humes was faced with a room holding as many as thirty people observing, talking and debating the procedure. He wished he could have '. . . thrown them all out . . . these other people, the Secret Service and the FBI who wouldn't normally be present . . .'

The casket was opened and the medical staff took their first look at the deceased leader. Dr Humes, his senior X-ray technician, Jerrol Custer, and twenty-year-old technician Edward Reed all gazed down upon the body. The 35th President of the United States was completely naked; all his clothing was missing. A set of exhibits vital to assist with bullet trajectory, calibre size and entrance/exit opinions, gone. In fact, the body was sheathed in a bloodstained heavy plastic sheet and the base of the coffin was saturated with blood and fragments of human remains. Quietly shaking his head at the sight, FBI Agent O'Neill glanced over at the Secret Service contingent and noticed that Agent Kellerman's clothes were speckled with JFK's brain matter; likewise Agent Greer's jacket, obviously from the original crime scene back at Dealey Plaza.

Shortly afterwards Dr Pierre Finck arrived. With many years of experience undertaking autopsies on military personnel killed in action, his expertise was in ballistic wounds. Questioning the anomaly of the missing clothing Dr Finck was told it was 'not available'. Secret Service Agent Greer failed to mention that the ER doctors at Parkland Hospital had handed him the President's bloodstained and bullet-holed garments in a brown paper bag.

The legitimate occupants of the room were to note down the number of persons present. Each count would differ, yet each number would tell the same story: there were far too many 'hangers-on' watching over the forensic procedure. Finck noted down the number '26' on his autopsy notes. O'Neill was running a log, requesting names and positions on entry; it was becoming a passing parade of Secret Service agents and military heads. His log showed twenty-seven men present, not including the immediate family. Jackie arrived to wait nearby along with JFK's brother, Robert Kennedy. There was also a four-man team of embalmers. Kellerman and his offsider Agent Greer stayed all night; even agents O'Leary and Youngblood dropped in, as did the head of the bodyguard unit, James Rowley. Another account had thirty-three men crowding into the suite. Possibly the only man unaccounted for in the push was George Hickey; he was in the land of the missing.

During the next few hours, the diligent Dr Humes was to see his medical authority belittled, his role, crucial to the success of the autopsy, largely reduced to that of a man who would do as he was told, by men not wearing hospital scrubs. He worked through his tasks suffering questions and comments, mostly from people with no medical qualifications. At times their behaviour degenerated into squabbling as they differed in their opinions. Dr Humes was to describe the mayhem by stating to the ARRB 'It was like trying to do delicate neurosurgery in a three-ring circus.' Assisting pathologist Dr Boswell, under oath to the ARRB, agreed with Humes's three-ring circus quote and added, the Secret Service 'were in such an emotional state, running around like chickens with their heads cut off . . . They misquoted an awful lot of things we said or did.'

FBI Agent Sibert watched the autopsy with a sense of duty and incredulity, considering it to be 'unusual'. He expected medical notes to have come from Parkland Hospital detailing the doctors' and surgeons' attempts to revive JFK. Such information is invaluable when first viewing a transported body, enabling a differentiation between the damage caused by bullets, that caused by emergency medical procedures and that caused by the oddity of transporting a body over a long distance in a non-medical facility such as Air Force One. No such information was forthcoming. It was going to be all guesswork for the pathologists at Bethesda. Sibert couldn't fathom why the body had been transported from Texas in the first place, believing the autopsy should have been undertaken at Parkland Memorial Hospital.

The autopsy got underway. Opinion had it that the first bullet to penetrate the President's body entered at the back of the lower region of the neck, below the collar line at the shoulder. Everyone seemed to be in agreement that it was a neat entry, a clean shot, passing through the body and exiting at the lower front neck region. The bullet left a hole consistent with a round measuring 6.65 millimetres in diameter. There was no evidence of any internal trauma or damage apart from the obvious track of the bullet itself. Such a wound is entirely consistent with the behaviour of a full metal jacket round, designed to pass efficiently and cleanly through the body. Three 6.65-millimetre full metal jacket spent cartridges had been located next to the rifle at the sixth-floor window of the Texas School Book Depository.

Meanwhile, back at the Parkland Hospital in Dallas, Governor Connally was receiving treatment for a similarly neat, clean wound. When the news was telephoned through to the Bethesda autopsy suite that a 6.65-millimetre full metal jacket bullet in near pristine condition had been located on the Governor's hospital trolley the team mentally ticked off their first 'missing' bullet. The news that it matched the spent rounds located where Lee Harvey Oswald sat on the sixth floor even had the Secret Service crack a smile. The autopsy was starting to look good . . . at least for a while.

JFK's 'second' bullet wound presented a completely contradictory scenario, one that would pepper the tone of conversation in the autopsy suite for the remainder of the evening. That round had hit the President in the back of the head, causing a massive wound, up to 130 millimetres or five inches in diameter. Nothing clean, nothing neat here. This rear shot to the head, clearly shown in the Zapruder film, was devastating and explosive by nature.

On first seeing the head wound Dr Humes believed it to be the entry wound of a bullet that had exploded. He concluded that the damage done to JFK's skull and brain was caused '. . . partially by the projectile [the bullet] and partially by the explosive force of the missile . . .' Dr Humes observed within the brain and towards the front of the skull cavity '. . . little tiny fragments of radio-opaque material which we thought to be bullet fragments . . . sort of granular-looking material, went almost as far forward as the frontal bone . . . they were small and irregular . . . flat irregular, two or three millimetres . . .' Some of the metal fragments were larger, one measuring seven millimetres by three to four millimetres. Dr Humes observed at least thirty to forty tiny fragments within the brain and organised a series of slide tissue cells showing the metal fragments when viewed on a light box. 'I didn't need a neuropathologist to see that the man's brain was blown,' Humes said.

When he saw the metal fragments, Dr Finck was keen to have multiple X-rays taken of the brain. He removed metal fragments from JFK's head, '. . . I recall many metal fragments were seen on the X-ray of the head and metal fragments being removed.' Dr Finck also recalled seeing a larger metal fragment measuring seven millimetres by four millimetres.

Agent Sibert heard the pathologists agree that the large wound to the back of JFK's head was an entrance wound. From what he saw of the gaping wound Sibert, too, agreed, believing it was caused by 'a bullet that disintegrated' and that 'part of the brain was missing . . . due to this explosion caused by gunshot wound to the head.' Sibert took custody of two metal fragments which had been removed from the skull and placed in an exhibit jar. He signed for the exhibit and later deposited the jar with his FBI laboratory. During this time he recalled Dr Humes looking at an X-ray and seeing metal fragments. Sibert believed the fragments to look like a 'Milky Way of metal stars' once the X-ray was placed up against the light box.

O'Neill also saw the gaping wound and recalled that there was a general feeling in the room that a soft-nose bullet had struck the President. He felt that the bullet might well have been slowed by the entry and subsequent explosive reaction, then hit the inside of the curved skull wall and returned in the direction it came. Bullets often do strange things in homicides; there are countless examples of unusual bullet reactions!

There was not one suggestion from within the autopsy suite that the wound was the work of a bullet fired in front of the President. Not one word of a suspected shooter forward of the

President. Indeed, there was complete agreement of all in the autopsy suite, medicos and hangers-on alike, that the second bullet had been fired from behind JFK and his head suffered a massive wound caused by the explosion of that round. The surviving photographs of the autopsy show the President lying on the examination table looking oddly serene. His face bears no markings of any kind that would indicate he was shot from the front and the wound exited the rear of his skull.

X-ray technician Jerrol Custer was busying himself carrying out the instructions of Drs Humes and Finck. Once Jerrol had taken the X-rays he would rush upstairs to his photographic laboratory to process the exposures and bring them straight back for the pathologists to view. As time moved on and the work centred on the blast to the President's head, Jerrol noticed that the mood of the hangers-on intensified. He started to feel pressure from the Secret Service and military personnel. The assisting pathologist, Dr Boswell, also reported feeling the pressure and noted that JFK's personal physician demanded only a limited autopsy. It was left to Dr Humes to argue for a full autopsy.

Jerrol believed up to thirty people were in the autopsy suite and the chatter was constant. Each procedure was debated, discussed and he witnessed the doctors being harassed. 'The commotion level was astronomical. The decibel level was extremely high. You had to scream at people at times.'

An experienced man in autopsy X-ray procedures, Jerrol Custer had an explanation for the horrific damage to the President's brain. 'You look at the big portion of the scalp; those [metal] fragments are in the skin of the scalp. That's the only logical place they could be. They went through the brain, exploded and went out into the scalp, perforated the scalp, impregnated the scalp. When you have a fragmented bullet it hits. It blows. Pushes everything out.'

This was not the work of a full metal jacket bullet. This was the work of a bullet designed to explode, fragment or disintegrate on impact. A bullet such as a .223 hollow point or soft point high-velocity round.

Jerrol observed Dr Humes's search. 'The body was literally butchered . . . there was body fluid everywhere . . .', Jerrol recalled. 'Bullet fragments throughout the temporal region' of the skull showed up in his X-ray images, '. . . also bullet fragments in the C3/C4 area of the cervical spine.' (C3 and C4 are beneath the vertebrae at the base of the skull.) With reference to the number of metal fragments, Jerrol recalled 'there was enough . . . it was very prevalent'. So prevalent that Jerrol highlighted the fact to others in the room. 'I was told to mind my own business. That's where I was shut down again.' Jerrol recalled Dr Finck barking orders at his fellow doctors as the tension increased and the search for fragments continued. 'A king size fragment fell from [JFK's] back . . . Dr Finck took [it], that's the last time I ever saw it.'

Helping with the workload, taking X-rays of the entire body, was student technician Edward Reed. He, too, recalled seeing metal fragments.

Jerrol Custer would say under oath to the ARRB that on one occasion when he left the autopsy suite to develop his exposures, he was followed by two agents, down the corridor, up the stairs and along another corridor to the door of his photographic lab. As he entered the lab the agents tried to take the X-rays from him. Pushing himself and the X-rays free, Jerrol entered the safety of his lab and closed the door. Those same X-rays, which showed metal fragments, went missing subsequent to the autopsy. He told the hearing, 'The reason why they are not here [at the ARRB hearing] is because they showed massive amounts of bullet fragments.' The cloak-and-dagger performance Jerrol had to follow to develop his X-rays continued throughout the night as he did his best to support Dr Humes.

At one point during the evening, Jerrol's superior, Dr Ebersole, approached him. Ebersole had been seen coming and going from the autopsy suite, conversing with the Secret Service agents and others. Dr Ebersole gave Jerrol a stern warning, saying, '. . . everything you see from now on you should forget.'

Medical photographer and drawer John Stringer was also called to the autopsy to photograph the various stages of proceedings and sketch the wound details. He recalled taking numerous exposures, mostly black and white. His intention was to place each film on a proof sheet so the pathologists could then pick the images to assist their report. He thought he took fifteen rolls of film, mostly of JFK's head wounds, some of metal fragments, even photographs of the three-ring circus and the dour men watching over. Stringer also observed the doctors discussing the two bullet wounds, hearing a consensus that the first shot entered the President high on the back and exited at the throat and that the second shot entered at the rear of the head. He felt that the Presidential party were pushy, trying to hasten the procedure. 'There [were] a lot of people hurrying. They wanted to get it over with. From the Presidential party . . . let's get it over with . . . let's get going . . .'

As the facts and shocking conclusions were being revealed, Dr Humes and his staff were put under extraordinary pressure to hurry up and finish the autopsy. Secret Service agents declared the family wanted the autopsy completed and that Jackie and Bobby Kennedy didn't want the President's body incised below the neck. Jerrol recalled one of the agents stepping forward and saying to the autopsy team, '. . . the Kennedy family would not allow . . . you [to] pursue that path any further. We do not want you to go any further in this direction . . .' A four-star Army general was pacing about; Kennedy's own physician seemed just as worried. With this pressure shrouding the autopsy suite, the pathologists worked on and the X-ray technician and medical photographer attempted to support the process. Jerrol would give his impression to the ARRB of how he saw the interference by the Secret Service: '. . . the autopsy was something that had to be done. It didn't have to be done correctly, it had to be done for records purposes only . . . finding out facts, forget it . . .'

From this author's reading of the ARRB testimonies it was like the elephant in the room. It was obvious the President had been killed by a head shot that had blown his skull apart leaving metal fragments but nobody mentioned a bullet that was designed to explode on impact – a soft nose or hollow point frangible round. Nor did anyone mention that if a second weapon was involved then a second shooter was also involved.

The autopsy had given Stringer an opportunity to bring in a trainee photographer to gain some valuable experience. He encouraged student medical photographer Floyd Reibe to work alongside him, offering support and supervision as young Reibe took his pictures. The student recalled seeing the brain of the President: '. . . it was less than half a brain there . . .', an observation that indicates the damage done by the explosive round. Reibe also recalled taking 'around one hundred shots' on 'eight to nine' separate film packs. The Secret Service put a stop to that by confiscating his camera and removing the film. The film was never seen again. This vital evidence was only obtained more than thirty years later. Reibe was then asked to recall if he could have taken any films out of the autopsy suite. He replied, 'No, no. Couldn't have got out [of] there with them. They even took unused rolls of film . . .'

The FBI evidence log for the shift showed twenty-two colour rolls and eighteen black and white rolls of film were shot and their care entrusted to the Secret Service. Agent O'Neill clearly recalled handing the film to Roy Kellerman and Chief Rowley. The head of the Secret Service promised to forward a copy of all photographs to the FBI. He never did. At the naval photographic laboratory days later, technicians Saundra Kay Spencer and her superior Robert Knudsen were interrupted in the course of their daily routine by the unannounced arrival of a Secret Service agent. In his possession were 'eight to ten' rolls of unprocessed film. The agent insisted they develop the films immediately while he waited in the hallway and stressed that they must not look at the printed pictures. With the sound of muffled footsteps pacing outside their laboratory door, the two technicians worked through their task. Curiosity got the better of them and they carefully studied each image. Images they would never forget, photographs of their deceased President on an autopsy table, etched in their minds forever.

What happened to the other rolls of film in the possession of the Secret Service is a mystery. In 1966 John Springer went to a meeting to discuss and view the autopsy photos and again confirmed that many were missing, never having seen the inside of the Warren Commission. And not seen since. Neither Saundra

Kay Spencer nor Robert Knudsen was called to give evidence at the Warren Commission.

Some years later, the two technicians were able to tell their bizarre tale at the ARRB hearings into the development of the film. Both Spencer and Knudsen were adamant that the photos submitted to the Warren Commission were different from those they had developed for the Secret Service agent on the weekend after the assassination. They believed it highly likely that select images had been altered for the Commission – in other words, falsified.

Although Dr Humes was dissatisfied with the autopsy process, he knew he managed to achieve as much he could under the conditions. He stored the brain of President Kennedy in a stainless-steel pail for later dissection and forensic analysis, a process that required the brain to sit in a particular solution for a number of days so as to harden. Analysis on both the metal fragments and the bullet wound would then be undertaken. Dr Humes gave the fragments recovered earlier from the brain to the Secret Service, but despite his efforts he never saw them again.

Dr Humes had found himself a part of a process that was not only unorthodox but against any practice acceptable in a court of law. He was troubled. Exhausted, he went home in the wee hours of the morning to complete his notes. For reasons that defy any medical or investigative logic, he burnt his handwritten autopsy notes. Reading Humes's cross-examination I received the impression that he had become scared of ramifications or riddled with shame.

At the time of the autopsy, Lee Harvey Oswald was well and truly alive and playing the Dallas detectives for fools with his smart-ass manner and arrogance. As the pathologists were working away with their scalpels and cutting tools on the seventeenth floor of Bethesda, the big Captain Fritz and his boys were working away on the third floor of Dallas police headquarters interviewing an assassin. That's the situation. That's the plot in real time: an autopsy and a man in custody, a classic homicide scenario. All that was required from the pathology team was a thorough examination of the body and determination of the cause of death, coupled with the recovery of bullets used and any other facts that would assist the interview and subsequent prosecution of Oswald. It doesn't get any more basic than that.

If everything in the autopsy suite was on the up and up, then within a few hours the cause of death would have been confirmed. The lone, near pristine full metal jacket bullet that passed through the bodies of JFK and Governor Connally would have been legitimised. The entrance wound to the back of the President's head would have been photographed and logged on the autopsy report and the facts would have been sent through to Captain Fritz, Oswald's interviewing officer. Through this process, each stage, each discovery would have been noted and all exhibits would have found exhibits bags and a chain of continuity log. Just like Dr Rose at Parkland Memorial Hospital wanted. So why were the Secret Service and others trying to confiscate X-rays, documentary evidence vital to the case against Oswald? Why did the Secret Service destroy photographs of an official autopsy? Why did they take custody of Stringer's many photographs? Why did they push and pressure the medical team to end the autopsy prematurely?

What went on within the autopsy suite that night was anything but an exercise in proper gathering of evidence.

Indeed, it was more akin to a mission to remove or destroy evidence concerning the wound to the rear of JFK's head, the final shot, the explosive round. Chain of custody rules on the handling of exhibits were tossed aside. Logging and labelling of exhibits never took place. It was all about ridding the President's body of any evidence that could point to the type of bullet used in the head shot. Clearly the Secret Service had taken a dictatorial position in the process. It started in Dallas with the body and travelled to Washington. All exhibits had to be handed to them, but why? If forensic principles were to be upheld, the Secret Service agents should have been excused from the process. As noted by FBI Agent O'Neill, Kellerman and Greer were still clad in garments bearing the human remains of JFK. Both Secret Service agents should have been disqualified from entering the autopsy environment, for fear of contamination. Certainly, their clothing should have been seized and photographed as crucial to the prosecution case. Instead, they pushed on, and no one stood in their way. Obviously they did have a part to play in the proceedings. Being present at the time of the assassination, indeed among the two closest to the atrocity, it would be paramount to safeguard their integrity as eyewitnesses, and not have their future testimony against Oswald tainted by participating in the autopsy. Certainly they had no business being present, let alone taking charge. Furthermore, for the chain of evidence to have any integrity, the only persons who should have handled the exhibits, photographs and X-rays should have been FBI agents Sibert and O'Neill, the exhibit officers appointed by J Edgar Hoover. By jurisdiction it should have been an FBI investigation, but in reality it became a Secret Service case, a mission which could only be to destroy any evidence associated with the head shot and to silence everyone within the autopsy suite, forever.

A couple of days after the autopsy, Dr Humes encountered JFK's personal physician, George Burkley, who happened to be his superior at Bethesda. Burkley informed him that Bobby Kennedy wished to inter the President's brain. Dr Humes understood that Bobby Kennedy was requesting custody of the brain. He would recall, '. . . he asked me would I give him the brain which I properly handed it to him . . . then the mystery really begins because what happened after that I don't know . . . What George Burkley did with the brain is the mystery of the century. And why I so easily acceded to his wishes, I don't know, other than he's talking about Bobby and the family and what they want . . .'

The brain hasn't been seen since, lost with its metal fragments and its clues.

Days later Dr Humes was then required to sign a gag order forbidding him to speak to any person of his work in the autopsy suite, including anything that he observed or heard.

There was no love lost between senior X-ray technician Jerrol Custer and his supervisor Dr Ebersole, but they seemed to tolerate each other. Days after the autopsy Dr Ebersole walked into Jerrol's office. Like something out of a matinee movie of the day, Ebersole was on a mission – he'd been to a clandestine meeting with the Secret Service at the White House. He called it a 'de-briefing' with 'high-ranking people'. Gripped by the intrigue of it all, he blurted out his request. In his hand were a few metal fragments, looking a lot like fragments of a bullet. Jerrol had never seen them before. Ebersole asked the technician to create an X-ray using pieces of skull from the autopsy. Jerrol recalled Dr Ebersole saying, 'I want these bone fragments X-rayed with metal fragments attached.'

There was no doubt Jerrol was being asked to falsify an X-ray. Although he was deeply concerned about the situation he deferred to the authority of his medical superior and undertook the task, an incident he would regret forever. He, too, signed a gag order, waved in front of him by Ebersole. Jerrol would keep his copy of the gag order in a drawer at home for the rest of his life. He was told, '. . . everything I see from now on I should forget . . . I was told if anything – no matter what – got out, it would be the sorriest day of my life. I'd spend the rest of my time behind prison walls.' He believed it.

Dr Ebersole obviously enjoyed his stroll on the sordid side of the street, as he continued to spout falsities well into his later career. Anyone who would lend an ear heard that he took most of the X-rays during the JFK autopsy. At the ARRB hearing in 1997, Ebersole summed up the autopsy result: '. . . the path of a missile which appeared to enter the back of the skull and the path of the disintegrated fragments could be observed along the right side of the skull . . .' Knowing that, he must have understood the level of corruption he was entering into by ordering the falsification of an X-ray for the Secret Service. It seems Ebersole had become a misguided patriot. Neither he nor young X-ray technician Edward Reed was called to give evidence at the Warren Commission.

A few days after the autopsy, trainee photographer Floyd Reibe would tell the ARRB, he was also asked to sign a gag order, forbidding him to ever talk of what went on in the autopsy suite. He was told the gag order was under the *National Security Act* and that he would be court-martialled should he breach the order. This threat was reinforced verbally a few days later. And of course he was not called to give evidence at the Warren Commission. Similarly, medical photographer and drawer John Stringer was not called. His exposures were confiscated by the Secret Service, many went missing, and he, too, was forced to sign an order of silence. Indeed, neither Stringer nor Reibe was asked to tell their story to any level of officialdom until thirty-four years later when he was called to the ARRB hearings.

There were so many potential witnesses, so many stories going unheard. Pathologist Chester Boyers entered the autopsy suite and made similar observations to those of the others. He was not called to give evidence at the Warren Commission, yet he was forced to sign an order of silence. There were many busy ballpoint pens that weekend – another signature came from Robert Karnei, a second-year resident doctor at Bethesda. Karnei witnessed the longwinded search for the head shot bullet that was never found. And he was not required to give evidence at the Warren Commission.

Representing the Navy general in charge of the hospital during the autopsy was aide Richard Lipsey. It was his first autopsy, and Lipsey also witnessed the frantic search for the bullet. Years later at the ARRB hearings he gave a graphic account of JFK's body being pulled apart, all organs, in the search. He missed the shortlist of the Warren Commission as well. What he didn't miss was the chatter about the missing bullet and numerous metal fragments. Those present considered this fact highly confidential. Why? From what he had heard and seen, Lipsey formed the untrained view that the 'missing' bullet had exited the same gaping hole that it had entered.

Laboratory assistant Paul O'Connor was not called to give evidence at the Warren Commission. Harold Rydberg, who sketched the drawings of the cadaver of JFK, likewise, not called, yet he was in the ideal position to see the head wound and form an opinion. The Bethesda's chief surgeon, David Osborne, popped into the proceedings to see if all was going well. From what he saw he believed there was no question the third round entered the back of JFK's head and blew the top off. Osborne was not required at the Warren Commission. On and on, the list gets longer, so many voices from the autopsy silenced. Virtually everyone who entered the suite on that bloodied 22nd day of November, 1963, was forced to sign a silence order, their testimony kept from the people of America.

As a veteran detective I am flabbergasted at the arrogance shown to the proper process of probing into a death, in this case the death of an extremely prominent global figure.

My reading of the ARRB files staggered me, it is such a Pandora's box of skulduggery on the part of those in charge of the corpse of JFK. But my dismay would not end there, I would learn something else within the bound pages of the ARRB hearings that would stir worry. To explain my concern is to outline the hearing process of the ARRB. The review board was set up after legislation had been passed, known as the *President John F Kennedy Records Collection Act of 1992*. What followed was a series of ARRB hearings, behind closed doors and in public, as the Board spent most of 1994 until late in 1998 gathering evidence, records, documents and papers. These could then be studied and verified and logged into a definitive collection of records relating to the assassination of President Kennedy and released to the fullest extent possible to the American people.

In doing so, the ARRB hoped to '. . . shed new evidentiary light on the assassination of President Kennedy, enrich the historical understanding of the tragic moment in American history, and help restore public confidence . . .' It was a monumental task and required all agencies involved in the investigation into the assassination of JFK, or government departments and law enforcements agencies who played a role in the events in Dallas on 22 November, 1963, or any other persons with evidence, to pass such material to the ARRB. In effect, an inquisition the likes unseen since the Warren Commission.

In all, sixty-three hearing dates were set aside as the evidence mounted up. The five person Review Board methodically waded through the documents and interviewed witnesses. *The JFK Act*, as it became known, held certain powers that directed federal agencies to surrender their records to the ARRB. Without exception, agencies complied. *The JFK Act* also gave all potential witnesses the freedom to respond to the questions by the ARRB interviewers, despite any previous gag orders.

In early 1995 the ARRB set about drafting a request to the Secret Service for further and better particulars related to the President's Dallas tour. Everything related to that day in November 1963. Obviously, it would contain information that was not offered to the Warren Commission, and documents and log sheets on the agents' duties for the days before the tour, during and after. One can only imagine the volume of information – notes, diary entries, memos and, most of all, duty sheets and firearms reports. A week before the written demand could be finalised and served on the Secret Service the administration of the Secret Service 'destroyed' all the files and reports.

This destruction of material was met with a demand from the ARRB to the Secret Service to explain. Apparently other documents related to the Dallas case, outside the immediate scope of the ARRB, were also destroyed. The Secret Service administration would only offer a verbal explanation as to why they destroyed such vital evidence. The explanation was tendered in a closed hearing, and was never made public. The ARRB sought a written explanation but it never came.

To destroy such vital information smacks of only one thing: a last-ditch effort to cover up the behaviour and mistakes of the Secret Service agents in Dealey Plaza on 22 November, 1963, and later at the Parkland Memorial Hospital and the autopsy suite at Bethesda hospital. Such disregard of the process undertaken by the ARRB is, to this author, unforgivable.

CHAPTER 13
THE TRUTH HAS MANY FACES

The role of a prosecutor, district attorney, lawyer or counsel assisting an enquiry such as the Warren Commission is to search for the truth. It's that simple. The process is a lot like digging for gold on a landscape that can be vast, rugged and at times unforgiving. The Warren Commission dealt with 552 witnesses, a vast landscape indeed. A good lawyer will put his or her head down and work tenaciously towards the truth, keeping on digging until he or she finds the lucky strike, the facts. Careers are built on lucky strikes in the legal world. A good day in court, an acquittal or conviction, can hold an ordinary lawyer in good stead for years. Mediocrity in law firms means one thing: never to be invited into the boardroom, never to share the real gold, a partnership in the firm, or in the case of the public defender, the office of District Attorney. It's a ruthless game and often the only way to get ahead is to keep searching, keep trying for a breakthrough.

Chairman Earl Warren had fifteen counsel assisting. Lawyers handpicked to uphold truth, justice and the American way, all from a diverse range of careers. Some were more clever than talented. One or two were so clever it was almost as if they didn't want certain facts to be aired within their courtroom. Others were just average, the also-rans, lawyers who asked dozens of questions about a witness's personal history, domesticity, residency, schooling, working background and much, much more, pages of nonsense with little bearing on the search for truth.

Dallas patrolman Earle Brown came to court and raised the Bible. He had a great story to tell. Earle had been standing on the overpass looking down on the approaching motorcade. It was getting closer, a hundred metres away. In no time the vehicles would disappear underneath him, underneath the roadway as it headed for the scheduled Trade Mart Presidential luncheon. As the limousines approached, Earle heard the three shots. His position offered him a perfect view of a Secret Service agent in the follow-up car: '. . . he had this gun and was swinging it around, looked like a machine gun and the President was all sprawled out.' Not only did Patrolman Brown's eyes work efficiently but also his nose. '. . . Then I smelled this gunpowder . . . at least it smelled like it to me,' he said to Counsellor Joseph Ball. The issue of where the gunpowder smell came from was to hang for a further fifty years, as a short time later Counsellor Ball excused Earle from the witness box. On reading the patrolman's testimony, the most fascinating detail wasn't necessarily his smelling of gunpowder or his observation of the machine-gun-swinging Secret Service agent, but his mentioning of two other policemen who were standing alongside him on the overpass at the time, patrolmen James Lomax and Joe Murphy. Here were two other officers in a position to have possibly seen what Earle Brown saw and to have been questioned on these key issues.

Anyone savvy to the ways of witnesses would know the value of a police officer's testimony, as opposed to that of a nervous civilian. Cops raise the Bible weekly; they know the rules of evidence and the need to be accurate and concise. The Commission would have known this too, yet many patrolmen were omitted from the Warren Commission's witness list. Lomax and Murphy were called, yet neither was asked about smoke, the smell of gunpowder or the story of a Secret Service agent swinging a machine gun around. This is an inconceivable omission by counsel assisting the commission.

Counsellor Ball merely queried Murphy as to what the railway men standing nearby were doing. Murphy's brief appearance in the witness box was of little value in terms of corroborating Earle Brown's testimony. Thankfully, though, he did explain the echo effect to the Commission. As a patrolman he knew the area well and offered a credible insight as to how the echo created by the overpass could confuse a person's hearing.

Following Earle Brown, Signal Supervisor Mr S M Holland stepped into the witness box to be cross-examined by Counsellor Samuel Stern. Holland recalled taking a group of his railwaymen to the overpass and standing near Patrolman Brown and his fellow officers. The railway contingent also had a perfect view of the assassination. Mr Holland testified that '. . . after the first shot the Secret Service man raised up from the seat with a machine gun and then dropped back down in the seat . . . and immediately sped off . . .' Holland recalled the last two shots were '. . . so close together . . . I have no doubt about seeing

that puff of smoke come up from under those trees either . . .'
Mr Holland informed the Commission that he had told 'six
federal men . . . that I definitely saw the puff of smoke . . .' He
also stated to the Commission that of the rounds he heard fired,
there were '. . . different sounds, different reports [the sound of
a bullet being fired] . . .'

Here we have two professional men in positions of
responsibility, one a police patrolman and one a supervisor of
railway signals, both reporting the same set of observations. Mr
Holland then offered testimony that could easily have taken
the Warren Commission on a very different path. He named
eight other men who were also standing on the overpass and
who had all witnessed that which he and Patrolman Brown
had seen. He spelt out their names to the Commission. He
told them their positions at work and what yards they worked
in. He told the Commission that he observed the patrolmen
record these workers' personal identification details in their
notebooks after the incident. Holland recalled the names of
Messrs. Dodd, Potter, Winborn, Johnson and Cowzert, and
added that a railwayman from the Katy yard and a railwayman
from Texas and Pacific rail yard were also present.

None of these men were called to give evidence before the
Warren Commission. Interestingly, Mr Holland would later
complain to the media of 'persons' browbeating him during
the Commission proceedings on what he saw and where he
saw smoke. He suggested they were trying to manipulate his
observations.

It was not only Patrolman Earle Brown and Mr Holland
who witnessed the group of railwaymen watching the motorcade.
Secret Service Agent Lawson, who gave sworn testimony that

he saw an agent with an 'automatic weapon' and thought he
had 'fired' the gun, also mentioned seeing the men on the
overpass. He told the hearing that as his car approached the
overpass he saw the group watching the motorcade: '. . . they
were spread out one or two deep, and as I say between five
and ten of them to my knowledge, and I noticed that police
officer . . . in the middle of the group . . .', perhaps referring to
Patrolman Brown. Agent Lawson watched the railwaymen on
the overpass for a considerable time but he didn't suggest they
be called to testify; nor did anyone else.

Following Mr Holland was Frank Reilly, who was also in
the group on the overpass. He told the Commission he believed
the three shots came out of the trees on Elm Street. This
observation is perfectly logical from his vantage point, high
above the ground on the overpass, and clearly suggests gunplay
at street level, not six storeys above from the Texas School
Book Depository. Yet all the Commission's counsellor asked of
this important witness was, '. . . did you see any pigeons fly?'
And seconds after that bizarre question the counsellor ended
with, '. . . I think that is all Mr Reilly . . .' Frank suggested
that the Commission call a man with him on the overpass, a
Mr Skinney. Yet another man who didn't see the witness box
at the Warren Commission. In all, at least eight sets of eyes,
eight noses, eight more citizens who could have swelled the
number who smelled gunpowder and saw the Secret Service
agent swinging his 'machine' gun around.

Royce Skelton, a twenty-three-year-old mail clerk with the
Texas Louisiana Freight Bureau, was watching the motorcade
with co-worker Austin Miller. Royce heard the first two shots
as the President's car was travelling towards him. He stepped

up before Counsellor Ball to be cross-examined. '. . . I thought that they were dumballs that they throw at the cement because I could see smoke coming up from the cement . . .' The counsellor asked, 'Did you see smoke come off of the cement?' Royce replied, 'Yes.' Counsellor Ball suggested that the smoke had come from the building, to which Royce responded, 'No: on the pavement . . .', making it clear that he saw the smoke on the street. Ball asked of the shots, 'Where did it seem to you that the sound came from, what direction?' Royce replied, 'Towards the President's car . . .' Ball suggested, '. . . from the President's car?' and Royce clarified, 'Right around the motorcycles and all that . . .' Royce was to reiterate towards the end of his brief time in the witness box that he saw smoke and that he had also heard '. . . other people say they did . . .'.

The Governor's wife, Mrs Nellie Connally, was in the Presidential car on that day. She heard the three shots and after the first round her gravely injured husband fell onto her lap. With regard to the last shot, Nellie said, '. . . the third round I heard, I felt, it felt like spent buckshot falling all over us.' She would then give a vivid description of the blood and brain tissue spraying over her. Anyone close to a high-powered weapon when discharged understands the description, 'I heard, I felt [it]'. It's all to do with velocity. A high-velocity bullet creates shockwaves as it roars through the air. This is called the 'shock front', an audible wave travelling away from the centre of the charge. Also known as a stress wave, it is 'felt' by persons closest to the weapon firing the round. In a theatre of war, soldiers 'feel' bullets whizzing past.

Nellie Connally's description needed astute cross-examination, verification. Yet her description was left hanging, unexplored. Counsellor Arlen Specter changed the subject and asked what seemed like an irrelevant question about how fast the car was moving, then a series of questions about Parkland Memorial Hospital with a definite tone of sympathy. Mrs Connally was in and out of the witness box in minutes, her testimony amounting to a mere three pages. But not before she mentioned seeing men at the Parkland Hospital, when she and her bloodied husband arrived, carrying 'machine guns'.

Likewise, Jackie Kennedy spent only minutes in the witness box, with no attempt from anyone in the Commission to probe.

The Commission did interview the five patrolmen closest to the President's vehicle, most of them motorcycle police. Although two were so close to the President that they were splattered with blood and human flesh after the head shot, their day in court would amount to only a few minutes each. These officers, street-savvy cops who could offer a bird's-eye-view account, were asked little of any consequence. The lack of attention to detail in the cross-examination of these key men was glaring. It was if the Commission considered their appearance pointless. Following their testimony, Counsellor David Belin questioned Captain Lawrence, the head of traffic policing for the city of Dallas. Lawrence had nothing to offer by way of evidence; he wasn't in the position to be considered a vital witness. Yet Belin took an extraordinary amount of time asking question after question regarding administration, mostly related to the days leading up to the assassination and immediately after. This onslaught of futile information would fill pages of the Commission report, and the 'facts' were never heard.

Forty-five-year-old Howard Brennan also took the stand to encounter Belin's cross-examination. Howard recalled standing on a retaining wall overlooking the motorcade as it rolled along Elm Street at a slow pace. He had an extraordinarily clear view of a white man he later identified as Lee Harvey Oswald pointing a high-powered rifle from a window of the sixth floor of the Texas School Book Depository. His view was so clear he could even see the boxes stacked up behind Oswald. Brennan watched Oswald point and aim his rifle and he heard the shots. He thought the first shot might have been a firecracker, the second a rifle shot. Of the third, Counsellor Belin asked if Howard could see Oswald's rifle 'explode . . . cause a flash . . . see the discharge of the rifle . . . see the recoil . . . or the flash?' Howard's reply to this volley of questions was negative on all occasions. Yet Howard Brennan heard the last shot.

One can almost hear the collective courtroom audience's intake of breath in expectation of the next obvious cross-examining question: 'So, where did the shot come from? If it was not Oswald's rifle, then whose weapon did fire that shot?' Belin let the question stand unasked, then Howard Brennan left the witness stand.

In Belin's cross-examination of Barbara Rowland, the young married woman standing in the crowd with her husband, he posed eighty-six different questions about Barbara's marriage, schooling and domesticity. Eighty-six questions about nothing! He could have saved pages of transcript, cut to the chase and simply asked if the young lady was on Elm Street on the 22nd day of November with her husband. A good portion of the entire 8000-plus pages of transcript material known as the twenty-six volumes of the Warren Commission is nothing more than twaddle created by ineffectual lawyers who seemed to have forgotten how to dig for gold.

Counsellor Arlen Specter questioned Barbara's husband, Arnold Rowland. He recalled standing on Houston Street with his bride, watching the crowd, waiting for JFK to arrive. They both observed a man leaning out of the sixth-floor window of the Book Depository building pointing a rifle. They studied him closely until the motorcade came and passed by. Then the shots started. The couple ran towards the Book Depository, in the direction of the first two shots. On the third shot Arnold insisted that they change direction and run the opposite way. 'It sounded like it came from this area "C" [the Dealey Plaza] . . .', so they ran down Elm Street into the Dealey Plaza, from where they believed the shot had emanated. All that was down there apart from a smattering of bystanders was the motorcade, now accelerating at high speed. The interview ended a short time later without exploring the reasons for the Rowlands' change of direction in running towards the motorcade, away from the Texas School Book Depository.

Newspaper journalist Robert Jackson was also on Houston Street, travelling in a car full of TV and newspaper journalists, cameramen and photographers. He recalled of the third shot, '. . . it never sounded like it was high or low . . .'. He also recalled seeing a man leaning from the sixth-floor window of the Texas School Book Depository, pointing a rifle. Oddly, Specter failed to seize on the opportunity to ask Jackson the names of all the other journalists, with cameras – a handy lead, one would think, for photographic evidence and first-hand eyewitnesses.

And on it went, witnesses giving hardboiled testimony of what they saw, what they smelt, and what their opinions were. Clues were dropped in a courtroom where counsellors seemed clueless, or reluctant to ask. A courtroom where counsellors would blatantly lead witnesses with suggestive questioning, where gathering comments from those in the best position to tell of their observations, of what they heard, what they saw, what they smelt, was sadly lacking.

Some of what was placed before the Commission seemed coordinated by Arlen Specter. Was it his job to pick and choose which witnesses the Commission would hear from? Certainly some witnesses tell of Specter's behaviour, outside the hearing room. An experienced district attorney, he had adopted the practice of interviewing witnesses privately, assessing the value of their evidence before they were called. He would then make a personal decision to excuse the witness, or log them onto the witness list.

Jerrol Custer had such a meeting with Specter, alone and outside the hearing of the Warren Commission. There was little doubt that Jerrol's observations at the autopsy and his involvement in falsifying an X-ray for the Secret Service was explosive evidence. The X-ray technician raised his concerns, then went home and waited. Specter never called. Jerrol Custer's evidence was never to see the witness stand.

Many others who had a story to tell suffered the same fate. Mary Moorman, the friend of Jean Hill, should have been called. Only a few metres away from her President, Mary snapped one of the last pictures of JFK before he was murdered, but she never saw the witness box. Specter cross-examined Jean Hill. He would have known the importance of Jean and Mary's evidence. At one point Specter asked Jean Hill, 'And you had the general impression that the Secret Service was firing the second group of shots at the man who fired the first group of shots?' Jean answered, 'That's right.' Specter went on to ask, 'But you had no specific impression of the source of the shots?' Jean answered, 'No.' Jean would go on to tell the Commission, 'At the time I thought there was more than one person shooting as I said before . . .' If there was ever a reason to call Jean's best friend Mary Moorman, it lay in Jean's reference to the Secret Service returning fire. If the Warren Commission or Counsellor Specter had been confused by Jean's comments or felt her comments to be ambiguous, Mary would have been the ideal witness to assist. And because of Jean Hill's dramatic revelation, every witness from Elm Street or Dealey Plaza should have been asked as to whether they felt the Secret Service was returning fire.

Midway through the Warren Commission proceedings, Specter instigated a private meeting with FBI agents Sibert and O'Neill. At a nondescript government office he proceeded to assess what they knew, what they believed, and if they had made any notes during the autopsy. Sibert and his partner had indeed made very comprehensive notes, known as exhibit FD 302. Five pages of typed notes, which came from many more pages of handwritten notes. They comprised a chronology of events, from the arrival of JFK's body at Bethesda until the end of the autopsy. They listed who took custody of photos, X-rays and exhibits, noting that Kellerman claimed copious rolls of film and X-rays and that he had promised to supply a copy of each item to the FBI. These were never forthcoming. The notes also indicated that O'Neill and Sibert had taken custody of some metal fragments for examination by the FBI laboratory, and that Dr Humes had advised the agents that '. . . approximately forty particles of disintegrated bullet and smudges indicated that the projectile had fragmentized while passing through the skull.'

Both agents were unimpressed with Specter, describing him as full of self-importance and lacking in investigative know-how. O'Neill believed 'Specter tried to mischaracterise me and Sibert and take things out of context.' He saw the Warren Commission counsellor as a 'flunky' and the interview as 'a farce'. Records within the Warren Commission concerning Specter's unorthodox discussion are clear, stating in Specter's own notes that Sibert and O'Neill 'made no notes during the autopsy'. Was this a misunderstanding or an outright lie?

And of course, after their meeting with Specter, FBI agents James Sibert and Francis O'Neill were not called to give evidence before the Warren Commission.

One has to wonder if Arlen Specter spoke with each of the Secret Service agents from the follow-up car, especially George Hickey and the field agents either side of him. And if the chat was like that of the two FBI men, in a nondescript location. And, if so, why Specter decided the bodyguards to the President of the United States had nothing to offer the hearing. Certainly someone kept these men from raising the Bible. The absence of more than ten men, all closest to the killing, all staring at the back of the President's head, all with a bird's-eye view of the entire scene, is not only neglectful, it is telling. That the observations and recollections of these highly trained men were missing from the Commission denied the American public their right to answers. Perhaps Specter feared what may have ensued had the car full of suits with their AR-15 assault weapon provided the truth behind the death of the 35th President of the United States.

Texan Senator Yarborough, the 'people's senator' was an army veteran with fifty years' experience handling firearms. As part of the Presidential motorcade he was seated in the open-top convertible immediately behind the follow-up car containing George Hickey and the large contingent of Secret Service agents. When the first shot rang out the Senator ducked down momentarily, then looked up again, towards the follow-up car.

In breaking news the morning after the assassination, the *New York Times* quoted Yarborough: '. . . the shots seemed to have come from the right and the rear of the car in which he was riding, the third in the motorcade.' The third car of the motorcade was the follow-up car containing the Secret Service agents. Yarborough's first-hand account to the media is ambiguous – does he mean 'he' to be JFK? Surprisingly this account managed to find its way into the prologue of the front volume of the Warren Commission report which was released to the general public. Yarborough went on to say in the *New York Times*, '. . . [he] saw a Secret Service man in the car ahead beating his fists against the trunk deck of the car in which he was riding, apparently in frustration and anguish . . .'. Another ambiguous statement in need of clarification. Later, at the Parkland Memorial Hospital, Yarborough was with Jackie Kennedy when she received the news that JFK had died. Yarborough recalled Jackie's words to him: 'They've murdered my husband, they've murdered my husband . . .' What did she mean by this, considering the likelihood all anyone at this point was proffering was the lone gunman theory?

A peep into the Warren Commission Executive Sessions memorandums, which were notes from meetings chaired by Earl Warren and attended by senior counsel Gerald Ford and the executive members, offers an intriguing snapshot into the worries and concerns of the men who steered the hearing, the men responsible for listening to the evidence. Most of the Executive Sessions were held before the hearings got underway, to discuss the complexities of what lay ahead and to chart an intended course. Each meeting was recorded and the minutes were then transcribed before being stamped 'Confidential', never to be read. As an added precaution they were marked 'Top Secret', indicating *in camera* discussions, held in absolute privacy. The Executive were of the understanding that the transcripts would not be made public for seventy-five years. But thirty years later, Congress had passed *The JFK Act*, legislation that lifted the secrecy provisions on documents and allowed the release of information, including the Executive Sessions minutes. With full access available, the Executive Sessions notes make compelling reading. They tell of a frustrated chief justice, adamant in one session that Senator Yarborough be called to his courtroom. Knowing that the Senator was in the car behind the follow-up car, Earl Warren was keen to hear his story. The Senator had written to Warren claiming to have smelt smoke at the scene and wanted to give his evidence before the Commission. Certainly Yarborough's story needed clarification and his firearms experience and position in the motorcade made him a vital witness. Yet no one subpoenaed him.

If asked, Senator Yarborough would speak as he often did to the media of 22 November, 1963, in scathing tones. His opinion of the Secret Service agents' behaviour on that fateful day was low. He stated, '. . . the secret service men seemed to me to respond very slowly, with no more than a puzzled look. I had been lulled into a sense of false hope for the President's safety, by the lack of motion, excitement, or apparent visual knowledge by the Secret Service men, that anything so dreadful was happening. Knowing something of the training that infantrymen and Marines receive, I am amazed at the lack of instantaneous response by the Secret Service, when the rifle fire began.'

Of the Warren Commission, Yarborough later recalled, 'a couple of fellows from the Warren Commission' called on him at his office, requesting that he sign a pre-typed affidavit. Naturally, the Senator refused: pre-typed affidavits are unethical. Such a practice is not only frowned upon but can damage the integrity of an investigation and arouse suspicions of corruption. Hence, the senator was never called. In time, he gave up waiting and wrote his own affidavit, albeit a limited one, touching on only some of the evidence he could have offered. Like his comments to the *New York Times*, his affidavit is ambiguous, in need of clarification. Although he seemed clear in his limited affidavit that the third shot was, 'about one and one-half seconds after the second shot', which is telling.

In reading both Yarborough's first-hand story in the *New York Times* and his limited affidavit, one is left with the overwhelming impression that he may well have been of great assistance to unravelling the truth behind JFK's assassination. He went on to tell his official biographer, Patrick Cox of the University of Texas Press, some three decades later that 'I could smell gunpowder very strongly and the rancid smell of gunpowder stayed in our nostrils for minutes as we raced towards Parkland Hospital.' This is consistent with his conversation with a journalist from the *Chicago Sun-Times*, while outside the hospital on the day of the killing: 'I heard three explosions like a deer rifle . . . you could smell powder on our car nearly all the way here [to the hospital].' This exact same quote appeared in

THE TRUTH HAS MANY FACES

another newspaper, the *Texas Observer* – again, notes taken by a journalist as Yarborough waited outside the hospital. A 1975 American ABCTV report into the killing of JFK quoted Yarborough as saying, 'You don't smell gunfire unless you are upwind from it, and it blows in your face.' He stated that he could not have smelled the gunpowder if the shots had been fired from behind the motorcade. I agree completely with the gunpowder smell theory by Senator Yarborough. Forty-five years' experience of handling weapons, firing rifles, hunting and using hand guns, as well as an extensive career investigating firearm-related crimes, allows me to form the same point of view as the Senator.

In 1983 Yarborough mentioned to a journalist 'the smell of gunpowder' drifting down his right side as Johnson's car rolled past the south-east corner of the Texas School Book Depository. Yarborough was travelling in LBJ's car, behind the follow-up car.

In 1992 Yarborough would tell another journalist, Gerald Strober, that he smelled gunsmoke and that some Dallas police had said to him, '. . . we all smelled that gunsmoke.' Still, of all the comments Yarborough would offer to journalists and writers, the one that caught this writer's attention, far and above anything else, was what Yarborough was quoted as saying to the *Chicago Sun-Times* reporter Carleton Kent, printed the day after the killing: 'The third shot [Yarborough] heard might even have been a Secret Service man returning the fire.' This comment was like diamonds to me! After I read the newspaper clipping over and over, I finally understood why the 'people's senator' was persona non grata at the Warren Commission. His jigsaw piece was far too big and would never fit their puzzle.

Clearly, someone within the Warren Commission felt Yarborough could be a can of worms, too risky to open . . . à la Jerrol Custer and FBI agents Sibert and O'Neill. So Senator Yarborough's evidence was reduced to a limited affidavit. In reality, what he smelt was explosive and the only way to defuse it was to ignore him and hope he blew away, like the gunpowder smells on the day.

Also missing from the list of witnesses was Congressman Ray Roberts, seated in the car behind Yarborough's. Roberts had smelt gunpowder and stated that, '. . . from out of nowhere appeared one Secret Serviceman with a submachine gun.' The Congressman was angered that he was not asked to tender his evidence in the enquiry into the death of his colleague. He held strong opinions on the smell of gunpowder that day until his death, mentioning it on many occasions to journalists, writers and JFK aficionados.

Certainly Arlen Specter's name is associated with not calling important witnesses, individuals who would have shed a very different light on the crime scene. Specter must also take the award for the greatest number of missed opportunities during questioning. Witness after witness raised the Bible and tried their best as Specter cross-examined. But to read his work, to follow the transcripts, to see the leads that were made available to the former Yale Law School graduate and not exploited, is to see mediocrity.

The first of only a few Secret Service agents to take the stand was Roy Kellerman, the architect of the removal of JFK's body from Dallas's Parkland Memorial Hospital to the Bethesda Naval Hospital in Washington DC. Kellerman was seated in the President's vehicle, the closest agent to the action, and described the first shot as 'like a firecracker, pop'. Then Kellerman surprised the Commission by describing the second and third shots as being close together 'like a plane going through a sound barrier, bang, bang'. A graphic and sensational description, consistent of a high-powered weapon being used in close proximity, when the sound can be frightening. In cross-examining, Specter chose to reiterate the words 'pop' and 'firecracker' as if to reinforce the less dramatic while failing to flesh out the 'sound barrier' comment. The question of why not begs to be asked.

Kellerman mentioned that he had human remains from JFK 'all over my coat', to which Specter said nothing. Sensible cross-examination would have included questions as to why the coat wasn't surrendered as an exhibit or why Kellerman hadn't excused himself from the autopsy. Instead, the comment, like so many others, was left to hang.

Kellerman was the closest agent to both male victims, the President and Governor Connally. So close that he wore the signs of death, his jacket covered in brain matter. He saw it all and heard it all. Kellerman knew exactly the number of rounds fired and exactly the number of wounds sustained by both men. It was he who rushed both victims to the hospital and stated under oath at the Commission that he never left JFK's side, even during the autopsy. Kellerman was present when the pathologist tracked the shoulder wound to the exit hole at the throat. Yet he stated under oath that JFK 'had entry [wound] in the throat' and earlier claimed that he did not see the throat exit wound at all. 'I saw nothing in his face to indicate an injury, whether the shot had come through or not.' He insisted that JFK had suffered 'four wounds . . . two in the head and [one in] the shoulder and [one in] the neck . . .' and suggested to the Commission that 'there have got to be more than three shots'.

Let's not forget that Kellerman was less than one metre away, and that the President grabbed his throat after the bullet exited. Indeed, the world saw what Kellerman knew, via the Zapruder film. So why the story of four wounds, why the suggestion of more bullets? Was this an attempt to confuse the Commission, create doubt and thereby invite any number of theories, conjecture or conspiracy angles?

The treating surgeon, Dr James Carrico, at Parkland Memorial Hospital had used the throat exit hole as a tracheotomy in an attempt to revive the President. He recalled to the Commission that there were no signs of gunpowder present at the exit hole, and that he had fully briefed the Secret Service of this fact on two occasions. Furthermore, the President's own physician observed this procedure at Parkland and he was later in the company of Kellerman at the autopsy. Surely they would have spoken.

Kellerman claimed he didn't recall seeing any blood 'anyplace in the front of JFK's body'. Yet Agent Clint Hill, who jumped onto the rear of JFK's convertible, recalled of the blood that 'there was so much blood you could not tell if there had been any other wound or not . . . there was a large amount of blood in the lower abdominal area.'

So what was Kellerman playing at? And why wasn't Specter working on the witness, getting him back on track, back to the facts? Specter was privy to the hundreds of affidavits from witnesses who had stated there were 'three shots'. Why didn't he confront Kellerman and demand an explanation for his statements?

Kellerman went on to tell the Commission that he wasn't informed of the discovery of bullet fragments within the President's car until the following day, yet those same bullet fragments were brought into the autopsy room during the night of 22 November and were the subject of much discussion by all in attendance. Kellerman was there, alongside FBI Agent Sibert and Secret Service Agent Greer.

When asked by Specter about being in the autopsy suite and viewing X-rays as the medical staff searched for bullet fragments, Kellerman offered, '. . . when you placed the X-ray up against the light the whole head looked like a little mass of stars, there must have been thirty, forty lights where these pieces were . . .' Each piece of metal [fragment] was the size of the 'tip of a match head a little larger'.

Amazingly, Specter probed no further into this startling piece of sworn testimony. No enquiry as to what the fragments may have been before they disintegrated. No exploration of the sort of bullets that disintegrate upon impact. A soft nose or hollow point bullet from an AR-15 assault weapon would be about the equivalent size of 'thirty to forty match heads', albeit in the shape of a bullet. Here was the missing bullet, the lost round that penetrated the President's head, now shattered into thirty to forty little pieces, and the main lawyer for the Commission isn't probing, isn't searching for answers. The most vital piece of evidence from the Commission lay silent on the pages of the transcript for fifty years.

During his testimony Agent Kellerman claimed to have called his colleague Agent Clint Hill to view the President's body. Kellerman commented, '. . . after the completion of the autopsy and before the embalming I summoned Agent Hill down to the morgue to view the body and to witness the damage of the gunshot wounds . . .' Bear in mind that this was well past midnight. What possible reason could Kellerman have to summon another agent for one last look, moments before the embalming? Both Hill and Kellerman had been in the presence of the deceased President's mutilated remains for well over twelve hours, never leaving his side, even during the autopsy procedure. Police know too well the stench that emits from a gaping wound, the smell of coagulating blood. During such an autopsy escaping gases heighten the stench with the opening of the skull and inspection of brain matter, as well as the removal of the heart and liver in the search for bullet and fragments. As Jerrol Custer recalled, the body was '. . . literally butchered . . . there was body fluid everywhere . . .'

To witness an autopsy is a harsh experience; it carries a smell and sights that you never forget; it lingers, seeps inside you, never seeming to subside. Wanting to take another look, up close and personal, is difficult to comprehend. It defies reason that both Hill and Kellerman would want to spend more time with the now dissected corpse. FBI Agent Sibert recalls Kellerman being present in the autopsy suite for the duration, along with Agent Greer. Was the last-minute 'viewing' a time for planning? Was it a time to strategise how to keep the news of the shocking Secret Service error from the American public? Thus far it seemed that Kellerman had been party to the evidence-destroying mission, so what further gems were he and Greer considering at the final viewing?

Upon the arrival of the dying President's motorcade at Parkland Memorial Hospital Kellerman mustered his Secret Service staff. At a time of extreme alert, the President's bodyguard contingent was charged with sealing off and securing the hospital. In his testimony Kellerman detailed the duties of each man in his command. Every man, that is, except George Hickey. The man with the perfect defensive weapon for such a situation, the AR-15 assault weapon, was missing from the roll call. When asked before the Commission who was present on board Air Force One before it left Texas, Kellerman again rattled off a list of names; again, there was no mention of George Hickey or the AR-15 assault weapon. When asked a similar question concerning his personnel and their duties in Washington and the Bethesda Hospital, most in the follow-up car got a mention, but not George Hickey. In isolation, the absence of Hickey might not be considered odd, but on all three occasions throughout the entire day, night and following days is telling.

FBI firearms expert Agent Robert Frazier was called to the Warren Commission three times. The skilled ballistics man confirmed the finer details of the Carcano rifle and the spent full metal jacket rounds located on the sixth floor of the Book Depository. At the request of the Commission Frazier had visited the scene of the shooting to ascertain if the three shots could have been fired from Lee Harvey Oswald's vantage position. He noted some difficulty with pipes near the window; nonetheless, he observed a line of sight. As he looked down onto Elm Street, to the area where JFK's convertible would have been, he noticed mature trees and assessed that, dependent on the aim and shot, the trees may well have hindered Lee Harvey Oswald's accuracy, at least in part. He also told the hearing that the Carcano rifle was '. . . a very low velocity and pressure [weapon].'

Agent Frazier's comments got me thinking laterally on the issue. I found his weapon description at odds with the effect of the final shot, the shot that caused the head of the President to explode so violently. I also found the presence of mature oak trees in Elm Street intriguing. Many witnesses had mentioned the trees and some of the film footage and photographs taken on the day showed the maturity of those trees even then. There were also traffic lights, overhead cables and a freeway sign, all additional obstacles to hinder a would-be assassin.

At this point I decided to set the facts aside momentarily and apply logic to the case. When stuck for a solution, detectives often suspend the rules and guidelines they work under and allow logic to tell its own story. This was one of those occasions. I cashed in my frequent flyer points and caught a 16-hour flight from Sydney to Dallas, Texas, to see the holy grail of all crime scenes for myself.

Stepping from my taxi at the intersection of Elm and Houston streets felt like walking into a time warp. Everything was there: the gardens, shrubbery, trees and gentle slopes, and the big red brick Book Depository building. It was exactly as I had expected, a credit to the local authorities and business owners who had obviously chosen to preserve the integrity of history's most talked-about crime scene. I paced around for hours, criss-crossing Elm Street, checking my notes, walking into and out of Dealey Plaza, identifying the landmarks. Pacing, sketching, looking up and down, I even took up a position behind the famed picket fence at the head of the 'grassy knoll' and thought about the wild conspiracy theories proffered by Mark Lane. I let much of my research wash over me, story after theory, proposition after so-called fact. I had read them all. It was a great day for a former detective, time to forget all the theories I had digested over the years, time to fall back to what I knew. Detective work.

It was a quiet day in downtown Dallas and traffic was light. I stood in the centre of the roadway and commenced walking down Houston Street, imagining I was in a slow-moving Secret Service follow-up car. My eyes scanned the façades of the businesses lining the street until I reached the Book Depository. Undeniably imposing, it stood almost regally, like a beacon, with no other structures abutting it. I stopped in the dead-centre of the roadway and stared at 'the' sixth-floor window. I had great difficulty understanding how two dozen trained agents hadn't seen a man with a rifle, or at least a rifle, protruding from that window. To me, the tip of the rifle as Oswald sighted his weapon would have presented as a gift to alert eyes. I looked around at the route the Secret Service had chosen; there were possible escape routes everywhere. Had Oswald been observed there would have been many ways to avoid his firing range. Both a right turn at Elm or travelling onward along Houston would have avoided the would-be sniper. Pulling hard left onto the lawn of Dealey Plaza and under the cover of trees would also have the President safely away, out of sight of a sniper. I walked on.

I recalled the many witness statements I had read, how they had seen the rifle. Some had even seen the man himself, bobbing up and down in the window frame as JFK's car got closer.

What I saw on my visit overwhelmed me. Not in the negative sense – it was the realisation of how difficult it would have been for an 'average' lone gunman to get off three shots, all within less than six seconds. I thought of Howard Donahue, and his efforts all those years ago, down in his cellar, playing ballistics. I saw first-hand the complexities involved in the lone gunman theory. First, the street known as Elm Street, which cuts through Dealey Plaza, has a significant fall, a downward gradient. And it's quite steep. A stationary ball would gather momentum without assistance, its speed increasing as it rolled down the asphalt slope. Secondly, Elm Street bends to the left, then turns to the right, all in the same distance that the shots were in play. In simple terms, the road snakes along as it dips. This stretch of roadway would require a high level of concentration for any driver, and an inordinate level of precision for a marksman attempting to fire three bullseye shots with a second-hand $19.95 bolt-action rifle that was prone to being sticky to work – the bolt action mechanism tended to be clunky and stiff. And it had a dodgy telescopic sight.

I observed all the obstacles in play back in 1963. The mature oak trees that have stood for decades offer a natural canopy over the roadway – good for pedestrians, bad for snipers. Logically, for Lee Harvey Oswald to fire a shot from his vantage point, he would have to compensate for the canopy as well as the obstacles of traffic lights and road signs while factoring in the snake-like twist and turns in the roadway and the dip on Elm Street. All this would be on his mind as he focused. He would know that his bullet might hit a tree branch, a sign, a street light pedestal, a twig or a clump of leaves, causing the bullet to ricochet and deflect away from the intended target, all this in ideal weather conditions. I remembered from my research that weather records from the day stated the wind was around thirteen knots, increasing to seventeen knots by 1pm, blowing northward along Elm Street, into the faces of the approaching motorcade guests. In lay terms the wind was gusty and noticeable, blowing in the face of the shooter, the President, the Secret Service guys and most witnesses. The breeze would also cause the branches to move around, exponentially increasing the degree of difficulty involved in getting off three quick shots.

To compensate, Oswald would need to readjust his aim, perhaps duck and weave, move his position to find a clear shot. Logic was telling me it would have been difficult to get one clear shot in. I started to understand how the first shot missed the target and hit the roadway.

I climbed the stairs to the sixth floor of the most known book warehouse on the planet and inspected Oswald's stook. A cramped space, covered in boxes, tighter and smaller than I had envisaged from old images and TV reports. The crime scene had been preserved *in situ* all this time, a fabulous piece of archival work! I appreciated Oswald's inaccuracy all the more clearly. He only had a cardboard carton and window ledge to brace, feeding ammunition into the breech of his clunking rifle as he worked his weapon in incredibly cramped conditions, and let's not forget the nerves, the adrenaline, the sheer pressure he must have felt, trying to kill his nemesis, the man who had his wife's affections. Or so his twisted mind had thought.

My visit to Dallas had been worth every point in my frequent flyer program!

I sat with my back against the glassed-off wall to Oswald's workstation and thought long and hard, letting all that I had learnt roll through my mind. I studied the salient points of the killing in my notebook. To fire one shot cleanly from this position, through this obstacle field, would be lucky work from a shooter with only average skills. The task would be next to impossible if you handed that shooter a sub-standard

low-velocity rifle and put him under extreme pressure. To fire
three shots cleanly through the same obstacle path, with the
target moving, the roadside bystanders (by then) becoming
panic-stricken and Secret Service agents readying their weapons,
is unimaginable. Not in 5.6 seconds. Especially as the intended
target was going downhill and, after shot two, the crowd was
screaming. The proposition of Oswald being successful with
any of his shots was remarkable. However, he obviously got off
one lucky round: the one that hit the President in the back of
the neck and wounded Governor Connally.

I had come to embrace Howard Donahue's ballistic position
on the death of the 35th President of the United States. Oswald
could not have fired the third and fatal shot from where he
crouched. The line of the trajectory was all wrong. The third
shot to the back of JFK's head would carry on across to the
left side of his head, and pass through, exiting on the left side.
The altitude of Oswald's stance would cause any bullet to travel
in a downward, angled position, at least sixteen degrees. Yet,
amateur film footage captured by bystander Orville Nix showed
a fascinating sequence of frames when the head shot first hit.
Once the bullet had hit the target (JFK) a pinkish mist is seen
to push forward towards the front and past JFK's head. The
mist travels parallel to the roadway, not in a downwards motion,
which negates the theory the final shot was from above.

The third round could only have come from directly behind
the President.

I recalled evidence that I had read a year or so earlier,
given to the Warren Commission by three top-rate marksmen
who attempted to replicate the 'three shots by Oswald theory',
regarding the wounds to JFK's head and neck. Under 'exact'

conditions, each marksman shot 18 rounds using the same calibre Carcano rifle, ammunition and telescopic sights. None of them hit a bullseye. None of the 54 shots hit the intended target. This made sense to me.

And I hadn't forgotten that in 1967 the CBC Television network staged a similar experiment using eleven of America's most skilled riflemen. None of the best marksmen in the country were able to achieve the same result on their first volley of shots as did Lee Harvey Oswald. And none of the riflemen from any of the tests were under the stress of actually shooting to kill the most important political figure on earth.

I recalled the evidence put before the Warren Commission that, months prior to the assassination of JFK, on a dark night, Oswald had taken careful aim at retired US General Walker with his Carcano rifle. He had stalked the General for a long time, knew the General's home well and was familiar with the countryside surrounding his target. In fact he had photographed his prey's home and undertaken surveillance to learn the General's movements and ascertain the best time to strike. On the night he chose to kill, Oswald found his prey standing motionless at his window, staring into the night. The perfect quarry. The General was unaware that an assassin was pointing a rifle at him. Yet Oswald missed his target outright, the bullet lodging in the timber frame of the window. All the evidence I had read indicated Oswald wasn't much of a shot; his army records show him as merely average. Surely here was more evidence of the standard and quality of Oswald as a marksman.

Additionally, as must be understood, the General's shooting would not have carried remotely the same level of pressure for the assassin. Not the same level of stress and intensity that would be expected when sighting up the President of the United States, on the move, travelling away from the assassin, indeed, 50 metres away, through the trees, only his head and upper torso visible, his image getting smaller through the dodgy telescopic sights of the rifle as the limousine carried him away . . . 55 metres away . . . 70 metres away . . . 80 metres away, and accelerating. And, if this isn't difficult enough, Oswald fires three rounds, two of which find their target, one in the back of the neck and the other causing the head to explode?

When stacked against the evidence of ballistics expert FBI Agent Frazier that Oswald was using a 'very low velocity' weapon, this theory was even more unacceptable. I was increasingly bemused at how the Warren Commission had ignored the proverbial elephant in the room. How they missed the logical argument that Lee Harvey Oswald could not possibly have achieved such results with his low-velocity weapon and his ammunition. And certainly not from his chosen vantage point, six floors above a moving target. Still, the lone gunman theory was left to stand, without the slightest scintilla of scrutiny. I walked from the crime scene, went into a famous Dallas steakhouse and ordered the best cut of meat they could plate, along with one of America's finest bottles of red. I was off-duty!

•

During his testimony before the Warren Commission, FBI Agent Frazier positively identified the near pristine bullet found on the hospital gurney alongside Governor Connally as coming from the Carcano rifle. He also positively identified the two metal fragments from JFK's car that found their way into the autopsy room as coming from the Carcano rifle.

Sixteen hours after the assassination he searched the President's vehicle, still covered in blood and speckles of human flesh. He found three lead particles on a rug near where JFK had been seated and performed a spectrographic analysis of the particles. They failed to match the rounds attributed to Lee Harvey Oswald's Carcano rifle. Indeed, Frazier said a match was 'highly improbable'. This was a startling revelation, one that screamed out that another round had been used in the shooting, but Counsellor Specter failed to take the answer any further. And that is how it would had been left had another counsellor not stepped in and asked the ballistics man about Exhibit 843, two metal fragments taken from JFK's head wound and handed to Frazier by FBI Agents Sibert and O'Neill immediately after the autopsy. Frazier then explained that the two fragments had a 'similar lead composition' to those fragments found on the rug near where JFK had been seated, and that they had a 'similar lead composition' as fragments found on the inside of the President's car.

At that very moment, 1.30pm on 13 May, 1964, the Warren Commission became undeniably aware of the presence of a different type of bullet. One that had disintegrated on impact, one that was not fired from a Carcano rifle and, therefore, not one of Lee Harvey Oswald's rounds. Specter's reaction to this shattering revelation was to instantly excuse the witness. Ballistics expert FBI Agent Frazier stood down and left the courtroom. I was starting to see a commission uninterested in the truth, a commission more focused on telling their public a version that might stick. A commission of omissions.

Following Frazier on the stand were three doctors who had conducted tests on behalf of the Commission. Who actually authorised these bizarre tests is not known; this thread seems to have been lost over the passage of time. But Specter led the cross-examination as this 'evidence' unfolded. The doctors were all from the US Army, with an assortment of expertise, and each gave sworn testimony.

Leading the way was Dr Alfred Olivier, a research veterinarian whose specialty was to perform macabre tests on horsemeat, live goats and other animals to understand the reaction of ammunition. As I have stated before, bullets can do strange things when they find their target, and this vet was presenting evidence to support a theory. His team had crafted gelatin blocks, then draped each block with horse-meat, goat meat and pig skin, in an attempt to replicate human skin and body tissue. He then dressed these wobbly, fleshy ensembles in gents' suits, complete with shirt and tie, to replicate the bodies of Governor Connally and the President. Olivier then blasted each 'victim' with bullets identical to those used by Oswald. Reminiscent of the famous watermelon shots where the fruit is blown away, it is all very theatrical, but what does it prove?

The Carcano rifle employed by Olivier's team resulted in rounds that were 'very stable . . . passing through the body and muscle . . . a straight line shot'. Dr Olivier believed the 'pristine' bullet (the one taken from Connally's hospital gurney, still in near perfect condition) had caused injury to both JFK and Connally. He further claimed that the wrist injury to Connally was not from this same round but was caused by ricochet from the round that penetrated the President's skull. His rationale was personal opinion, without a scientific or ballistic basis, and he offered no test results or notes to substantiate his belief. Nor did he offer any qualification that could support such a theory.

He then testified about a second set of tests, which were similar to the first in that the rounds employed were identical bullets. However, Olivier explained that his team had used human cadavers in this experiment. A level more worrying than the first test, but with the same result, every bullet passing cleanly through. Nothing surprising there, as full metal jacket rounds are designed to pass cleanly through a target, even though the target in this experiment was not a live human.

Dr Olivier went on to detail his third round of tests. He filled ten human skulls with gelatin, draping each skull with a further layer of gelatin to replicate President Kennedy's skin. His team then shot bullets into each of the ten skulls, again the type of bullets matching the spent casings found alongside the Carcano rifle. It was then that an oddity appeared in the vet's evidence. In his reporting of his findings, Olivier focused on the alleged damage to only one of the skulls. He omitted any evidence of damage to all the skulls, as a group or as a pattern. The other nine skulls, the damage caused and any pattern of damage was not offered to the Commission. Olivier's evidence was now in the category of selective, as well as being subjective. Bearing in mind that the tests were conducted in the early part of the 1960s when forensic science was a relatively new methodology, it's worth commenting that Olivier's tests were proffered as being forensic, that is, tests conducted by a scientific means to assist a legal process, the Warren Commission. Yet, the leading forensic bodies of that time, the Federal Bureau of Investigation and the American Academy of Forensic Science, played no role in the tests.

Olivier opened his evidence stating, 'I thought [the bullet] would go through, making a small entrance and exit [hole] . . .'

Instead, the bullet caused a 'massive head wound'. Olivier claimed that he hadn't thought such damage '. . . could be done by this type of bullet . . .'

Dr Olivier was suggesting to the Commission that the head shot wound to JFK was caused by a full metal jacket round, thereby showing that Lee Harvey Oswald could have been the shooter of all three rounds, and in particular the round that hit JFK on the back of his head, causing a massive explosion of skull and brain matter. The fact that the Commission brought in the research veterinarian is in itself fascinating.

Questions were begging to be asked, especially whether the bullets fired into the other nine skulls also exploded. Had the other nine bullets caused the skulls to explode, the evidence of Olivier would have been not only riveting but conclusive of the premise that Oswald's weapon (and rounds) could have caused the President's final and fatal wound. But the Commission never heard of the results of the missing nine rounds. The omission of these results is more telling than the selected results of one bullet's work. The blatant absence of any evidence on the missing nine bullets strongly suggests the rounds passed cleanly through the skulls, as would be expected from a full metal jacket round, the rounds used by Oswald. Logistically, had the result been any different, and the bullets caused massive damage, one would expect that they, too, would have been shown to the court 'exploding'.

The evidence was (at best) open to criticism, should anyone want to test its veracity. Equally worrying was that there was no ballistics expert involved in the tests, no one to verify the calibre of the rounds, the grain weight of each bullet load, the velocity of each projectile, and on it goes. Interestingly, no film footage of the tests was tendered, just a small number of black and white photographs.

All scientific tests placed before courts of law, particularly those open to malpractice or inferior testing regimes and those that might be seen as controversial, need to be validated. For tests to be used as evidence, the integrity of the 'scientific' process must be scrutinised. Prove the tests, prove the veracity, show the science and integrity of the studies and the tests themselves gather credibility.

In this process a court might want to know what consistency was the gelatin used? Was it rock-hard, soft or otherwise? And what age were the skull bones (skulls are known to harden over time) and how brittle? Indeed, what pre-existing fractures were on the skulls at the time of blasting them with a high-powered bullet? Bullets are known to shatter hard objects, particularly if they're dry and brittle, so shattering doesn't necessarily mean it was the actual round, but merely the projectile hitting a brittle surface.

To introduce scientific tests into a complex homicide enquiry is to tread with absolute caution. Specter's questioning of the 'expert' witness failed to focus on the tests themselves; he seemed to just accept the outcomes. Indeed, no one questioned if the tests were scientifically reliable or whether they had a scientific connection to the killing of JFK. Sure, in one of the tests the bullets were fired into cadavers, which probably had a similar mass and look to that of JFK and Connally's bodies, but no one bothered to question the mass, weight or thickness of the cadavers compared with the two victims' body mass, etc.

And, more importantly, no one asked why a ballistics expert wasn't overseeing the tests, and why a team led by a vet had no independent expert assessing the procedure. Or, most troubling, why FBI ballistics expert Robert Frazier wasn't involved.

There was no inquisition of any sort into the validity of the tests. In an era where such forensic evidence was so new, so green, the Commission just accepted the findings and moved on to the next phase of Olivier's evidence.

The 'expert' veterinarian witness, Dr Olivier, had difficulty answering a few minor questions, deferring to his notebook. Expert witnesses tend to keep comprehensive notes of their tests and studies. Their notes are vital to proving their theories. Doctors, surgeons, scientists, particularly forensic scientists, are known for their notebooks, the basis for their assessment of a case. Dr Olivier had no notebook with him in court, no record of the tests he undertook or his outcomes. When asked, he told the Commission his notes were outside the courtroom, not within his reach. No one from the Commission told him to step down and get his notebooks. With the results on the other nine bullet shots to the other nine skulls still up in the air, the veterinarian's notebooks would have been crucial to the matter under consideration. In fact, Olivier's notebooks should have been passed around the Commission, as a way to assist Earl Warren and his tribe of lawyers to understand the evidence and form their own conclusions on what was really subjective evidence, at best. There is not one legitimate reason for an expert to stand noteless in a witness box, particularly as Lee Harvey Oswald was not legally represented, therefore Olivier could not be in jeopardy of rigorous cross-examination that might expose his theory. A burning fascination as to what happened to the other nine skulls remains. Does the omission of this evidence mean the full metal jacket rounds passed cleanly through the skulls? And just as troubling, what was the original condition of the one and only skull whose gunshot result was tendered at the Commission?

The objectivity and integrity of the witness's testimony was starting to falter.

Oddly, Specter moved on, eventually excusing Olivier from any further testimony. Unusually, the other two army doctors who were part of his tests were allowed to sit in and hear Dr Olivier's evidence and cross-examination. In many jurisdictions around the world, a witness testifies to his or her own recollections, own involvement and own opinions. All other witnesses are outside the courtroom, so as to be able to give their own, untainted views. However, in American courts, experts involved in the same tests or studies are able to hear the initial evidence by the leading expert witness, so as to shorten a lengthy process of going over the same ground twice. Olivier's collaborators, doctors Dziemian and Light, sat, listening, in the court.

Once Olivier left the witness box, the next to raise the Bible was Dr Dziemian, a physiologist in the army's chemical laboratory. He was in the witness box only long enough to confirm the results of the tests and the accuracy of Olivier's testimony. Again, no one pried, no one questioned, no one queried the missing results on the nine skulls.

The final witness of the trio was Dr Frederick Light, a specialist in the pathology of wounds and co-supervisor to the tests. When asked by the Commission to confirm Olivier's evidence, Dr Light stated, 'I am not quite certain about some of the things . . .' Dr Light disagreed with Olivier's findings with regard to the wounds to Connally, believing the pristine

bullet passed through JFK and then through Connally, as put
forward by the autopsy report.

When asked his opinion of Olivier's view on the reaction
of a bullet, related to Connally's wounds and JFK's wounds,
Dr Light responded that he 'did not feel justified in drawing
a conclusion one way or the other . . .' Dr Light went on to
say that Olivier's theory relating to JFK's head wound and
Connally's wrist wound was 'barely conceivable'. Yet, counsel for
the Commission never pressed Light for his own theory, given
that he had difficulty with Olivier's theory. Nor did anyone
within the Commission ask Light about the results of the
missing nine skulls. During Light's testimony Specter initiated
an 'off-the-record' discussion with the Commissioner while
Light was still under oath (the detail of which has never been
made public), before reconvening the court only long enough
to excuse Dr Light from any further questioning. Dr Light
stepped down from the witness box, leaving behind serious,
unanswered questions as to the veracity of Olivier's testimony.
If testimony and its value is to be summarised in the number
of pages in the witnesses' Q&A court transcript, Dr Light's
evidence consisted of three and a half pages, a good portion
dealing with who he was and his qualifications. Dr Dziemian's
testimony was merely half as long, minutes in actuality.

It is difficult to comprehend why such tests were called for.
And why the FBI themselves hadn't been involved, since they
ran the country's leading forensic unit. I couldn't help but feel
sceptical that the US Naval medical facility, Bethesda, having
ruined and manipulated the autopsy, was now offering up US
Army scientists to convince the Warren Commission that the

lone gunman theory was correct, by way of their macabre tests on cadavers and dead pigs.

The next witness called was J Edgar Hoover, who was asked nothing of the tests. All Hoover would do was launch into myriad statements concerning Lee Harvey Oswald's Russian, Cuban and communist connections. Completely out of context with the evidence heard so far, the Commission was now tilted back on a path of conspiracy theories – more nonsense, more hi-jinks. It was as if this day in the hearing room was reserved for anything other than factual evidence from the crime scene. Interestingly, though, J Edgar Hoover was scheduled to follow the bizarre evidence of Dr Olivier for perhaps another reason. Bearing in mind Hoover would have been privy to the evidence of Olivier's tests, as he was the next witness waiting to be heard, Hoover never mentioned in any of his following evidence that his own FBI had undertaken a series of tests, on gelatin blocks, testing ammunition, to observe the reaction of bullets once they hit the gelatin 'models'. These tests by Hoover's laboratory were independent of Olivier's tests. The telling aspect of Hoover's tests was that the bullets fired into the gelatin 'models' were frangible rounds. Lee Harvey Oswald wasn't using frangible rounds on the day. So, why the need for Hoover's men to test the reaction from frangible bullets (exploding rounds) when the official version of the truth at the time was a 'lone shooter' with full metal rounds? The FBI also found 'minor variations' in their analysis of the bullet fragments found in the Presidential vehicle. The report on this analysis was accidentally located in 1973, nine years after the Commission hearings.

●

The idea of walking into a courtroom is daunting for most. Experienced lawyer and Commission counsellor Wesley Liebeler would have been well aware of the difficulties involved in extracting evidence from nervous witnesses, in this case the many men and women on Elm Street that day. Such cross-examination can be like taking baby steps, little by little; it can be painful, but extremely rewarding. Salesman James Tague was heading downtown to take his wife to lunch. He decided to stop his car near Dealey Plaza, get out and take a look. Forward of the motorcade, James had more reason than most to recall the events on the day JFK was shot as he, too, was hit, in the face, by a ricochet fragment. He was adamant he hadn't heard an echo and was clear in his recollection of the shots. James thought one of the bullets sounded like 'it was just a loud, oh, not a cannon but definitely louder and more solid than a rifle shot . . .' James Tague was a crucial witness particularly because he had a clear view of both the motorcade and the Book Depository. Liebeler asked Tague from where he believed the shot had originated, prefacing the witness's answer with, '. . . of course now we have other evidence that would indicate that the shots did come from the Texas School Book Depository, but see if we can disregard that.' 'Leading' a witness means asking a question that suggests an answer or puts words into the mouth of the witness. By employing this method an attorney is suggesting a pre-planned story. Liebeler should have been stopped from doing this, leading witnesses. The counsellor continued with a volley of suggestions that the shots Tague saw had emanated from an area known in the hearings as 'area No 7', the Texas School Book Depository. Tague did not acquiesce, stating that he thought the shots came from a different vicinity, down low, near Dealey Plaza.

Leading a witness is prone to interjection from the judge. Strangely, this was not the case at the Warren Commission, where leading questions were commonplace.

The next to raise the Bible before Counsellor Liebeler was Emmett Hudson, groundkeeper for Dealey Plaza. An ordinary man in the street, Emmett knew the plaza better than anyone and was standing close by when the fatal shot hit JFK in the head. Emmett was certain the shots came from 'behind the President's car, towards the back . . .' In fact, he gave this description twice.

An astute counsellor would have nurtured his evidence, taken him slowly through the events. However, Liebeler led the witness with, 'But you are quite sure in your own mind that the shots came from the rear of the President's car and above; is that correct?'

Emmett: 'Yes.'

Liebeler: 'Did you have any idea that they might have come from the Texas School Book Depository Building?'

Emmett: '. . . Well it sounded like it was high, you know, from above and kind of behind like – in other words, to the left . . .'

Liebeler: 'And that would have fit in with the Texas School Book Depository Building, wouldn't it?'

Emmett: 'Yes.'

Liebeler: 'Did you look up there and see if you could see anybody?'

Emmett: 'No, sir; I didn't. I never thought about looking up that way, to tell you the truth about it.'

Of course he didn't! The witness wasn't stating he thought the shots had come from the Texas School Book Depository, he was trying to say something very different.

Emmett's earlier responses indicated the area behind JFK's limousine. To a good counsellor this would have opened a myriad possible locations and possible questions. Perhaps even behind the President's car and at the height of a Secret Service agent standing in the follow-up car. Emmett would never have the opportunity to expand.

This was the strange tactic of Counsellor Liebeler, one witness after another. If he wasn't leading a witness he was ignoring their value. By this stage in the hearings much had been heard about the timing between each of the three shots. The most consistent description was of a single, less explosive first shot, then a gap of approximately two to three seconds, followed by shots two and three, '. . . close together . . . simultaneous, together . . . much closer than the first and second shots . . .', and on the descriptions went. Of the critical mass of the people who heard the shots – at least those who gave sworn evidence – it is undeniably clear that shots two and three occurred too close together in time to have been from the same weapon. Yet no one explored the possibility of another shooter.

•

Fifteen-year-old schoolgirl Linda Willis and her parents were standing in the Dealey Plaza admiring the President. Linda gave graphic testimony, keeping to the facts of what she saw. She described how the hit to JFK's head was like seeing a 'red halo'. Such is the innocence of kids giving evidence. Answering Counsellor Liebeler's question regarding the shots, Linda recalled, 'I heard one. Then there was a little bit of time, then there were two real fast bullets together . . . When the first one hit, well, the President turned from waving to the people, and he grabbed his throat, and he kind of slumped forward, and then I couldn't tell where the second shot went . . .' Liebeler's only comment was to let the witness know that the Texas School Book Depository was near where she had been standing. Liebeler asked Linda nothing further of consequence. No question as to what 'two real fast bullets together' meant. Linda offered no evidence about the Book Depository and Liebeler did not ask this articulate teenager from which direction she thought the shots had come. Her entire testimony amounted to just thirteen questions. It was as if Liebeler didn't want to know, just in case the answer was more explosive than the final shot on 22 November, 1963.

The same can be said for Liebeler's cross-examination of bookkeeper Virgie Rachley. Virgie was standing on Elm Street as the motorcade passed by. She heard the shots and was trying to explain to the Commission from where she believed they had emanated. When she was a tad ambiguous in her explanation, Liebeler seemed to seize on it and blatantly led the witness, trying his hardest to suggest the area of the Texas School Book Depository: 'Now you have subsequently heard I'm sure and from reading in newspapers and one thing and another that it appears the shots actually came from the Texas School Book Depository building: is that right?' When Virgie refused this proposition as her answer, Liebeler tried a second time to lead the witness towards the Texas School Book Depository building. Virgie was adamant with a flat 'No Sir' and explained in her answer that she didn't look at the Book Depository. Liebeler would persist, again suggesting to the witness the shots she heard came from the Depository, to which Virgie stated under oath, 'It sounded like it was coming from along in here – it didn't sound like it was too far away . . .'

Virgie had been standing on Elm Street out the front of the Book Depository watching the motorcade. It seems to explain that the shots were in front of her, or on Elm Street. Virgie would later state to Liebeler that she was getting confused. Any wonder. Both would persist with the Q&A for no measurable outcome. Towards the end of Virgie's testimony Liebeler asked, 'The FBI report [which Virgie signed under oath two days after the assassination] indicates that after the second shot you began to smell gunsmoke: is that correct?' Virgie agreed. Despite her mention of gun smoke she was never asked to explain further why, how, when or where.

Liebeler kept newspaper journalist James Altgens in the witness stand for an inordinate period of time. The journalist was taking pictures 'fifteen feet' away from JFK's car when the shots rang out. The counsellor was keen to hear from what direction Altgens thought the shots had come, but the journalist was unsure. Liebeler persisted with question after question, mentioning the Texas School Book Depository ten times as he framed his cross-examination. The best Altgens could do in reply was to say that the shots came from his left, behind the motorcade, towards the corner of Elm and Houston streets. On the issue of how many shots were fired Liebeler turned to his usual chestnut of suggesting the answer to the witness: '. . . as you well know – there were supposed to have been three shots, but how many shots did you hear?' The crusty old reporter with twenty-six years' experience wasn't about to fall for that one, answering, 'Well I wouldn't like to say . . .'

The work of many of the counsellors assisting Earl Warren is best summed up by their cross-examination. Their transcripts speak volumes.

One newspaper reporter who never got a look-in was Connie Kritzberg of the *Dallas Times Herald*. She had been reporting on the assassination on 22 November, scouting about for stories, trying to get an angle. An editor on the paper, she had gleaned information from her contacts at the Parkland Hospital about the injuries suffered by JFK and was rushing to file her story. In essence her story, which went into the next day's edition, related to the neck wound and the separate wound to the back of JFK's head. Once she'd logged the article to her news editor, Connie went chasing another angle, another story. The next morning she reeled in shock as she read her story. Someone had tampered with her copy, changing the thrust of her article. The line '. . . a doctor admitted that it was possible there was only one wound . . .' was the line that offended her – it was wrong, a lie. Connie had never received such a comment from her doctor contacts at the hospital; indeed, the breaking story related to a massive head wound and the neck wound. She contacted her editor, demanding to know who included the false comment in her story. She was told it was the FBI who had tampered with the wording. Until as late as 2011, Connie Kritzberg stoically held the position that the FBI falsified her story and were from day one touting a lone gunman theory. She appears as angry in recent times as she did back in 1963 when she first discovered the FBI manipulation.

Another incident that smacks of interference by the FBI relates to a family man named Charles Brehm, who was standing with his wife and five-year-old son on Elm Street as President Kennedy's car went past. Charles was a unique witness insofar as he had been in military service and had experience with rifles. He was quoted on page one of the *Dallas Times Herald* that evening, a quote that detectives would say was uttered close in time to the incident. Contemporaneous evidence is always the best sort of evidence. 'The first shot must not have been too solid, because he just slumped. Then on the second shot he seemed to fall back . . .' The article went on to state that, 'Brehm seemed to think that the shots came from in front of or beside the President . . .' An extraordinary revelation, on day one, that suggests the shots were close by, at ground level.

The oddity in Brehm's revelation came two days later when the FBI took his statement. All of a sudden Brehm was saying in his affidavit that '. . . shots came from one of two buildings back at the corner of Elm and Houston streets . . .' The story had changed dramatically. Gone was the evidence of shot(s) coming from 'in front of or beside the President.'

The Warren Commission never heard of the FBI's role in tampering with Connie or Charles's words. The truth seemed to have many faces.

•

The twenty-six back volumes of the Commission are well laid out, listing the hundreds of witnesses from day one of the hearing. As would be expected, Volume One contains the evidence of Marina Oswald, wife of the lone gunman. Marina supplied the hearing with a graphic history of her relationship with the dysfunctional loner who had a fascination for guns and a want to be important. Her testimony is both vivid and fascinating, giving the American people a word picture of an assassin. Following Marina was her close friend Ruth Paine, who offered further insight. Ruth knew Lee Harvey Oswald and also appeared candidly honest.

Once the 'family' evidence relating to Lee Harvey Oswald was over it was time to get into the observations and facts to do with the crime scene itself. Volume Two is devoted to such evidence.

To cast an eye down the witness list is to be flabbergasted by the inclusion of the first witness called, one who was nowhere near Dealey Plaza on the fateful day. Thirty-seven-year-old Mark Lane, a lawyer from New York City, is the man who went on to champion many conspiracy theories regarding who killed JFK, all of which were then, as they are now, baseless in truth and useless under the rules of evidence.

It's incomprehensible that a hearing charged with finding fact would allow a theorist to start the proceedings, especially when the eyes of the world were glued to the media coverage. Why not have an open invitation to all and sundry to stand in the witness box and have their say – it would amount to the same level of relevance as that of Mark Lane. To allow him to ramble on for thirty-two pages of transcript over two days defies logic! Lane's 'evidence' reads like that of someone who had heard a whisper or gathered a snippet and wanted to place himself in the thick of things. At one point he tried to argue a seat for himself on the Commission, to represent the rights of Lee Harvey Oswald, his client, he claimed. Yet Oswald was long dead and had never met the New York lawyer. So why had the Commission allowed Mark Lane to bounce the ball and start their game?

The only explanation seems to be that whoever fashioned the witness list wanted to colour the investigation into the death of JFK right from the beginning. Having Lane proffer a theory about a forward shooter, international intrigue, double agents, a grassy knoll, wrong gun used by Oswald and government cover-up, would stir sufficient doubt in the public arena that no one would discern the real reason for the President's head being blown away. A simple case of: throw in the conspiracy theorist, get the media writing stories, fill the newspapers and TV sets with sensational headlines, then start the real evidence. By this stage the masses are already thinking 'cover-up', 'double agent', 'intrigue', 'grassy knoll' and no one's thinking 'follow-up car'.

Fascinatingly, the witnesses to follow Mark Lane were Roy Kellerman and a few select Secret Service agents.

Not all agents have elected to remain silent – a few have actually spoken out, over time. But it's the content of what they say that is more important than their breaking of the silence. With the 50th anniversary into the assassination drawing near, a few retired agents pulled themselves away from their retirement villages to write memoirs. One of the most widely read comes from retired Agent Gerald Blaine, who penned *The Kennedy Detail* in 2011. The centrepiece of the book concerns the assassination of their president and the minutes, hours and days surrounding the tragedy. Offered as a truthful account of life in 'the detail', the 400 pages of quotes and verbatim comments recalls all the players and their movements – from the Secret Service team to JFK himself and Jackie, right down to words spoken during the six seconds in Dealey Plaza. Trouble is, retired agent Blaine wasn't there, in Dallas, at all. He had missed out and was attending to duties elsewhere. He explains to his readers that he compiled the accounts from the other agents' notes, yet many of the agents had been deceased for many years. And some of the quotes relating to conversations differ dramatically from words the actual agents said as witnesses under oath at the Warren Commission.

What he said about George Hickey was interesting, if not odd. He recalled Hickey having raised the AR-15 at the time of the shooting; indeed, he recalled the weapon by saying, 'God have mercy on you if you were the target of the AR-15.' He then told how George, '. . . picked up the rifle as soon as he registered that shots were being fired and immediately pulled back the lever to inject a shell from the clip into the chamber. He was just about to lift himself off the seat when the fatal shot hit the President . . .' In this same passage of his book he told how Hickey was a newish member to the staff of the Secret Service, that he was actually a 'driver', not one of the Secret Service agents, the men who watched over the President and Vice President. Blaine tells of Hickey's job description as being attached to the garage, and how the driver team were trained strictly as 'drivers'. The small team of drivers was under the control of a separate unit, nothing to do with the field agents. In fact, they were not updated on threat subjects and did not travel with the field agents. The drivers would be responsible for maintaining the cars, getting them to and from the appointments in the various cities and washing and cleaning the cars before being used. Also, that the motorcade on the 22nd day of November was Hickey's first ever ride in the follow-up car and that the only duties Hickey seemed to undertake prior to his actual presence in the follow-up car (holding the AR-15) were to wash and polish the President's car hours earlier.

Blaine also mentioned that as soon as the motorcade arrived at the Parkland Hospital, the gravely wounded JFK was rushed inside among the 'chaos', and a short time later Hickey was told by his superior to lock the AR-15 away in its case. Soon afterwards he was told to drive one of the motorcade vehicles back to Love Field Airport. A fascinating set of directions from the superior: at a time when the presidency is under fire, with blood on the streets and death on the hospital stretchers, the most powerful weapon among the security contingent is locked away. And its operator banished to sit it out, at an airport.

Throughout his memoir Blaine left no doubt that on the morning of the parade everyone was exhausted and there was a drastic shortage of manpower for key positions on the motorcade. He confirmed that the agents went out till the wee hours the night before to a hotel for scotch and beer and later to the Cellar Bar 'where scantily clad waitresses doubled as singers'. But, he adds, they only drank soda and coffee in the company of the scantily clad.

Blaine also recalled discussing staff shortages before the parade with Emory Roberts, the agent in charge, who was struggling to find sufficient manpower. Emory spoke at length about the concern and then advised Blaine that George Hickey would be part of the parade. Blaine was stunned by what Emory told him.

At the start of the parade, field agents were being moved around as seats in the follow-up car and President's car were filled. Blaine stated some field agents were working shifts far in excess of twenty hours and getting only an hour or so, or a few hours', sleep at a time. And one of the manpower had no experience as a field agent, protecting the President. Some were mere drivers. It is a riveting insight into the one day in history that the agency would wish to erase, even though Blaine himself was many miles away at the time.

An interesting aspect of Blaine's book is the many photographs he includes. A great many of the photos are of fellow agents, especially those who worked the 'detail' on 22 November, 1963. The only one missing from the book is that of driver George Hickey.

CHAPTER 14
KILL FOR AN ANALYST

By the middle of 1964, Earl Warren was slouch-backed after seven months at the bench, one witness after another. A one-time chief justice of the United States Supreme Court, the seventy-two-year-old was on the last lap of a mammoth task, the biggest of his long career, and decent help was thin on the ground. This fact aside, the single greatest problem facing him was the mountain of paperwork. The computer age had not yet arrived; there were no personal computers, no computer programs, IT storage capabilities, search software, link programs or the like. America's most significant investigation came at a time when the most advanced pieces of technology were the telephone and the lie detector. And neither of these held any importance for an investigation that centred on crime-scene analysis. The Warren Commission worked in an environment that would eventually smother itself, a paper jungle. Everything uncovered, spoken, found, heard, located and revealed ended up typed on a fading-ribboned Olivetti or handwritten on a card, report, slip of paper, index, register or file. In no time the paperwork became a monumental haystack more than large enough to bury the fine needles of fact. To add to the impossible nature of the task, the Commission was bereft of a finder of needles.

In any task-force office there are investigators, the detectives who uncover the leads and chase down the perpetrators. Working quietly alongside them are highly skilled specialists to assist the process: the criminal analysts. Every competent modern-day task force has at least one of these analysts, to catch the gems that fall from the lips of witnesses and polish them into diamonds. Then, offering up those with the finest clarity and colour, they steer the direction of the task force, thereby allowing the investigators to get on with gathering evidence and getting to the bottom of the matter under investigation. The notion of having a task force without an analyst or two today is incomprehensible. It's about as unthinkable as running a massive investigation like the Warren Commission without computers.

At the time of the death of JFK, the analyst had not yet revolutionised the domain of the investigator. It would be some years into the next decade before the art of investigation incorporated an independent mind to assess the collected data. I know the importance of a good analyst, having worked many task forces, as a detective and as a team leader, investigating rapes, murders and the criminal activities of crime bosses. It would be inconceivable for me to undertake a complex investigation and Crime Scene Investigation study without a talented analyst or two.

The Warren Commission Executive Sessions memorandums reveal Earl Warren discussing the need to 'get someone with a most sceptical nature, sort of a Devil's Advocate who would take this FBI report and this CIA report and go through it and analyse every contradiction and every soft point in it . . . get some man to look for the weaknesses and possible contradictions and study it, just as if he were prosecuting them or planning to prosecute . . .' There was a suggestion that such a person should study the reports to the highest level, '. . . as if he were going to prosecute J Edgar Hoover . . .' The next comment was telling. Clearly, since this was the early stages of proceedings, some two months before actual evidence was heard, the Commission members were becoming sceptical of the relationships between the main investigative bodies involved in the production of evidence. Senator Russell, on the Executive, suggests, 'I think one study should be made just from the standpoint of every one of these reports, if we are ever to reconcile all of this contradictory rumor, the relationship of the Secret Service and the FBI and the police departments . . . get some man to look for the weaknesses and possible contradictions, and study it solely from that standpoint.' Earl Warren replied, 'I agree with you one hundred percent . . .' So, from December 1963, the Warren Commission were onto it: the Executive wanted everything cross-checked and analysed. They also decided at that same meeting to hear from the Secret Service first.

Despite their wisdom in realising they needed someone, they just didn't know who they actually needed – a criminal analyst. Indeed, they could have done with a few of these clever professionals. Earl Warren seemed to understand the need to analyse the material before him, to appoint a devil's advocate. Unfortunately, the men selected for the roles of Warren's 'devil's advocates' were lawyers. Anyone who has worked on a task force will tell you that lawyers are no more analysts than analysts are lawyers.

The hearings commenced without the clever analytical brain who can sift responses and decipher the how, why, when and where. A small team of analysts would have had a dramatic effect on the hearings. Having read each of the witness affidavits and subsequent sworn testimony or Q&A, they would have provided the Commission lawyers with the much-needed 'links' between the stand-alone testimonies, guiding the Commission's line of questioning.

Were an analyst to have reviewed the witness statements regarding the number of shots fired, they would have seen the overwhelming number of times that 'three shots' were mentioned. Furthermore, they would have noted the numerous occasions 'gunpowder' and 'gunsmoke' and 'smoke' were mentioned, both on the street and in the immediate location of the follow-up car. A good analyst would have linked these snippets of evidence to other testimony, in which witnesses saw a Secret Service agent in the follow-up car with an automatic weapon, to witnesses who saw that Secret Service agent stand, wave the weapon around and fall backwards. Of the ninety-five persons who gave evidence at the hearings regarding the number of shots fired, over forty stated that two of the shots were close together, almost simultaneous. Almost certainly an analyst would have surmised that (in the opinion of many witnesses) at least one of the shots had to have come from another weapon. In a detective's world this is known as a 'back to the office' moment, where an analyst discovers something so important that it changes the entire course of an investigation and all the detectives are called back to the muster room to hear the revelation. In reality, such moments are rare, but exciting. And once they occur, the crime is invariably solved.

Surely an analytical team would have queried the omission of the nest of evidence I call 'Decker's deck of lost witnesses'. On the day of the President's assassination a gentleman by the name of Bill Decker was riding in the lead car alongside Secret Service boss Agent Lawson. As the Sheriff in charge of Dallas, Decker had scored one of the best seats in the house. Somewhat of a local legend, old Decker's career stretched as far back as the days of bank robbers Bonnie and Clyde, whom he had chased until their bloody end. He still ran a good team of deputies. Immediately after the killing of JFK, in classic detective style, Decker gathered his boys together and began scouring Elm Street and Dealey Plaza for witnesses. The result was highly successful. By night's end the Dallas Sheriff's office had pulled in several dozen witnesses, all claiming to have seen the shooting, to have heard shots and who were prepared to sign sworn statements for the Public Notary. Signed up on the very day of the killing, Decker had sourced the best sort of eyewitness accounts: those taken before memory can be affected by media or outside influence.

One of those witnesses was nineteen-year-old Marvin Faye Chism, who was standing extraordinarily close to the President's car at the time of the assassination. She saw the head shot and '. . . the two men in the front of the car stood up, and when the second shot was fired they all fell down and the car took off . . .' Why did they fall down and what had happened to make them fall over? Her statement was undeniably ambiguous, one requiring clarification and exploration, yet Marvin was never called to give evidence at the Warren Commission.

Likewise, the observations of Hugh Betzner were ignored. Twenty-two-year-old Hugh was running alongside the motorcade taking photographs with his wind-on camera. He offered a vivid description of '. . . a flash of pink like someone standing up then sitting back down in the car . . . I also saw a man in either the President's car or the car behind his and someone down in one of those cars pull out what looked like a rifle . . .' Three photographs Betzner had taken at the time were seized and sealed by one of Decker's deputies. Yet no one from the Warren Commission wanted Decker's witness or the photographs.

Decker's men also found Austin Miller and committed his observations to paper. Miller's sworn statement attested that, 'I saw something which I thought was smoke or steam . . .' at the time of the shooting. For reasons that defy logic, while the Commission did call Miller to testify, Counsel David W Belin failed to follow this line of enquiry. Why on earth didn't he ask the witness to expand his memory on what the smoke or steam was? The witness also told Belin that there were 'ten or twelve people' standing with him, sharing the observations, seeing the tragedy unfold. Yet Belin asked not one single word of the identity of these persons. In fact, Austin Miller was out of the witness box within a minute or so after this revelation.

Bill Decker was also responsible for recording the words of Jean Hill, arguably the closest civilian to JFK at the time of his assassination. On her original Sheriff's statement, Jean said, 'I saw the President grab his chest and fall forward . . . I thought I saw some men in plain clothes shooting back . . .' Arlen Specter was to cross-examine Jean during the Warren Commission hearings. Perhaps an analyst would have been able to draw his attention to the fact that for the thousands of spectators lining the streets on that sunny afternoon, most would have been dressed in their Sunday best to greet their President. The only men in 'plain clothes . . .' were the Secret Service, a fact that Arlen apparently didn't grasp. Men 'shooting back' is a riveting comment, one that demands answers. But for answers to come, questions need to be asked, and none were asked by Specter.

From his position in the lead car, seated next to Decker, Agent Lawson claimed to have seen '. . . an agent standing up with an automatic weapon in his hand, and the first thing that flashed through my mind was, this was the only weapon I had seen, was that he had fired.' It would have been interesting to hear what the experienced law enforcement officer seated next to him had observed, but Decker was never called to give evidence at the Warren Commission.

If Bill Decker and his quick-thinking deputies were disappointed with the Commission's disinterest in so many of their witnesses, it's worth sparing a thought for the Dallas office of the FBI, who undertook the majority of the foot-slogging. In a sea of people, all nervous, all uncertain, it can be tough going picking through the stories. Memory recall is painstaking work and fear of losing everyday folk to shock is also a concern and real possibility. Some witnesses close to a gunshot murder can become too shocked to recall facts. Best to grab whatever facts they have, quickly, before they dwell on the event, or venture home to worry. Time constantly works against the investigator. It's a case of get in, get a quick statement and get going, on to the next witness.

The FBI was instrumental in achieving the majority of the witness statements placed before the Warren Commission;

however, just as many fell through the net. And some, it appears, were altered by the FBI from what the witnesses first said on the day of the killing of the President.

Luckily a few important statements got through the system. These statements offered dramatic evidence, such as the words of George Davis, who had been standing on Elm Street admiring the passing parade when the shots came. He saw, '. . . guns in the hands of the Secret Service agents . . .', a brief comment that begged to be cross-examined. Any number of questions arise. What sort of guns? Did any of the Secret Service have hold of an automatic rifle or, more pointedly, did any of the Secret Service men fire their weapon? He was never called to the witness box.

The FBI agents were lucky to find a husband and wife standing close to the motorcade, smiling, enjoying the moment until the shots, the exploding head and the blood. William Newman was staring at the face of JFK when all three shots were in play. He stated that two of the shots were fired in rapid succession. William's wife, Frances, saw the 'blood flowing from his body'. She, too, heard two shots in succession, as well as a lone shot. The couple were not called. Jean Newman (no relation) was also on Elm Street, walking towards the overpass, when the shots were fired. She was as close as her namesakes yet was also never called to the hearings.

Another couple close to the motorcade admiring Jackie Kennedy were Jack Franzen and his wife. Both made statements to the FBI that they heard three shots and witnessed the head shot to JFK. Mrs Franzen also saw the Secret Service men 'behind the President's car were holding guns in their hands'. Jack recalled looking at the Texas School Book Depository at the time of the shooting, and that he saw nothing suspicious there. This couple should have been asked a list of pertinent questions, but no one called, no one asked and their observations faded into the dark reaches of law enforcement history. Standing near the Franzens was Clemen Johnson, who also witnessed the catastrophe. He saw 'white smoke' near where the motorcade had passed. There were police motorcycles and the President's cars in the parade. One would expect that vehicles used in a parade involving the 35th President of the United States would be in pristine condition, but perhaps they emitted exhaust fumes that might have been misconstrued as smoke? Questions needed to be asked and memories should have been tested to the fullest to find the cause of the 'smoke'. Yet, if we are to believe the findings of the Warren Commission, there was no mention of smoke down on the street. Of course, Clemen was not asked.

That same fate would befall Nolan Potter, who stood on Elm Street with his workmates from the railway yard. He watched as the Kennedy car cruised by and saw the horror. He recalled to the FBI that he saw 'smoke in front of the Texas School Book Depository rising above the trees'. Apart from the observation of 'smoke', a fascinating feature of this evidence is that it was 'rising' up, from the street, above the trees. This could only mean that it emanated from the street. Nolan's fellow worker James Simmons also witnessed the 'smoke', yet neither was called to the Commission.

Local law enforcement officers interviewed Dallas citizen Walter Winborn, who had been standing on the overpass. Walter believed he saw smoke, 'it looked like a little haze . . . but it was a haze there . . . at least ten feet long and about two or three feet wide . . .' He gave this graphic account sometime later, in the time of the Warren Commission hearings, but he was not called.

Patrolman Joe Smith was interviewed by the FBI in December 1963. Joe claimed to have smelled gunpowder, 'a distinctive smell of gunsmoke cordite', as he moved along Elm Street towards the grassy section of Dealey Plaza. This was never addressed by the Warren Commission.

Home-movie buff and clerk at the Old Red Courthouse, Patsy Paschall brought her Bell & Howell 8-millimetre colour movie camera to the parade. Filming from her third-floor office window, she claimed to have captured an image of 'smoke' near the motorcade as it travelled down Elm Street and past the grassy knoll. Her film has been the subject of much conjecture but was never offered to the Warren Commission.

A reporter for the *Fort Worth Star/Telegram* newspaper, Ed Johnson wrote in his newspaper the following day, '. . . some of us saw little puffs of white smoke that seemed to hit the grassy area in the esplanade that divides Dallas' main downtown streets . . .' The reporter was never asked for a statement despite the newspaper carrying the story.

Even at face value each of these statements is telling. Some are in need of clarification or further explanation yet they all share elements that should have set off alarm bells for any person or group investigating the shooting: the presence of 'gunpowder' and/or 'smoke' at street level.

An FBI statement from Dallas citizen Thomas Murphy gave his description of what he saw of the shooting, and how President Kennedy and Governor Connally slumped in their seats. In 1966 he stated in an interview that he saw 'smoke' near the motorcade.

Years later, Secret Service Agent Rufus Youngblood consented to an interview with writer Gary Goettling. The subsequent published interview in the *Georgia Tech* magazine was entitled 'Eyewitnesses to the Death of a President' published in 1992 is a revelation. The telling segment is quoted verbatim.

> . . . From his position Youngblood noticed, '. . . a greyish blur in the air above the right side of the President's car . . .' right after the third shot. '. . . There were shouts from ahead then the cars in front of us lurched forward under the underpass. I yelled to our driver, '. . . Stay with them and keep close!' From his uncomfortable sprawled position on the back seat, Johnson [Vice President] asked what happened. Youngblood replied that the President had been shot, and that they were headed to the hospital. '. . . My God! They've shot the President . . .' exclaimed Sen. Yarborough who shared the backseat of the limousine with the Vice President. Lady Bird Johnson, seated between the two men, cried out, '. . . Oh no, that can't be!'

This verbatim account is remarkably in context with evidence surrounding gunpowder/gunsmoke and the Secret Service agents, particularly from railway signalman Mr SM Holland's observations, and those of Virgie Rachley, Elizabeth Cabell, Tom Dillard, Congressman Ray Roberts and so many more. The evidence suggests one thing: that the 'greyish blur' was gunpowder or gunsmoke. Yarborough's alleged comment, 'My God! They've shot the President . . .' is telling, and Lady Bird Johnson's remark needs to be further defined. If only Ralph Yarborough had been called to the stand at the Warren Commission. And of course, if only Tom Dillard had been able to elaborate fully on his gunpowder smell to the Commission . . . and his twelve negatives were never destroyed in later years.

In total, this brings the tally to twenty-two persons, some with expertise in firearms, who claim to have smelt or seen 'gunpowder' or 'smoke' at the time of the shooting at street level. The six who were seated in open-topped convertibles as a part of the motorcade are the most compelling group within this growing number of 'smokers'. Senator Ralph Yarborough and Agent Rufus Youngblood were occupants of the Vice Presidential car, travelling only metres behind the follow-up car. Congressman Roberts and the Mayor's wife Elizabeth Cabell were two cars behind them in the Mayoral car. Towards the rear of the motorcade sat Thomas Dillard and Robert Jackson in the open-topped press convertible. All six smelt gunsmoke or gunpowder, all six were adamant and all six moved into the road and air space occupied seconds earlier by the follow-up car, the car with the Secret Service agents and the AR-15.

If ever there was a blatant omission of key witnesses then the occupants of the motorcade would be it. Behind the follow-up car as part of the formal motorcade tailing JFK and his wife were an additional twelve vehicles plus a bus at the very back of the parade. Almost all of the cars were open-topped convertibles. In all, excluding the bus, which mostly contained hangers-on from the police department and press gallery, the number of officials travelling in convoy was more than forty persons. Forty pairs of eyes, forty noses, forty senses honed, all scanning the surrounds as the parade moved along, all catching glimpses of the attractive First Lady alongside the man many saw as the most powerful political figure in the world. Of these forty persons, only six were called to give evidence at the Warren Commission. Of that six, four would go on to tell of their recollection of gunsmoke or gunpowder at street level. One only has to recall how adamant Elizabeth Cabell was in her recollection of smelling gunpowder. Was this the underlying reason why the Warren Commission omitted calling the others? For fear of more stories of gunsmoke?

Hurchel Jacks, a Texas highway patrolman and the driver of the Vice Presidential convertible, made the briefest of statements shortly after the shooting in which he said, 'I was looking directly at the President's car at that time . . .' Hurchel, a man who by his job description was metres from the follow-up car and by his own admission had his eyes glued to the back of the President's convertible – like the other dozen drivers of as many cars – was absent from the Warren Commission.

The eighth, ninth and tenth vehicles in the parade were convertibles, each containing an assortment of professional photographers using both 35-millimetre film and movie cameras. Many were filming the parade from their vehicles. Dave Weigman, an NBC cameraman, was filming the action in front of his car when the first shot rang out. He jumped from his car and proceeded to run down Elm Street, still filming as the last shots were fired. Likewise Thomas Craven of the CBS television network, who alighted his vehicle following Weigman's lead. He, too, was filming as he ran. Indeed, shortly afterwards all the professional photographers spilled onto Dealey Plaza, Elm Street and the grassy knoll filming and photographing anything and everything.

I searched the Warren Commission documents for any investigative appraisal of the work of these professionals in the seconds and minutes surrounding the shooting of the President.

There was no concerted assessment. What I did come across was an independent report by Richard Trask. The author of an in-depth study of the photography associated with the assassination of President Kennedy, Mr Trask's exhaustive work is best summed up in his own words: '... during the assassination a minimum of nineteen spectators in Dealey Plaza recorded some of that event, while at least fourteen professional photographers took scenes from the motorcade or after exiting their vehicles. Within a short time of the assassination over a score more photographers were in the Plaza recording all sorts of activity. Those photographic materials which were collected, utilized, and kept by the FBI and subsequent Warren Commission investigation are quite scanty. There are copies of some photographs though most are dramatically cropped and multi-generational. A number of photos, films, and video tapes possibly part of the original Commission record often do not show up in archival or freedom of information search requests ...' It appeared I wasn't the only one who felt that the Commission had failed.

It seems that those coordinating the witness list for the Warren Commission gave the dignitaries, Secret Service agents, press and hangers-on with a ticket to ride the parade a bonus ticket to excuse them from giving any evidence. One can only guess at how many of them suffered the same frustration as Senator Yarborough and Congressman Roberts at not being able to have their day in court. A team of analysts would have found the missing three dozen or more witnesses from the official motorcade. Their discovery would have shaken the tree of the Warren Commission and made dramatic amendments to the witness list. Again, without these witnesses, the Commission was merely a commission of omission.

During the hearings the recalled seventy-two-year-old Justice Earl Warren acted as his own analyst and for all his good intentions, he would be a fool to himself. He would plough through a veritable mountain of evidence, tens of thousands of pages, thousands of exhibits and documents, pictures and affidavits. The trouble was that the trees now hid the forest. The transcripts, affidavits, documents and facts were piled high. Some witnesses needed to be recalled, others postponed, and at times Warren and his team had to take evidence off site, to other states. It was as if he had half a dozen balls in the air, people on standby and corridors full of waiting witnesses, as his investigation intensified. Then there was the media, following his every move, demanding answers and suggesting theories. Warren was being buried by documents, smothered in his own achievements and responsibility. The perfect environment for a cover-up, the ideal theatre for evidence to be lost or ignored, manipulated or massaged.

No dill when it came to asking the tough questions, Warren often took on the interrogating himself, especially when something bit into him. He was capable of extracting evidence from the most reticent of witnesses. Except for the occasional moments of vigour by his sometime stand-in Gerald Ford, none of the counsel assisting seemed to push for the truth or take on the hard questions as competently as the Chief Justice. In the month of June, he placed himself up against his equal and opposite number as he cross-examined the chief of the Secret Service. Chief Justice Warren had Chief James Rowley held up in the witness box for hours. The latter was attempting to justify why none of his agents had been dismissed or removed from the agency, under Section Ten of their manual, for their blatant alcohol infringements on the eve of the assassination, only hours before the motorcade. It was a war of two old minds. Rowley stood by his men, stating his rationale was not wanting to 'upset the wives and children of his agents' with dismissals. Not wanting the American people to think that the agency might have contributed to the death of their President. He didn't want the wrong message out there. Yet Section Ten of the Secret Service Manual is clear: '. . . the use of intoxicating liquor of any kind . . . by members of the White House Detail . . . while they are in a travel status, is prohibited . . .' Furthermore, '. . . violation or slight disregard of the above paragraphs or the excessive or improper use of intoxicating liquor at any time will be cause for removal from the service . . .'

Rowley's justification for not admonishing his men or sacking those known to have consumed alcohol (they all did) was possibly the most poignant comment from within the vipers' nest of the Secret Service, to the point of being flabbergasting. The future of the Secret Service was centre stage and Chief Rowley was ducking and weaving as Warren sized up his scalp. As the questions were asked it became evident that alcohol was indeed a problem within the secret squad. Only the previous month an agent had been in strife with his administration when an incident of alcohol usage came to their notice. And three months earlier a court action had been listed against a whistle-blowing agent who made eleven claims against fellow team members, some to do with alcohol, while away on a mission. Warren gave it his best shot, targeting the drinking at the press club and beatnik bar in the wee hours of the final day in the life of the President.

He pressured Rowley, asking if there was an expectation 'that men who did what these men did, being out until early morning hours, doing a little, even a small amount of drinking would be as alert the next day as men should be when they are charged with the tremendous responsibility of protecting the President?' Rowley's return was an embarrassment: '. . . but these men are young, they are of such age that I think that they responded in this instance adequately and sufficiently as anyone could have under the circumstances . . .' It was becoming like a heavyweight boxing match as both men sweated it out.

Unconvinced, the head of the enquiry got specific, citing a glaring difference between supposedly alert close personal protection officers and the smiling public idling in the midday sun on the day of the killing: '. . . even some people in the crowds saw a man with a rifle up in this building from which the President was shot. Now, don't you think that if a man went to bed reasonably early, and hadn't been drinking the night before, he would be more alert to see these things as a Secret Service agent than if they stayed up till three, four, five o'clock in the morning going to beatnik joints and doing some drinking along the way?'

Rowley agreed with the proposition, but went on to describe past shifts when his agents worked overtime, often past midnight, and were still required to be up for an early start, as if to somehow justify their behaviour. Warren instantly retorted with, 'there were three of these men [agents] actually on night duty protecting the life of the President. And around four o'clock in the morning when they were protecting him at the Texas Hotel they said that they had a coffee break, they went from the hotel over to the beatnik joint . . .' Rowley's only contribution apart from agreeing with Warren was that the hotel where the agents were sitting was a 'stuffy hotel . . . and the men were in need of fresh air'. Chief Rowley was a company man. In the face of defeat, his tactic was to keep denying, keep supporting his men. No doubt Rowley was also aware of an issue that could have smothered him: vicarious liability. That is, in simple terms, a legal doctrine that pushes liability up the line, assigning the liability and responsibility to a person who did not cause the injury but who had a legal relationship to the person who did act negligently. Such a doctrine is there to ward against senior management sanctioning bad behaviour, or being tolerant of behaviour that might cause injury by negligence. In other words, a boss not putting a stop to bad practices or encouraging bad practice might be a case to fit a claim for vicarious liability. Chief Rowley was remiss in not stamping out after-hours drinking or drunkenness among his agents while on 'away' duty.

Despite his efforts, Earl Warren failed to ask Chief Rowley one key question: 'Why are only a few of your Secret Service agents who were on duty that day giving sworn testimony at my Commission?' The fact that Earl Warren didn't demand that all agents present themselves at the Commission is puzzling. Furthermore, one has to wonder why the Commission didn't seize the firearms of all Secret Service agents for testing – a normal procedure for law enforcement officers involved in a fatal shooting. That opportunity is lost to time.

It was the interrogations of Rowley, Sorrels and Kellerman that really highlighted a worry. Each man was able to control his cross-examination, keeping the enquiry on matters that were either administrative or non-specific to the actual shooting. Even when the finite detail of the number of shots fired or the wounds sustained by the victims was discussed, the Secret Service was able to deflect answers or twist facts. The cross-examination of the few Secret Service agents who gave evidence was fair at best. But fair doesn't get admissions. Fair doesn't break down a wall of untruths, deflections and uncertain memories. Fair doesn't find the misleading statements, uncover the lies. The entire Secret Service testimony amounted to less than 150 pages of transcript, a mere 2 per cent of the total affidavit and exhibit pages of more than 8000 pages. And without an analytical team to follow the deliberate course in which these supervisors were leading the Commission, they simply got away with it, leaving the minute detail of the most crucial seconds in Presidential history to the mercy of conspiracy theorists.

Like the head shot the Commission was investigating, snippets of information flew in all directions. Without a team of clever analysts there was no cross-referencing, no matching words, locating holes, finding carefully worded statements, or similar facts. No suggesting lines of interrogation or investigation. No one to point to the obvious. Each night, the lights would be turned off and everyone would go home tired, believing they'd had a good day, only to return the next and do it all over again. Building a room of paperwork that became the twenty-six back volumes of the Warren Commission, a paper mountain.

As a past team leader to numerous major crime and homicide task forces I knew at times there can be bewilderment at the sheer volume of information. And I worked in an age of computers and analysts. I can't help speculating if Earl Warren, under the weight of so many documents, ever found himself wanting to scream, 'My God, I'd kill for an analyst!'

CHAPTER 15

THE SMOKING GUN

Could so many people standing on the pavements and manicured lawns of Dealey Plaza on that sunny Texas afternoon have all got it so wrong? Could what they saw and heard, individually and collectively, have been a mass of errors? Could what they had smelt been an illusion? Let's not forget, this was middle America, watching a passing parade in a socially conservative town at a socially conservative time. The closest many of the bystanders would have ever been to violence and killing would have been the thirty-minute Friday night episode of 'Dragnet'. Then the shots rang out. And the blood sprayed as the crowd fell, some jumping for cover. Just as fast as it happened, it was all finished. Dozens of stunned faces with mixed memories were all that was left as the motorcade disappeared into the sunset. Some of the recollections were graphic, a few poignant, some extraordinary, many definite, and all blended together into one giant mosaic that gave a totally different impression to that which the front volume of the Warren Report offered to a waiting world. Why?

Just prior to the commencement of the Warren Commission hearings, the Executive Sessions Committee declared itself confused by the question of how many shots were actually fired at the crime scene, how many hit JFK and how many hit Governor Connally. Believing their discussions were 'Top Secret', they mentioned bullet 'fragmentation' and the need to 'ask for help from the ballistic experts'. This important point seems to have vanished in the subsequent months of evidence gathering. A pity, as specialist ballistic help may well have uncovered the anomaly of the final bullet, the last shot, and delved further into what causes fragmentation of a round. All the Commission seemed to be concerned with was proving the lone gunman theory, that Lee Harvey Oswald with his second-hand 'clunky' Carcano rifle was the sole perpetrator. It was as if they had their man, albeit dead, they had their gun, and they needed to close off the puzzle. Had they looked into what causes fragmentation they would have uncovered hollow point rounds designed to fragment on impact, and other frangible rounds. Detectives worldwide have a saying: 'Failure to search is failure to find.' The Sessions notes show (again) that the inner-sanctum, Earl Warren and Gerald Ford, had many questions about what actually occurred on 22 November, 1963. To read the notes is to see their meetings laced with uncertainty, fine legal minds not privy to the complex ways of law enforcement and principles of investigation, flagging concerns from the start. While Warren and Ford had suspicions, ultimately they failed to search and failed to find the real answers.

At one of the Sessions meetings, with the approval of the Chairman, Gerald Ford suggested calling for the autopsy evidence. Sadly, the only evidence presented to the Commission was that of the pathologists. Jerrol Custer's name was not on the witness list, neither was FBI agent Sibert nor O'Neill, nor photographer John Stringer nor Floyd Reibe, and on it went. These forgotten men formed the core of a group of more than a dozen professionals gagged by silence orders. Some suffered threats of incarceration, others were left in fear of court-martial should they speak of what they knew or what they saw. And what was it that they knew? Each of these professionals bore witness to between thirty and forty metal fragments located in the brain of the President, a veritable 'Milky Way' of metal specks within the brain and skull. They were aware of the unanimous agreement of those within the autopsy suite that the head shot to JFK was initiated from the rear. They had knowledge pertaining to the disappearance and doctoring of X-rays and photographs, to the extreme pressure to hasten the procedure by worried men in suits and military uniforms, to a secret debriefing at the White House and the eventual disappearance of the President's brain. Could this group of professionals be like the many citizens standing on Dealey Plaza on the afternoon of the assassination? Could they all have got it so wrong?

In 1978 the House Select Committee on Assassinations launched an investigation to find out where the brain was and who last had custody of it. It was determined that Dr Burkley transferred the brain in the pail on 26 April 1965 but to where is unclear. The brain was then locked in a footlocker and never seen again. The enquiry was told that JFK's brother Robert

Kennedy took possession of the contents of the locker (the pail and brain and other exhibits) and as the brain has never been seen since, the conclusion was drawn that it was he who had disposed of same. At the time, Robert Kennedy was Attorney General, the most powerful legal man in the country. Yet he took possession of an exhibit crucial to understanding the cause of his brother's death. Why? Was it his knowledge that the brain was speckled with metal fragments and, if so, what did he fear might eventually be revealed?

The autopsy didn't appear to be the work of a group of people striving to see justice served. And definitely not what one would expect from the highest level of officialdom charged with responding to a nation's outcry. The Commission was never to hear what really went on behind those closed doors despite its star counsel, Arlen Specter, having a fair inkling via his knowledge of facts from Jerrol Castor, FBI agents Silbert and O'Neill, and the Secret Service agents. With so much evidence going missing and the threats of incarceration and court-martial, the only conclusion that can be drawn is that someone was filtering the witnesses, ensuring that only certain evidence entered the Warren Commission hearing room.

With the majority of the key players now deceased – virtually every Commission member, almost every one of the citizens on Dealey Plaza and the medical experts within the autopsy suite – and with no chance of viewing the personal diaries of the lawyers involved in the Commission, conjecture is all that remains as to who was overtly blocking evidence to the Commission. Fortunately, each of the Dealey Plaza witnesses left behind a sworn affidavit, and in the case of the autopsy staff, transcripts of lengthy testimony from the rigorous cross-examination by the ARRB lawyers in 1995 and onwards.

When considering who the culprit may have been, within the Warren Commission or the Secret Service, or both, who could have held back witnesses from giving testimony, it is worth remembering the era in which the killing of the President took place. It was the height of the Cold War, a time of spies and intrigue, an age of wild imaginations. It was also the dawn of an era of new age writers telling tales of mysteries and carefully crafted cover-ups. Cover-ups, like conspiracy theories, were nouveau, creations of vivid minds, tools of a new way of thinking, a new way of approaching and solving problems. Then along came the killing of JFK, the assassination of the leader of the free world, laced with mystery and blanketed in uncertainty. An official cover-up may well have seemed a feasible solution to place before the naive millions expecting answers. At the end of a lengthy enquiry such as the Warren Commission, surely the public would accept whatever their government set down. And just as sure was the play by the Secret Service in 1995 when they were required to surrender documents to the ARRB finding, but instead chose to destroy all records of their involvement on 22 November, 1963. Cover-up is the only logical explanation for such actions. Instead of letting the people know the truth, the whole truth and nothing but the truth. But by the mid-1990s the American public were a tad wiser, more attuned to the ways of officialdom, and cover-up. Still, in the case of the ARRB snub, no one questioned the destruction of evidence. It was let slide. Perhaps a sign of the times, of a new generation that weren't invested in one of the most talked about tragedies in American history.

But, back in the Warren Commission days, officialdom was just as cunning, and almost certainly had a mole or moles within its ranks committed to sanitising the evidence, who personally and systematically, page by page, witness by expert, worked at keeping the truth behind the death from the American public. The perpetrator/s must have been confident in the knowledge that the cover-up would be hidden for seventy-five years under the secrecy provisions of federal legislation. But, only thirty years later, a Senate under pressure from a freer-thinking populace repealed the clause that held the secrets and opened a can of worms, for all to see.

A lawyer can toil all day in search of answers, striving to find the vein that can lead to a gold strike. They can pose question after question in an attempt to get at the truth, but if the witnesses who have the answers are not on the stand, their work is futile. In the case of the Warren Commission, the search for answers lasted ten long months. Under the glare of fluorescent tubes, lawyers rolled up their sleeves and started digging, alongside a mole. The cross-examination certainly looked good, appeared to be the real thing, but the end result was a farce. The mole/s worked away, ensuring which witnesses were called, and which were not. So the gold stayed hidden despite twenty-two eyewitness accounts of gunpowder or smoke in and around the motorcade; despite thirteen good people telling of an agent standing and waving an automatic weapon; despite testimony that there were six additional railwaymen who could have given supportive evidence as well as the potential witnesses from the Decker deck and FBI list; regardless of forty-eight people asserting that the last two shots were too close to have come from the same weapon. Whoever the mole was, they ensured that the Commission failed to locate the smoking gun and that any strike was well and truly covered up. Indeed the presence of a second gunman never entered the Commission's domain as the counsellors ran their one-man shooter investigation.

Any detective who has been in a courtroom, any investigator who has raised the Bible and stood before a jury, hoping, praying, that their prosecution will convict a rapist, murderer or crime boss, knows only too well that the truth has many faces. Evidence can bend and twist in that hallowed environment, dependent on who's wearing the wig and who's wearing the robe. And there are as many disappointments in the world of lawyers as there are in the world of law enforcement officers. It happens on any team when random selection is applied; there are stars and there are duds, just as there is mediocrity. After reading the 10 000-plus pages of ARRB files, the Dallas Sheriff reports, the Dallas FBI dossier and the Warren Commission back volumes, it was clear who were the stars. It was also clear which lawyers consistently missed or ignored opportunities, for whatever reason.

Maybe it was the relentless pressure of the Commission itself and the constant media scrutiny that affected their individual performances? Perhaps they held an unshakeable belief that the atrocity on 22 November, 1963, was the work of a lone gunman and they simply stopped looking for the gold strike. Or, as I came to believe as I read the material, perhaps they were blinded by patriotism, not wanting the truth of the real tragedy to blow away America's global prestige. A year earlier the Russians had suffered a most humiliating backdown against the Americans in the Cuban Missile Crisis. A world of media satirists mocked the big bad Soviet bear and a global community witnessed the might of democracy. JFK was on a roll, towards a second term in office, and the media loves a winner! But then came the tragic incident that could have painted the American political machine as the laughing stock of the world. One only has to contemplate the Russian propaganda had the truth behind the shooting ever seen daylight. The global front-page headlines would have been running for months, ridiculing the American administration. A deflection of massive proportions was needed, so a Commission of enquiry was pulled together to probe the assassination. But, in the end, fool's gold is only gold to fools. Maybe the Warren Commission lawyers were happy to keep panning, keep sifting until their licence ran out and everyone eventually went home. Everyone except the conspiracy theorists.

As for so many cold cases, especially the investigation of a homicide that took place decades earlier, time can be a detective's biggest adversary. Facts can be easily eroded; a salient point at the time of a crime can recede into a foggy memory or, worse still, can be embellished, altered or corrupted. A detective has enough to contend with when the case is hot, where a body is still the dominant aspect of the crime scene, where a gun or bloodied knife lies nearby, teasing forensic experts. That's what a detective excels at – joining the dots, solving the puzzle and catching the villain. To be successful, the scene of the crime must be preserved. There is no room for error. Treating the assassination of JFK as a cold case poses innumerable issues. The trail is not just cold, it is glacial. The location of the slaying has changed – insofar as it has been contaminated by 200 weather seasons, millions of cars and trucks, and just as many passers-by and tourists. New grass at Dealey Plaza has altered the location irrevocably. JFK is long buried, as are Governor Connally and a large percentage of the witnesses. So where does an investigator start?

Ask any seasoned detective, 'How do you know what actually happened at a crime scene?' and most will offer one unanimous comment: 'Listen to your witnesses.' Blessed are the witnesses, a detective might say, for without them crimes could go unsolved. Forensic science, microscopes, latex gloves, dust-proof suits, exhibit logs, fingerprint powder and ultraviolet lights are all useful when gathering exhibits, but the old-fashioned witness remains the investigator's best friend. Invariably, the critical mass of witness accounts is an accurate summation of what occurred at a crime scene. At the very least, it's a damn good place to start looking. And the more witnesses you have saying and hearing the same things, the greater the likelihood that yes, indeed, that is what actually happened.

On 22 November, 1963, there were hundreds of witnesses lining Houston Street as well as sprawling out along Elm Street and onto Dealey Plaza. A detective of the time should have seen this number of people as a veritable smorgasbord. All these people eagerly standing in rapt attention, waiting for their once-in-a-lifetime glimpse of a Presidential motorcade, then, all of a sudden, *bang . . . bang, bang*!

More than one hundred witnesses heard that same sequence, three shots. A few heard four shots, but also admitted to being confused by the echo effect from the overpass. And forty-eight witnesses on the ground heard two shots spaced close together, so close that their descriptions included: 'close together', 'rapid succession', 'quick succession', 'instantaneous', 'at the same time', 'fairly close together', 'closer together', 'close enough to be from an automatic rifle', 'rapid explosions', 'two real fast bullets together', 'quicker, more automatic', 'right behind the other', 'two real quick', 'pretty close together', 'followed very quickly', 'closer than the first', 'much shorter time', 'rapid shots' and 'simultaneously'.

Of all of the descriptions used by these forty-eight witnesses, the most common descriptions were, 'rapid succession', 'simultaneously' and 'close together'. These witness accounts speak as loudly as the gunshots themselves, as each witness (except for those not called) went through a process, a filtering known as cross-examination. The results of this process become a detective's critical mass. This is the stuff that solves crimes, a block of matching observations, matching evidence and matching comments that cannot be ignored. In the case of the Dealey Plaza incident, this 'matching' evidence was ignored, by the Warren Commission and every other commission or investigator, conspiracy theorist and individual that has studied the case since.

During my research I found other accounts from persons in Dealey Plaza not part of the official Warren Commission who heard shots and saw the motorcade; citizens that the FBI and local law enforcement personnel located and signed up as witnesses. And citizens who were quoted in the media. Though they weren't tracked down by the Commission it is fair to say that what they saw and heard was consistent with the aforementioned Commission witnesses. So, a conclusion on the number of shots fired that day is simple: there were three, and two close together.

The answers to the shooting of JFK were always going to be found within the recollections of those who saw the atrocity, all senses honed, anticipating the passing parade. The Warren Commission back volumes are the key to the door that locked away those many eyewitness accounts. In studying the testimonies, the evidence given under oath and the cross-examinations, an opportunity presented to understand what really happened on that day. There were three shots and they rang out in quick succession. The first shot, impotent, hit the roadway and ricocheted, hitting an onlooker, salesman James Tague. The second penetrated the President at the back of his neck and exited cleanly at his throat. This was a full metal jacket round. The same projectile passed through Governor Connally. The third and fatal round hit the President in the back of the head causing devastating results, the work of a frangible round, designed to explode on impact. Of those closest to the killing, many recalled that the last two shots resounded virtually simultaneously, making it impossible for both to have come from the same weapon. Research into the hundred or so witness comments on the issue of the three shots and in particular the last two shots could be best summed up by the matter-of-fact comment of fifteen-year-old schoolgirl Linda Willis, watching, admiring, smiling, so close to the action, standing near her father. Of the last two shots, she said 'two real fast bullets together'. There had to be another shooter.

Bystanders reported having seen a man aiming a rifle from the sixth-floor window of the Texas School Book Depository, aiming a rifle then retreating. They watched the motorcade unsuspecting, eyes glued. The horror came minutes later. They saw the work of the bullets, the action and inaction of the Secret Service agents. They saw men in suits turn to look towards the Book Depository. Some saw an agent stand with an automatic weapon and some heard a weapon fired. Others believed a weapon was fired, some saw an agent fall back into his seat, and twenty-two persons either saw smoke or smelt gunpowder. A number of the Secret Service agents concurred with the observations of these witnesses, that the agent had brandished his weapon; some even believed the weapon had been fired. Yet most of those observations were kept from the public volume of the Warren Commission, as were the observations of the twenty-two witnesses who either saw gunsmoke or smelt gunsmoke at street level, in or around the motorcade. This evidence, crucial to understanding what really happened in those final six seconds in the life of a President, was ignored. Many of the witnesses were either not called to the Commission or, for those who were, the lawyers simply passed over their observations with complete disregard for a process they were meant to be serving. To a detective, to this author, this lack of integrity by the lawyers at the Commission is unforgivable, especially as the standing of the witnesses, in each and every case, was exemplary, all respectable, working Americans. Some of these people had significant experience with long arms – journalists Tom Dillard and Robert Jackson definitely smelt gunpowder; Signal Supervisor Holland saw a puff of smoke, Patrolman Brown smelt smoke. Virgie Rachley smelt smoke as the motorcade passed by and Lady Mayoress Elizabeth Cabell was adamant about smelling gunpowder, as was her travel partner in the motorcade, Congressman Roberts. Then there were the stunning comments of police officer Martin: 'You can smell powder burning, smell the gunpowder in the street.' Equally important is the comment from fellow policeman Joe Smith, who smelt 'gunsmoke cordite'. Newspaper reporter Ed

Johnson saw a puff of smoke, as did bystanders Austin Miller, Royce Skelton, Clemen Johnson, Nolan Potter, James Simmons, Walter Winborn, Thomas Murphy, Patsy Paschall and Richard Dodd. Simple folk who made a simple observation. Yet their stories were not called to action by the Commission. The men in the courtroom with their suits and impressive law degrees just brushed over their words or failed to even probe the observations. Even the senior postal investigator, watching the parade from a distance through binoculars, saw smoke at the motorcade. But, of all the observations, none was more dramatic, more in need of a public hearing, than the 'people's senator's' observations of smelling gunpowder, the rancid smell of gunfire, at the exact moment he believed a Secret Service agent had fired the third and final shot. He, too, was never called, never asked to raise the Bible and tell his constituents what he saw: 'You don't smell gunfire unless you are upwind from it and it blows in your face.' Words that would have stopped the Warren Commission and started the presses in every newspaper publisher in the world! Words that only mean one thing: there was a smoking gun, and it was very, very close to the President.

A fascinating adjunct to the observations of these ignored witnesses is a quirky characteristic of the early-model Colt AR-15, the model of AR-15 in use by the Secret Service in 1963. The rifle was prone to smoking; that is, due to its direct gas operating system, it would emit excessive levels of smoke each time a round was fired. A plume of smoke would waft around the shooter. This fault was eliminated in later years, with later models, but not before 1970.

To disregard the above summation from the witnesses standing nearby or travelling within the motorcade is to snub twenty-two reliable accounts, the testimony of unbiased Americans. To ignore the possibility of a tragic accident colliding with an assassination attempt is to run an investigation with blinkers on. To ignore the evidence of witnesses is to throw crime scene principles to the wind. No detective is that foolhardy. Yet that is exactly what seems to have occurred.

It almost seemed that one or more persons within the Commission was vigilantly making sure that any needles of truth stayed well and truly buried in the haystack.

The Zapruder film clearly shows the horror inflicted when bullet meets human flesh. The head of the President literally exploded. For that to happen, frangible hollow point or soft point rounds must have been in play. It's all to do with physics, velocity, ballistics and armoury design. It's nothing to do with grassy knoll theories, Russian spies, mafia hitmen or Cuban activists. The violent snap of the President's head is a classic victim reaction when a hollow point round shatters, in this case causing the head to explode and jolt back. Lee Harvey Oswald was using full metal jacket rounds that day – there is no doubt of that important fact. He was not using rounds designed to explode upon impact.

Seconds before the killing, in vantage points around Dealey Plaza, were a number of amateur photographers, some filming the motorcade with the latest fad home movie cameras. One such amateur, Orville Nix, captured a side view of the President as his motorcade travelled towards the overpass. In the background, Orville's footage also captured the tree-lined area known as the 'grassy knoll'; however, his black and white film stock was of poor quality and only offered shadows. It wasn't until 2011 that the latest technology was thrown at this priceless footage.

The now digitally enhanced Orville Nix film footage shows the head of JFK exploding, a pink spray of brain matter seen as a fine mist, leaving the skull and pushing forward. 'Pushing forward' means categorically that the shot came from behind. So, someone else had to have shot JFK from the rear. The answer is that simple, and Howard Donahue knew it. From 1969 to 1992 he was onto it, but no one listened, no one encouraged his work. Indeed, after the countless knock-backs to interview key people over many years, Howard, too, like the truth, was lost in a mountain of 'declined to be interviewed' letters and he eventually gave up. Perhaps his answer to 'Who killed JFK?' was too raw for the American public, too hard to accept and too damaging to national security and the good name of the Secret Service.

The enhanced Nix footage, part of the JFK Memorial Museum library of near-crystal-clear images, offers an added bonus. The enhancements give a clear look into the bushes and shrubs of the 'grassy knoll' with all the shadows removed. It is a remarkable achievement. Also remarkable is that there is no evidence of any man on the grassy knoll firing at the President. In fact, there is nothing in the new footage that any conspiracy theorist could use to suggest that the fatal shot to JFK came from the front. It smashes that theory and buries the macabre legacy of Mark Lane, the oddball who fathered the earlier conspiracy theories on shots from the grassy knoll. The enhancements extend to the Zapruder film footage, destroying any notion that the driver of the Presidential car turned and shot JFK. It also demolishes the suggestion that an 'umbrella man', standing nearby, shot the President using a James Bond type clandestine weapon hidden inside the umbrella. Indeed, almost all conspiracy theories are now invalidated by the enhanced footage!

•

Law enforcement officers spend a great portion of their careers in the witness box under cross-examination. They know the rules of evidence, the inadmissibility of hearsay; they know how to get to the point and not to exaggerate. They are trained at evidence giving. Every law enforcement officer, every investigator, carries a notebook. They are disciplined to take notes and to record what they see, what they hear, what they do. While reading the back volumes of the Warren Commission, one glaring omission worried me. Where was the evidence under oath and the cross-examination of the entire team of Secret Service agents? As trained and disciplined quasi-law enforcement officers and the closest people to the shooting, any evidence the agents, particularly the eight within the follow-up car, could offer should have been viewed as vital. The very nature of their work should have guaranteed a run of succinct and accurate accounts. The more I read, the more research I undertook, the clearer it became that there was a sound reason for their non-attendance at the Commission. They had too much to fear, both as a group and as individuals.

By the time the Presidential entourage arrived in Dallas, Texas, a galvanised culture of drinking and late-night partying existed within a core group of Secret Service agents. In the months preceding the visit, astute newspaper reporters were on to it. Articles appeared, tucked away among the financial and international headlines, short stories of a team of men partying and drinking during the previous tours of Hawaii and

Florida. By all reports the agents closest to JFK were becoming more undisciplined the longer they served in the Presidential detail. Also becoming evident was a schism, a growing level of friction within the team of agents. For as many men who were boozing, there appeared an equal number who were against such behaviour and thought poorly of the lapse in discipline. One such member was Agent William McIntyre, on duty in the follow-up car. In later years he was to criticise the team, believing them to be below the standard required to protect the President of the United States. Equally, some of the President's agents criticised JFK for his 'womanising and parties'. Latter-day reading on the subject of JFK is laced with interviews of agents complaining about each other and their poor discipline, particularly around 1963.

Let's revisit the events of the night of 21 November that year. Eleven agents were recorded as having left the President at his hotel to go drinking until the wee hours at the Fort Worth Press Club, then the Cellar Door bar in the company of strippers. Agent Rufus Youngblood went off alone to catch up with a 'friend'. At the 8am muster on the last morning in the life of John Fitzgerald Kennedy hangovers, sleepy heads and confusion prevailed as the two factions of the Secret Service came together for a Presidential parade.

The trouble brewing within the President's group of minders would be exemplified by two Secret Service agents after the motorcade left Love Field Airport that morning. A squabble broke out. Agent Hank Rykba was left behind as the motorcade moved towards Dallas. He drifted back to the airport to sit and await the return of his team. Agent Don Lawton was a well-qualified agent; he could easily have filled the role of sniper. However, he was known to have been drinking the night before. Still, he was part of the team, captured on black and white TV news film footage taken on the day. He moved from the follow-up car to take up a position jogging on foot alongside JFK's vehicle. The camera shows him looking very casual as he loafs towards the limousine. Then, for reasons never explained, Emory Roberts orders Lawton to move to the rear of the motorcade. An argument ensues. Lawton seems to challenge the instruction of his superior, standing his ground and raising his arms in the air, an obvious sign of frustration. The most telling move in this altercation is from Emory Roberts, who actually stood up in the follow-up car and gestured aggressively towards Lawton, as if to tell him to get away. Lawton waves his arms about three times as he stares at Roberts. Then he drops his arms and walks to the rear of the follow-up car. Whatever sting was in the disagreement between Emory Roberts and Lawton, it ended with Lawton leaving his post. He returned to Love Field Airport, taking no further part in the parade at a time when there was a drastic shortage of qualified and experienced agents to man the motorcade.

Oddly, Emory Roberts's log sheet, his record of what staff were assigned to what positions on the day, still recorded Agent Hank Rykba as positioned on the rear seat of the follow-up car, the position for the sniper. But he had been left behind at the airport. Emory Roberts's log made no mention of any altercation with his agents or their demotion from duty.

Criticism of Roberts over the way he handled his men came out at the Commission. It was reported that he often cut across the decisions of Agent Kellerman and was generally disliked. Yet, he was complicit in condoning the breaking of rules as far as alcohol consumption and partying went. Could the circumstances between Roberts and Lawton and the situation with Rykba have been the catalyst for one monumental error?

The man who finished up on the rear seat of the follow-up car was one George Warren Hickey. Forty-year-old Hickey had only joined the service four months earlier, assigned to the 'garage' as a driver and chauffeur. In the area of close personal protection of the President of the United States he was the least experienced, least qualified and least savvy of any member in the detail. Yet Hickey was given the task of sniper duty with the AR-15 assault weapon – a set of duties that would surely necessitate the selection of the most experienced sniper in the group. There is nothing in the records to suggest he was a boozer or partook in the partying, he was too new. And, as protocol would dictate, drivers were not allowed to mix with the field agents.

It seems that with so many men hungover, the bout of infighting at the beginning of the parade and Hickey being one of the few who had not been out till 5am, the new boy got to hold the gun. In hindsight this was a shocking decision by Roberts and arguably not the last on the day.

The demands upon the Secret Service once the motorcade had rushed the fatally wounded JFK to Parkland Hospital were extraordinary. Dallas was in a panic. The hospital had to be sealed off and the dignitaries guarded. The safety of Vice President Lyndon Johnson, Jackie Kennedy, the Governor and the Mayor were at stake. Every man was needed. A siege mentality prevailed among the agents as they gathered and deployed trusted colleagues from their team to surround the building as the President received urgent medical attention.

Yet at that same moment, under such pressure for manpower, George Hickey and the AR-15 assault weapon were sent to Love Field Airport. The most prominent politicians in America were under threat and Roberts sent his 'sniper' away to sit alone at an airport. Why?

Some years later, a report surfaced that I would not normally consider for the simple reason that it had not been validated before a court. However, in context, it may provide the smallest of pieces to the puzzle. At the same time Hickey was supposedly at Love Field Airport, a man also there claimed to have witnessed a Secret Service agent beating the trunk of one of the Presidential vehicles with an axe. On face value the story seems bizarre. But such a strange observation invites comment. Was it Hickey? The other agents were at Parkland Hospital or converging on Dealey Plaza. Or was it Don Lawton, banished to Love Field before the parade? Or was it Hank Rykba, also stuck at Love Field? Three men in the sin bin when manpower was needed most, and one AR-15 weapon locked away in its case. What was in the boot of the limousine, the smoking gun? We do know through Emory Roberts's testimony that Hickey was assigned to drive the President's car back to Love Field Airport, once JFK was secured in the intensive care ward at Parkland Hospital. Conjecture is all that remains.

The behaviour of the agent allegedy seen beating the limousine's trunk calls to mind the observations of Senator Yarborough, who wanted to tell his story to the Commission but was denied the opportunity. The Senator recalled in his affidavit that he saw an agent banging on the trunk of a vehicle as it raced to Parkland Hospital. A Secret Service agent banging on the body of the vehicle seconds after the President was shot in the head could easily be understood as an act of sheer frustration at their own performance or lack of performance, or monumental error. Why an agent at Love Field Airport was attacking the boot of a Presidential vehicle with an axe could have been explained the same way. In the absence of any further evidence, the Love Field actions remain bizarre.

The lack of testimony to the Warren Commission from the agents in the follow-up car is reprehensible, an assault of massive proportions on the hearings. All the men in the follow-up car offered concerning the death of their President was a few words typed on a piece of paper entitled 'Affidavit'. Words remarkably similar to each other, so similar it appears likely that they compiled their stories together. November 22, 1963, could easily be described as not only the day JFK was killed, but also the day the Secret Service's negligent behaviour came to a head and bloomed one almighty error in judgement.

The Secret Service agents should have been called to the witness box and sworn in, like Marina Oswald, Patrolman Earle Brown, Mr SM Holland, Linda Willis and hundreds of others. They should have laboured through their individual accounts. Then maybe the smoking gun might have been discovered. Instead, the missing-in-action follow-up car agents have left a gaping hole in a wound that will never heal, and will always smack of collusion. Let's just focus on the fundamental facts. There is no suggestion of malice aforethought on the part of any agent or, moreso, by George Hickey. No evidence of a deliberate, premeditated act by anyone within the agency to do harm to their President. It was just a terrible accident, the result of a series of events rolling together towards a tragic outcome. A lone errant shot from an inexperienced Secret Service agent, in reaction to the planned sniper work of a deranged young man on a mission. I am not looking to blame, just to know. Indeed, no one is trying to blacken the name of any individual or organisation. It's just about the truth, and a definitive answer into who killed JFK. An answer no more complex than a tragic accident colliding with a foolhardy assassination attempt.

What we have been left with is one massive internal conspiracy, a set of lies and omissions to cover up a truth. Lies that gained momentum a short time after JFK arrived at the Parkland Hospital and went on to create a life of their own after his death. Certainly it was an unplanned conspiracy; its birth was as simple (for a time) as the shocking error itself. But entwined in an assassin's attempt to kill, that simple mistake created a train of actions, manoeuvres, twists and turns by a select gathering of like-minded individuals.

Detectives have a saying for such a play: to be 'in on the giggle'. To be part of a team that could hold a secret, the darkest and most important of all secrets. In this case, to cover up an embarrassment that would have had insurmountable international consequences had the secret not been held tight. The game was on, indeed, the cover-up started at the Parkland Hospital as doctors, surgeons and nurses worked frantically on JFK. Just as frantically at work were the Secret Service agents, working out how to get their dead boss out of Texas and into an environment that was their own, an area that was safe and free of questions. And so it went; the 'giggle' was formed and a hasty cover-up gathered motion. A body, a hearse and a team of men headed for an aircraft with two bewildered first ladies.

The office of the President of the United States has a well-honed tradition of covering up facts that might embarrass an administration. There are many examples, however, like all cover-ups, the truth eventually seeps out and the embarrassment suffered through exposure of the cover-up is often far worse than the error itself. A case in point is the most infamous line ever spoken by a President, Bill Clinton's, 'I did not have sexual relations with that woman . . .' A modern society would, as the polls showed time and time again, have cared less about their leader's sexual dalliance than the murky mess after the concerted effort to cover up his error in judgement. The muckraking, over two years, the study and discussion of the forensic evidence and telephone tapes far exceeded the simple embarrassment that could have been dealt with by an apology. Instead, a brilliant President suffered irreparable damage to his reputation and to the credibility of his office.

Likewise, Ronald Reagan and his most senior advisors would spoil the name of the US administration after an almighty cover-up in what became known as the Iran–Contra Affair. Channelling ill-gotten funds from selling arms to Iran to rebels fighting the Nicaraguan government, the sordid affair was well aired in the mid-1980s, but not before a swathe of lies and denials.

Another case involved the scandalous and criminal activity undertaken by President Richard Nixon, known simply as 'Watergate'. A President condoning the unlawful entry into their political opposition Democratic Party's office at the Watergate Hotel is inexcusable. Yet all the American public heard from their President was cover-up after deflection as he wove a blanket of lies, until all that was left was a humbling, half-baked apology, accompanied by a resignation from office. Again, the embarrassment of constant lies, manipulation of facts, avoidance of the obvious and the theatre that travels with a cover-up far outweighed the end to a scandal.

In the case of the Secret Service in 1963, in the days following the death of President Kennedy, their task seemed to get easier. At the time of the shooting all eyes shifted from the smiling President and his beautiful wife to high in the air, up towards the sixth floor of the Texas School Book Depository. Stunned witnesses looked in the direction from which they thought shots had come. Fear spread as hundreds of pairs of eyes squinted at a nondescript set of windows on an unremarkable building. No one was looking at the follow-up car. No one had reason to. No one was looking at a Secret Service agent with far too much responsibility hidden among the wall of suits, all now standing, all turning and all looking at the same windows. Then an errant shot: a hellish mistake by an extremely inexperienced agent, who had turned back to check on his boss, AR-15 in hand. The only connection between the last two shots is the time; both seemed close together, too close to have come from the same weapon. But no one was making that observation at that exact moment. Everyone was jumping for cover, running, falling to the ground, hiding their heads, shielding their loved ones from the terror. By the time they looked up, nothing was the same. The motorcade was gone, as was their President and their day in the sun. All that remained was shock and amazement as confused witnesses stood and cried and police sirens began to wail. The major players in the crime scene simply disappeared. Just like that . . . as though it had never happened.

•

In the world of criminal investigations there are as many different characters and individuals as there are crimes. As a detective, most of your contemporaries are ordinary, unassuming people, men and women focused on the search for truth. There are not too many swashbuckling, dry-martini-sipping, tuxedo-wearing men of intrigue, solving crimes while kissing a bevy of pretty girls. More the in-need-of-a-shave, frayed shirt and tie, exhausted, near-to-divorce detective who dreams of a beer at the end of a twenty-hour shift. These people are quiet achievers, the type you could easily pass in the street, perhaps on their way to the murder of a century. Ballistics expert Howard Donahue was one such character, happy to idle away years in his workshop cellar, with just his reference books, instruments and calculations, all in a search for the truth; a man big on facts and low on rumour. Donahue spent years researching his theory; as a ballistics man his mission was to prove forensically that a second gunman was at the scene. He went to the US National Archives to read the Warren Commission back volumes, hours at a time, until the closing bell went and he was sent home. One could only wonder what he might have achieved had he been issued with a full set of the Warren Commission documents to study in his own time, and if his mind had been more crime-scene oriented than ballistics oriented. Regardless, his ballistic analysis and presentation is without fault.

Oliver Stone's film *JFK* was one of the biggest movies of the year in 1992, perhaps an indication of the level of interest in conspiracy theories, or perhaps just a well-made piece of scripted drama. Whichever, the marketing hype leading up to and following its release was so massive that it effectively drowned out the simultaneous release of a publication about

Donahue's work from St Martin's Press, entitled *Mortal Error: The Shot that Killed JFK*. While I was riveted by its forensic science and Donahue's tenacity, the book came and went without fanfare and the American people remained largely unaware of an explanation for the death of a President that still hangs. It's worth wondering what might have happened had Oliver Stone's movie bombed in the first week and Donahue's book caught the attention of Oprah Winfrey's book club or the *New York Times*?

Many of the agents in the follow-up car were never to speak to each other again. Agent John Ready from the follow-up car, a known heavy drinker and one of the party set, declined to attend any of the Secret Service reunions; he had fallen out with some of his colleagues and there were a few he never spoke to again. Agent Roy Kellerman, now long dead, left behind a quirky legacy. Following his death in 1984, his wife June reported to have once overheard Kellerman talking on the telephone about the assassination. June is quoted as saying Kellerman 'accepted that there was a conspiracy'. Nothing more is known of this ambiguous quote, which begs to be explored. One of Kellerman's daughters has also been quoted in the press as saying, 'I hope the day will come when these men [her father and other Secret Service agents] will be able to say what they've told their families . . .' As the years ticked on, Agent Kinney, also in the follow-up car, was reported as saying something similar, but no elaboration has ever been offered. What they knew and what they wanted to say has gone with them to their graves. Perhaps the Secret Service agents also had to sign silence orders, gagging them from any comment. Were they under the threat of incarceration, the same threats directed at the autopsy crew, should they speak out?

By the 1970s a good portion of the lawyers attached to the Warren Commission, including Earl Warren himself, are recorded in the media as saying that they believe they did not uncover all the evidence available and that some of them held reservations about their own conclusions. The man who set up the Warren Commission, President Lyndon Johnson, had no faith in the outcome, publically denouncing the result of the Commission hearings during the later years of his life.

CHAPTER 16
CLOSURE

In deciding to close off my crime scene analysis and cold case study into the death of the 35th President of the United States I saved two salient points for last. Individually, and without reference to each other, they are perhaps a mere curiosity. Together, they helped galvanise my thoughts on what happened on 22 November, 1963. Both issues relate to when the Presidential limousine arrived at Parkland Hospital, and JFK and Governor Connally were whisked inside. Within minutes of the critically injured men being taken from the vehicle a photographer captured a photograph of a metal bucket and wet rag beside the limousine. Unbelievably, the Secret Service had begun cleaning the car. A car that was the primary crime scene to what seemed the attempted assassination of the President of the United States. Without doubt there would have been crucial evidence in the car, with blood splatters, possible gunshot residue and, more importantly, the probability of bullet fragments. All this could prove key evidence in tracing a suspect and assist the FBI on the vital information of what type of round was responsible for the devastating head shot to JFK. Yet all was on the path of being destroyed, mopped up by an unknown hand.

The second issue that hovers loud and clear over the Presidential limousine relates to the AR-15 semi-automatic rifle. A state-of-the-art weapon, that day was the first time it was used by the Secret Service. And yet it was placed in the hands of the newest member of the team, the 'driver', non-field agent George Hickey. As it turns out, it would be the first and the last time that weapon was ever used by the Secret Service, as it was retired from their arsenal immediately. Why would such an efficient weapon be banished after only one outing is the obvious question I had to ask myself. What had happened to see this weapon removed, when the Secret Service had previously had such faith in its newest firearm? But, like so many questions that shroud that one day in Texas, it would never receive an official response, leaving this retired detective and a perplexed public to but wonder.

Pushing the evidentiary aspects aside, the story of the death of President John F Kennedy could not have been more theatrical if Hollywood had written the script. This tale had it all. A cast of characters headed up by a jilted jealous husband intrigued by espionage; secret agents; Ray Bans and strippers; a pretty Russian; a ten-gallon-hatted detective and an aged chief justice both past their use-by dates; and an astute district attorney. Then there was the new-kid-on-the-block agent with a way-too-powerful weapon; three presidents in various stages of office; a wannabe-helpful Jewish strip club owner; and an interfering, presidentially aspiring brother.

Late-night boozing, Soviet fascinations and Cuban dreaming, squabbling, uncertainty, suburbia and a parade on a sunny Texas day – the stage was set for the charismatic leading man to take a drive with his Chanel-clad first lady. And roll the cameras, Mr Zapruder! Throw in two bullets and three shots, a murder in parallel with an accident, a gust of gunpowder, body snatching, textbook uniform cops and lazy crime-scene protocols, a missing brain, a clever ballistics expert, a Milky Way of metal stars, missing photos, seized footage, lawyer bungling, destroyed negatives, omissions, alterations and negligence, manipulation of facts, the gagging of medicos, fudged witness lists and a mole inside a commission, 8124 pages of official diatribe and an inexplicable failure to allow smart voices to be heard. Even Hollywood would have to pass on such a complicated plot.

Yet this is what actually happened. Dozens of factors and hundreds of individuals came together in a six-second window of time that became one of the most talked about events in history. And this is where a retired detective from Down Under signs on for his cameo role. For all the complexities surrounding that pretty little thoroughfare in Dallas known as Elm Street, the countless enquiries, studies and books on the subject, like most stories, it is the end that really matters.

Long after a crime scene has been swept away, well after the hunt for a perpetrator is finished, the anguish of the deceased's relatives will remain. It's something most detectives find hard to forget: the grief etched on the faces of the bereaved accompanied by the gnawing question of 'Why?' 'Why did this happen?' 'Why did he do this?' To most, the loss of a loved one through an act of crime is the most harrowing of all losses. They need closure, a few words to take with them into an uncertain future, into a life without their beloved. Sometimes a single word is the perfect closure: 'Guilty'. Other times, solace comes with a straightforward answer to 'Why'. In searching for closure to the death of a President, I have chosen to leave the last words to voices often silenced by conspiracy theorists.

Riding in the jump seat of the follow-up car among the Secret Service agents was the President's secretarial aide, Dave Powers. A close friend and long-time confidant of the President, Dave knew of his boss's dalliances, saw the parties and even took part in some of them. He watched over the affairs and was known to have been complicit in arranging girlfriends for the nation's leader. Dave Powers carried the secrets. And entwined in those secrets was the Secret Service, guarding the perimeters of the late-night shenanigans. When ballistics expert Howard Donahue approached Powers with his theory about a second weapon and a second ammunition type – a conversation quoted in Bonar Menninger's *Mortal Error* – all Powers said was, 'You know I never talk about the tragic day in Dallas . . . I admire you for all the research you are doing and all that, but there is nothing I can say about, you know, the assassination. I'm awfully sorry . . .' His most telling comment, though, was in his parting words, 'I admire the pursuit you are doing . . .' Perhaps the President's confidant knew the real story behind the head shot as he was quoted as offering this response. '[it made] a sickening sound of a grapefruit splattering against the side of a wall.' Such a sound is consistent with a frangible round exploding upon impact.

Dave Powers sat quietly in the follow-up car on that fateful day, waving to a crowd that might help re-elect the young, handsome leader of the American political machine. Behind him crouched the newest member of the team, Agent Driver George Hickey. When the melee broke out, the inexperienced Hickey jumped to action, fumbling with his, 'ready to go' AR-15 assault weapon. He tried an unsteady turn, right then left. A shot discharged and the rest, as they say, is history. And that is how Dave Powers decided to treat it, as history. He made a conscious decision not to speak of what he may have heard or seen, offering only the most basic of affidavits to the Warren Commission. He kept himself from the courtroom, ensuring another secret held safe. But this time it wasn't a secret that would save his handsome mate from the tortuous grasp of the media. This was a horrific secret that would save a team of bodyguards from ruin and a nation from global embarrassment, a secret that would not only be the worst of his life, of his time, but would remain with him until death. Dave Powers need not have supposed who killed his friend – all he needed to do was turn around and see the man with the smoking gun, by all accounts a thoroughly decent man, middle-aged and embarking on a new career path. Yet, under the circumstances, too rookie-raw to be thrust into a sniper role for which he had no experience.

The wife of Lee Harvey Oswald, the pretty Russian who wished for much and was delivered little, knew her husband better than anyone else. Marina suffered more than thirty interviews with the FBI, the Secret Service and Dallas Police, and spent days standing under oath at the Warren Commission. In short, her efforts to assist in uncovering the answers were exemplary. In investigative terms her account read as frank and honest; she was rarely brought to error. Marina Oswald had no hesitation in stating under oath that she believed her husband had assassinated the President, '. . . to do something that would make him outstanding. That he would be known in history . . .' She believed his rationale had been the same in his earlier attempt to kill General Walker.

The man charged with presiding over the Commission, Earl Warren, held court for almost ten months. He ran a mixed bag of lawyers. How some ever got a brief on the Commission is a mystery; most were fair at best. Without exception, counsel assisting regularly lost themselves to long-winded questioning of witnesses on irrelevant subject matter. About one-third of many interviews were given over to the personal history, education, past employment and group associations of the witness. Why was there so much time-wasting? And why didn't the man who gave his name to the Commission put a stop to such needless questions and cut to the chase? In the end, seven well-chosen words from Earl Warren should have put a stop to the conspiracy theorists everywhere: 'There was no conspiracy, foreign or domestic.'

Alongside Earl Warren for a large part of the hearings was Gerald Ford, a brilliant Yale Law School graduate, a man who delved deeply and probed constantly and who would later become the 38th President of the United States. Reading the cross-examination undertaken by Gerald Ford is to understand a man trying his hardest to get to the truth. Stepping in as chairman of the Commission, should the Chief Justice need to excuse himself on other matters, Ford would often interrupt another counsellor and press for a better answer, a more detailed explanation. Following the hearings, Gerald openly stated that there was no credible evidence of a conspiracy of any sort, foreign or domestic. He publicly subscribed to the lone gunman theory;

however, one can only wonder what he thought privately. Either he didn't sense the problems within the Secret Service camp, or he simply chose not to tackle the problem.

Governor Connally, the survivor of the shooting, was a man who offered unflappable evidence and wisdom before the Warren Commission. He presented as articulate, accepting and level-headed. For a man who had suffered much himself, including gunshot wounds and constant pressure from a probing media and officialdom, and no doubt post-traumatic stress, he spoke candidly. When asked by the Commission for his understanding of the reasons for the shooting, he stated firmly and clearly that he believed Lee Harvey Oswald was an '... individual with a completely warped, demented mind who for whatever reason wanted to ... vent his anger, his hate, against many people and many things in a dramatic fashion that would carve for him, in however infamous a fashion, a niche in the history books of this country ...'

Perhaps it was the dignified demeanour of Mrs Jacqueline Kennedy that offered the most telling comment on those bizarre hours in Dallas. As the Vice President's wife, Lady Bird Johnson, alighted from her car at the Parkland Hospital, she recalled, '[I] cast one last look over my shoulder and saw ... a bundle of pink, just like a drift of blossoms lying on the back seat. I think it was Mrs Kennedy lying over the President's body ...' Once her husband had been pronounced dead, Jackie watched as his body was hurried away inside a casket. The medical report, written by one of the hospital's senior physicians, stated that 'The President's wife refused to take off her bloody gloves, clothes. She did take a towel and wipe her face. She took her wedding ring off and placed it on one of the President's fingers.

All the President's belongings except his watch were given to the Secret Service.'

My four-and-a-half-year project of researching the death of a President was all but over. I took off my reading glasses, rubbed tired eyes and leaned back in a chair that had served me well, a swivel chair that had lost its swivel. I glanced across my long writer's desk at the piles of notes stacked so high that my cat had long ago stopped trying to sleep on it. I gazed at my notepads, empty pen canister and the worn-out keys of a faithful laptop. Two books were propped nearby. Both had sat with me for the duration, one acting as a catalyst, the other as a seed. *Mortal Error: The Shot that Killed JFK*, the too technical, yet wonderfully detailed paperback about Donahue, an unassuming expert, was certainly the catalyst for my research journey. The pages are now worn, dog-eared and riddled with fluorescent highlighter marks and detective jottings. I glanced at the other book, leaning against *Mortal Error* like a heavy weight. A frightfully impressive looking hardcover, bound in leather, embossed with gold ink: The Warren Commission Report, front volume. Two more contradictory publications on the same subject could not exist – exacting ballistic analysis versus a government whitewash. All I could think as I considered each book was *vive la* paperback! And *vive* perseverance! Coming to the end of a twisting road, I realised my journey could be summed up with a simple set of numbers. After four and a half years of toil applying a forensic analysis to more than 10 000 pages and up to 15 million words, an exercise in many thousands of hours of reading, it all came down to three shots in much less than six seconds, and the succinct observations of more than one hundred citizens of Dallas, watching a four-vehicle motorcade pass by. Forty-eight witnesses were adamant that two shots were heard virtually together and twenty-two smelt or saw gunsmoke at street level. The lone gunman theory reaffirmed with, regrettably, one extra player in the game. Add forty-year-old Agent Driver Hickey and twelve people who saw him holding the gun and the entire picture finally, sadly, made sense. My work was complete.

The most fitting manner to close such a journey would be to recall a set of observations and words between two very fine First Ladies . . . By 2.40pm on 22 November, 1963, the outgoing First Lady, Jackie Kennedy, was left with nothing but horrendous memories and a flurry of suited men. Her last moments in Dallas were at an airport, where she stood beside her dead husband's casket, her pink Chanel outfit smeared in blood. The world's news cameras zoomed in as she looked at nothing but the tarmac. Then she boarded Air Force One. She turned back to briefly glance at a town she would never revisit, a town that had taken everything. As the Secret Service agents bustled around her, lifting her husband's casket onto the jet, bewildered reporters, some with tears in their eyes, politely asked her for comment. Jackie looked beaten, yet dignified. Obviously she was conscious of her husband's blood on her dress. No doubt her frailty was held together by pride. All she offered was, 'I want them to see what they have done.' Few photographers dared flash her sad portrait.

What exactly did she mean by the words 'them' and 'they'? It was the third time in two hours Mrs Kennedy had mentioned the same collective words when referring to the shooting, at a time when she and the world knew of only a lone gunman, and well before any conspiracy theories were unleashed. Or was there a conspiracy after all, one from within? One designed to cover up a fatal accident, an accident at the hands of the President's protectors?

Lady Bird Johnson eloquently summed up Jackie's last moments in Dallas as she and the newly widowed Mrs Kennedy boarded Air Force One: 'I don't think I ever saw anyone so much alone in my life . . .' On board, a deceased head of state and a newly sworn-in President. The two women moved past the casket, to the Presidential cabin. Lady Bird recalled, 'I looked at her; Mrs Kennedy's dress was stained with blood. Her right glove was caked – that immaculate woman – it was caked with blood, her husband's blood. She always wore gloves like she was used to them. I never could. Somehow that was one of the most poignant sights – exquisitely dressed and caked in blood . . .'

In 1964, Jacqueline Kennedy was called to give sworn evidence at the Warren Commission. They asked her almost nothing and she offered almost nothing; she was in and out of the witness box within a few moments. She stepped away from her role as First Lady, and from the American dream. Some years later, she left the United States, marrying Greek shipping tycoon Aristotle Onassis. In later years she would speak neither of her grief nor the skulduggery shrouding that fateful afternoon in the Texas sun. Those interested in the truth were left to revisit Jackie's words that echoed through Dealey Plaza, and will always be heard:

'. . . Oh my God, they have killed my husband. I love you Jack . . .'

EPILOGUE

No great whodunit ever fades; there's always something floating to the surface, another revelation, a theory that depending on its provenance either adds to the pile or stirs thought. During my detective career, I would often harbour a nagging feeling towards the end of a big job, a sense that I might have missed something along the way, or been unable to fully understand an action, or some words. When this sensation struck I would brood and wonder, but rarely did I resolve the reason for my ponderings – that's just the way it was.

I had spent so long on the JFK mystery, tapping on my keyboard, sweating the words, stopping only to glance at my cat on the windowsill and share her autumn view of gold and brown. I was at another end, closing off the final chapter, my tribute of sorts to Jackie Kennedy. More than pleased with the legitimacy of my conclusions in the manuscript, I was satisfied that I had missed nothing and impressed with the level of research achieved. Yet I couldn't shake a familiar nagging feeling, this time due to the ambiguous nature of the words spoken by Jackie Kennedy on that fatal day.

My maudlin musings were broken by what would be a wonderfully serendipitous occurrence, starting with a telephone call from my editor and co-researcher, Alison. I owed her dinner as some thanks for her exhaustive efforts, a promise made and now well overdue for delivery.

Pushing aside my half-uttered invitation, she insisted that I turn on my radio . . . now! Long-retired Secret Service Agent Clint Hill was in Australia doing the talk show circuit promoting his new book, *Mrs Kennedy and Me: An Intimate Memoir*. I stopped typing and tuned in to ABC radio 774, where *Afternoons* presenter Richard Stubbs was interviewing the man who had once watched over the First Lady. Listening to Hill's sad recollection of events at Love Field Airport a mere two hours after the assassination, I could picture the blood-splattered Jackie, the epitome of a wife in shock. Once on board Air Force One she called her bodyguard to the rear of the craft for a private conversation. A conversation now made public.

'Oh Mr Hill, what's going to happen to you now?' were the words the elderly Agent Hill recalled her saying to him.

The radio interview ended a short time later and my concentration was lost for the day as I contemplated yet another of Jackie's ambiguous comments. What did she mean by her question? And why did Agent Hill single out that one line, after all these years? Surely he had done nothing to cast a shadow over his role as bodyguard to the First Lady. To the contrary, he and George Hickey were the only agents to respond, and they did so simultaneously at the second shot, one on foot and one with a rifle. Their fellow agents remained lead-footed, unmoved. Further, Hill's response was so textbook, so efficient in a time of need, that he received a bravery award from the Secret Service administration three days later. Nothing, however, was ever mentioned of the other alert agent, George Hickey, standing tall in the follow-up car, assault rifle in hand.

So was there an inference in Jackie's words that something wrong had happened, apart from the obvious? There was purpose in her words on every other occasion she had spoken in the two hours after she was raced from Dealey Plaza, after the 'incident' or 'accident' had ripped her world apart. Her quoted words mostly referred to the collective, 'they' and 'them'. More ambiguity. And now, perhaps, an inference that something had gone wrong? I was left to ponder, staring out my window, as writers do, in search of the unknown. And all I had to aid my thoughts was the image (below) of a gallant Agent Hill desperately clinging to the back of the Presidential limousine, shielding his lady. And that of George Hickey, assault rifle in hand, in the follow-up car . . . only metres behind.

Colin McLaren
Ex-Detective Sergeant/Task Force Team Leader
cm@scuttlebuttmedia.net

A rare image: the raised AR-15 rifle, in the hands of George Hickey, also raised up, moments after the third and fatal shot hit JFK

ACKNOWLEDGEMENT OF THE DOYENS

Undertaking a research project such as *JFK: The Smoking Gun* requires constant support and near daily encouragement; it's a project that demands *belief*! I'd like to extend my heartfelt gratitude to the following clever and insightful people who shared my journey, all doyens in their own field, each making my arduous task a touch easier.

Alison Bruce: my writer's editor, and sometime researcher; you cut through the repetition and punched my paras into shape. You were there, night and day, with understanding and belief. I will never forget!

My literary agent, Selwa Anthony: from her first read, she was hooked and determined to find a publishing home for *JFK*. You are a national treasure. My manager and friend, Daniel Scharf, a film industry mentor and the man who kept reading the drafts and taking care of business, whilst I burnt the midnight oil. Professor Dave Barclay from Scotland, lecturer in forensic science and crime scene guru: your steady-handed advice was often appreciated. Andrew Rule, author and Walkley-winning feature writer extraordinaire: you read the roughs and became an instant believer, and when it counted your introductions opened doors. Vanessa Radnidge, publisher at Hachette Australia. My fifth book has found a happy home, and so have I. Let there be more, you run a sweet team. And thanks to your senior editor and fabulously accomodating Kate Ballard, and obliging editor, Jacquie Brown. Simon Egan, of Bedlam Productions UK: we kept meeting on *JFK* in different parts of the world, such was your fascination with my work. You were the push, the believer who could see my book as a film. And to publishing nice girl, Foong Ling Kong: you started me on a writing career, and your industry tips on finding the right publisher were appreciated.

And finally, I am indebted to arguably Australia's most skilled gunsmith and ballistics man; Roger Vardy, for his valued insight into the workings of the Carcano rifle and AR-15 assault rifle and their respective bullets.

INDEX